Anxiety & Depression Workbook

2nd Edition

Laura L. Smith, PhD

A Wiley Brand

Anxiety & Depression WorkbookFor Dummies®, 2nd Edition

Published by: **John Wiley & Sons, Inc.,** 111 River Street, Hoboken, NJ 07030-5774, www.wiley.com

Copyright © 2022 by John Wiley & Sons, Inc., Hoboken, New Jersey

Published simultaneously in Canada

For general information on our other products and services, please contact our Customer Care Department within the U.S. at 877-762-2974, outside the U.S. at 317-572-3993, or fax 317-572-4002. For technical support, please visit https://hub.wiley.com/community/support/dummies.

Wiley publishes in a variety of print and electronic formats and by print-on-demand. Some material included with standard print versions of this book may not be included in e-books or in print-on-demand. If this book refers to media such as a CD or DVD that is not included in the version you purchased, you may download this material at http://booksupport.wiley.com. For more information about Wiley products, visit www.wiley.com.

Library of Congress Control Number: 2022902721

ISBN 978-1-119-86742-5 (pbk); ISBN 978-1-119-86743-2 (ebk); ISBN 978-1-119-86744-9 (ebk)

SKY10079526_071224

Contents at a Glance

Table of Contents

Introduction

D o you worry too much? Are you often sad or down in the dumps? Do you have to drag yourself out of bed in the morning? Or maybe you avoid people more than you should. If so, you're probably dealing with some type of anxiety or depression. Everyone feels sad or worried from time to time because unpleasant feelings are a normal part of life. But when depression or anxiety interferes with your work, play, or relationships, it's time to act.

Good news! You can conquer these problems with the help of *Anxiety & Depression Workbook For Dummies*. Feel free to use this workbook on its own or as a supplement to counseling. In either case, studies show that self-help efforts work.

Experts estimate that almost a quarter of the people in the world will experience significant problems with anxiety at some point in their lives. And between 15 and 20 percent will succumb to the ravages of depression at one point or another. Unfortunately, many people suffer from both of these maladies. Recent events such as the pandemic have increased rates of both anxiety and depression among adults and children all over the world.

So if you struggle with anxiety, depression, or both, you're not alone. This book joins you in your battle by giving you research-based strategies and plenty of practice opportunities to help you defeat depression and annihilate anxiety.

About This Book

The purpose of this book is to give you a range of skills and tools for managing anxiety and depression. Although there's information here about the essential concepts of depression and anxiety, this book is action-oriented — in other words, you have the opportunity to actively apply research-based ideas to your life in meaningful ways.

There's no doubt you used workbooks while you were in school. A math workbook helped you apply math concepts to everyday problems. Or a reading workbook improved your ability to comprehend stories. Today, you can find workbooks on almost any topic, from selling your home and succeeding on tests to preparing your taxes and improving your memory.

The purpose of any workbook is to lay out the basics of a topic and then provide numerous opportunities to apply and practice the concepts at hand. Typically, books *explain* issues, and workbooks help you *master* new skills. In other words, *Anxiety & Depression Workbook For Dummies* is "less talk — more action."

Did you notice the "work" part of workbook? Don't let that scare you. You'll be well paid for your work in the form of increased life satisfaction and reduced emotional distress. And the work is actually rather interesting because you discover new ways to live your life and get what you want.

Unlike most workbooks, you don't necessarily have to read and use the chapters of this book in order, beginning to end. You can pick and choose what chapters to read and which exercises to do, besides where to start and stop.

This book is meant to be written in unless, of course, you've borrowed it from the library, in which case you'll need to write your answers elsewhere. Writing enhances skills and commits you to action, so I strongly encourage you to do the work required for your recovery by writing out your answers in the forms and worksheets. Don't worry about your handwriting or spelling — nobody's grading your work.

Throughout this book, you'll see sections labeled My Reflections. When you come across a reflection space, take a little time to ponder what you're feeling, what you've discovered, and any new insights you've achieved. But hey, this is your workbook — write down anything you want in My Reflections.

Foolish Assumptions

By the sheer fact that you've picked up this book, I assume, perhaps foolishly, that you want to do something about depression or anxiety. Maybe you suffer from some of these issues, or you think that a family member or close friend may have problems with anxiety of depression.

On the other hand, maybe you're a mental health professional who's interested in finding a resource to help structure therapy with your clients. I've had positive feedback from both clients and professionals who have used this book in addition to psychotherapy.

Icons Used in This Book

Throughout this book, icons in the margins alert you to important types of information:

REMEMBER

This icon marks particularly noteworthy information that you might record or write down so you can refer to it later.

PRACTICE

This icon tells you it's time to roll up your sleeves and get to work! It denotes a worksheet, form, or exercise for you to fill out.

EXAMPLE

This icon points to specific examples that show you the way through worksheets or exercises. Examples are fictional composites that represent accurate struggles, but they're not real people.

This icon appears when you need to take care; you may need professional help or should be on the lookout for possible trouble.

WARNING

 This icon alerts you to especially useful insights and explanations.

TIP

Beyond the Book

Throughout the book, there are worksheets that you may want to complete more than once. Go to www.dummies.com/go/anxiety&depressionworkbookfd2e to download them.

In addition, there's a cheat sheet with tips and information about anxiety and depression. To access this online cheat sheet, go to www.dummies.com and then type "Anxiety& Depression Workbook For Dummies Cheat Sheet" in the search box.

Where to Go from Here

Anxiety & Depression Workbook For Dummies can help you deal with your depression and anxiety. It's pragmatic, concrete, and goes straight to the point. As such, this workbook doesn't devote a lot of text to lengthy explanations or embellishments of basic concepts, so you may want to find out more about specific types of depression and anxiety, available medications, and alternative treatments elsewhere. For that purpose, consider reading one or both of the companion books: *Depression For Dummies* (Wiley) and *Anxiety For Dummies* (Wiley).

1

Dissecting Distress and Preparing a Plan

Chapter **1**

Sorting Out Symptoms of Anxiety and Depression

For people all over the world, these past years of unrest, divisiveness, and fear and uncertainty related to the devastating pandemic have increased stress significantly. Stress often precedes the emergence of emotional disorders, especially anxiety and depression. In the United States, recent surveys suggest that about 40 percent of the adult population suffer from notable symptoms of anxiety or depression. The rates of anxiety and depression among adolescents have also risen dramatically due to disruptions in their lives during these tumultuous times.

Everyone feels sad or worried from time to time. Such emotions are both natural and unavoidable. People worry about their children, bills, aging parents, jobs, health, and powerful social issues. And most people have shed a tear or two watching a sad movie or a news story about a poignant tragedy. It's perfectly natural to experience significant sadness when faced with loss, frustration, or pain. That's normal. Anxiety and depression are part of everyday life.

But when sadness fills most of your days or worries saturate your mind, that's not so normal. You may be experiencing a real problem with depression or anxiety. Anxiety and depression can affect how you think, behave, feel, and relate to others. The discussion and quizzes in this chapter help you figure out how depression and anxiety affect your life. When you understand what's going on with your emotions, you can start doing something to manage them more effectively.

TIP

This workbook is designed to help with troubling emotions. It isn't meant to be a comprehensive review of emotional disorders. Many people choose to use this book along with professional counseling or therapy. Some use this book on their own. If you want more information and an in-depth discussion about anxiety or depression, take a look at the latest editions of *Anxiety For Dummies* or *Depression For Dummies*.

REMEMBER

Don't freak out if the quizzes in this chapter reveal that you have a few symptoms of anxiety or depression. Almost everyone has struggles; that's human. However, you should be concerned when these symptoms significantly interfere with your life. See the later section in this chapter, "When and Where to Get More Help," for more information.

WARNING

If your symptoms are numerous and severe or your life seems out of control, you should consult your primary care provider or a mental health professional. These quizzes aren't meant to replace trained mental health professionals — they're the only people who can really diagnose your problem.

Dwelling on Negative Thoughts

If you were able to listen in on the thoughts that reverberate through a depressed person's head, you might hear, "I'm a failure," "My future looks bleak," "Things just keep on getting worse," or "I regret so many things in my life."

On the other hand, the thoughts of an anxious person might sound like, "I'm going to make a fool out of myself when I give that speech," "I never know what to say at parties," "The freeway scares me to death," "I know that the odds of a plane crash are small, but flying scares me," or "I'm going to have a nervous breakdown if my editor doesn't like what I write."

Thoughts influence the way you feel. The very darkest thoughts usually lead to depression, whereas anxiety usually stems from thoughts about being judged or hurt. And, of course, people often have both types of thoughts.

PRACTICE

Do your thoughts dwell on the dark, dismal, or the scary aspects of life? Take the quiz in Worksheet 1-1 to determine if your thoughts reflect a problem with anxiety or depression. Put a check mark next to an item if you feel the statement applies to you.

Although these thoughts can occur to someone who's depressed or anxious (or both), the odd-numbered items are most indicative of depression, and the even-numbered items reflect anxious thinking. There's no pass or fail mark on this quiz. However, the more items you endorse, the more you have cause for concern; specifically, if you check more than eight or ten items, you should think seriously about addressing your condition. At the same time, if you very strongly believe in or you frequently have any of these thoughts, you may have too much anxiety or depression. For example, if you worry all the time (item number 2) with no relief, you could benefit from working on that issue.

Worksheet 1-1   The Negative Thinking Quiz

- ❑ 1. Things are getting worse and worse for me.
- ❑ 2. I worry all the time.
- ❑ 3. I think I'm worthless.
- ❑ 4. I never know what to say.
- ❑ 5. No one would miss me if I were dead.
- ❑ 6. I'm afraid that I'll get sick.
- ❑ 7. I think I'm a failure.
- ❑ 8. My thoughts race, and I obsess about things.
- ❑ 9. I don't look forward to much of anything.
- ❑ 10. I get really nervous around people I don't know.
- ❑ 11. The world would be better off without me.
- ❑ 12. Thoughts about past traumas keep rolling through my mind.
- ❑ 13. I find it impossible to make decisions.
- ❑ 14. I can't stand it when I'm the center of attention.
- ❑ 15. My life is full of regrets.
- ❑ 16. I can't stand making mistakes.
- ❑ 17. I don't see things getting any better in the future.
- ❑ 18. I worry about my health all the time.
- ❑ 19. I'm deeply ashamed of myself.
- ❑ 20. I over-prepare for everything.

Take a moment to write down your results on Worksheet 1-2, and then reflect on whether or not you believe you have difficulties with anxiety, depression, or both.

PRACTICE

Worksheet 1-2   My Reflections

_____

_____

_____

_____

If you have any thoughts of suicide or utter hopelessness, consult your primary care provider or a mental health professional immediately.

WARNING

If you have symptoms of both anxiety and depression, don't be surprised. Anxiety and depression often occur together.

TIP

Blue and Anxious Behavior

If you were to follow a depressed or anxious person around, you might see some behavioral signs of their emotional turmoil. That's because depression and anxiety on the inside affect what people do on the outside. For example, a depressed person may look tired, move slowly, or withdraw from friends and family; an anxious person may avoid socializing or have a trembling voice.

Take the quiz in Worksheet 1-3 to see if your behavior indicates a problem with anxiety or depression. Check off each statement that applies to you.

Worksheet 1-3   The Distraught Behavior Quiz

☐　1.　I've been crying for no clear reason.

☐　2.　I pace around when I'm worried.

☐　3.　Sometimes I can't make myself get out of bed.

☐　4.　I avoid going into crowded areas.

☐　5.　I can't seem to make myself exercise.

☐　6.　I avoid risks because I'm afraid of failure.

☐　7.　I don't do things for fun lately.

☐　8.　I always stay away from activities that could be dangerous.

☐　9.　I've been missing work lately because I just don't have the motivation.

☐　10.　I'm really fidgety.

☐　11.　I feel like I am walking in quicksand; I can't get moving.

☐　12.　I avoid people or places because I feel anxious.

☐　13.　I don't care what I look like anymore.

☐　14.　I spend too much time making sure I look okay.

☐　15.　I don't laugh anymore.

☐　16.　My hands shake when I'm nervous.

☐　17.　I've been letting things go that I need to attend to.

☐　18.　I feel compelled to repeat actions to keep myself safe.

Again, there's no pass or fail on this quiz. The more items you check, the greater the problem. Once again, even-numbered items are most consistent with anxiety, and odd-numbered items largely indicate depression. And, of course, like many people, you may have symptoms of both types of problems.

Again, add up your answers and reflect on your results in Worksheet 1-4.

Worksheet 1-4   My Reflections

_____
_____
_____
_____

Physical Funkiness

Depression and anxiety inevitably produce physical symptoms. In fact, some people primarily suffer from changes in appetite, sleep, energy, or pain while reporting few problematic thoughts or behaviors. These symptoms directly affect your body, but they're not as easily observed by other people as the behavioral signs covered in the preceding section.

PRACTICE

Take The Sad, Stressed Sensations Quiz in Worksheet 1-5 to see if your body is trying to tell you something about your emotional state.

Worksheet 1-5   The Sad, Stressed Sensations Quiz

- ❑ 1. I have no appetite.
- ❑ 2. My palms sweat all the time.
- ❑ 3. I wake up too early each morning and can't go back to sleep.
- ❑ 4. I've been experiencing a lot of nausea and diarrhea.
- ❑ 5. I've been sleeping a lot more than usual.
- ❑ 6. I feel shaky all over.
- ❑ 7. I've been having lots of aches and pains for no good reason.
- ❑ 8. When I'm nervous, my chest feels tight.
- ❑ 9. I have no energy lately.
- ❑ 10. My heart races when I'm tense.
- ❑ 11. I've been constipated a lot more often than usual.
- ❑ 12. I feel like I can't catch my breath.
- ❑ 13. I'm eating all the time lately.
- ❑ 14. My hands are often cold and clammy.
- ❑ 15. I've lost my sex drive.
- ❑ 16. Sometimes I hyperventilate.
- ❑ 17. Every move I make takes more effort lately.
- ❑ 18. I get dizzy easily.

WARNING

The symptoms in this quiz can also result from various physical illnesses, drugs in your medicine cabinet, or even your three-cup coffee fix in the morning. Be sure to consult your primary care provider if you're experiencing any of the symptoms in The Sad, Stressed Sensations Quiz. It's always a good idea to have a checkup once a year, or more frequently if you experience noticeable changes in your body.

Although physical sensations overlap in anxiety and depression, even-numbered items in the quiz above are most consistent with anxiety, and the odd-numbered items usually plague those with depression. There's no cutoff point for indicating a problem. The more statements you check off, though, the worse your issue.

PRACTICE

Add up your answers and reflect on your results in Worksheet 1-6. Think about other physical problems you may have that don't appear on the list that may be related to your emotions and jot those down as well.

Worksheet 1-6   My Reflections

_____

_____

_____

_____

Emotions of Anxiety and Depression

Emotions erupt in response to what happens in the present, what happened in the past, and what might happen in the future. Emotional reactions involve physiological, cognitive, and behavioral responses. People across the world express six primary emotions:

> ≫ Happiness

> ≫ Sadness

> ≫ Anger

> ≫ Fear

> ≫ Disgust

> ≫ Surprise

From those basic emotions, more subtle expressions emerge. For example, from happiness springs joy, contentment, cheerfulness, or pleasure. From sadness, depression, gloom, despair, despondency, low self-esteem, or shame occur. Fear may bring anxiety, terror, worry, embarrassment, or panic. Disgust usually leads to distaste or feelings of grossness. Surprise is a brief emotion. What follows surprise varies depending on what brought forth the initial response. Surprise may turn into curiosity, amusement, disgust, relief, or fear.

Emotions guide behavior. Fear increases alertness and avoidance, anger produces aggression, and sadness involves withdrawal. Although most people have a variety of emotional experiences, those with anxiety or depression are likely to experience more sadness and fear, or possibly anger and disgust.

Which primary emotions do you experience the most frequently? Think about a typical day and reflect on what you're feeling. Think about what happened just before your feeling. Were you thinking about the past or the future? Record your experience in Worksheet 1-7.

Worksheet 1-7   My Reflections

_____

_____

_____

_____

Reflecting upon Relationships

When you're feeling down or distressed for any length of time, odds are that your relationships with those around you will take a hit. Although you may think that your depression or anxiety affects only you, it affects your friends, family, lovers, coworkers, and acquaintances. Even the strangers you interact with, such as waiters, flight attendants, clerks, and bank tellers, can suffer from your emotional state.

PRACTICE

Take the quiz in Worksheet 1-8 to see if your emotions are causing trouble with your relationships. Check off any statements that apply to you.

Worksheet 1-8   The Conflicted Connections Quiz

❑   1.   I don't feel like being with anybody.

❑   2.   I get very nervous when I meet new people.

❑   3.   I don't feel like talking to anyone.

❑   4.   I'm overly sensitive when anyone criticizes me in the slightest way.

❑   5.   I'm more irritable with others than usual.

❑   6.   I worry about saying the wrong thing.

❑   7.   I don't feel connected to anyone.

❑   8.   I worry about people leaving me.

❑   9.   I don't feel like going out with anyone anymore.

❑   10.   I'm plagued by visions of people I care about getting hurt.

❑   11.   I've withdrawn from everyone.

❑   12.   I feel uptight in crowds, so I stay at home.

❑   13.   I feel numb around people.

❑   14.   I always feel uncomfortable in the spotlight.

❑   15.   I feel unworthy of friendship and love.

❑   16.   Compliments make me feel uneasy.

You guessed it; there's no cutoff score here to tell you definitively whether or not you're anxious or depressed. But the more items you check off, the more your relationships likely suffer from your anxiety, depression, or both. Odd-numbered items usually indicate problems with depression, and even-numbered items particularly accompany anxious feelings.

REMEMBER

Many people are a little shy or introverted. You may feel anxious meeting new people and may be uncomfortable in the spotlight — these feelings aren't necessarily anything to be concerned about. However, such issues become problematic when you find yourself avoiding social activities or meeting new people because of your shyness.

PRACTICE

Reflect on your results and write about which relationships are most affected by your emotions in Worksheet 1-9.

Worksheet 1-9   My Reflections

_____

_____

_____

_____

Plotting Your Personal Problems Profile

The Personal Problems Profile provides you with an overview of your problematic symptoms. (If you skipped the quizzes in the previous sections of this chapter, go back and take the time to complete them; your answers to those quizzes come into play in this exercise.) The profile exercise in this section helps you identify the ways in which anxiety and depression affect you. One good thing about this profile is that you can track how these symptoms change as you progress through the rest of this book.

EXAMPLE

Tyler, a middle-aged chemical engineer, doesn't consider himself depressed or plagued with any emotional problems. But when he sees his primary care doctor, Tyler complains of fatigue, recent weight gain, and a noticeable loss in his sex drive. These feelings predated the pandemic but became more noticeable while he was quarantined. After ruling out physical causes, the doctor suggests that he may be depressed. He reluctantly agrees to meet with a social worker.

When Tyler fills out his Personal Problems Profile (see Worksheet 1-10), he lists the following top ten symptoms and notes whether they indicate anxiety or depression (A or D).

As you can see, Tyler suffers primarily from symptoms of depression. And most of these symptoms are physical in nature. Filling out his Personal Problems Profile helps Tyler see that he has a depression he wasn't even consciously aware of. He reflects on his discovery (see Worksheet 1-11).

REMEMBER

This is the *Anxiety & Depression Workbook For Dummies.* You can't feel better without doing a little work. Don't worry; the work isn't that difficult. Of course, you can skip a few exercises, but the more of them you complete, the sooner you'll start feeling better. Odd as it may seem, writing things down does a world of good. Writing helps you remember, clarifies your thinking, and increases focus and reflection.

Worksheet 1-10   Tyler's Personal Problems Profile

1. I have no energy lately. (D)

2. Every move I make takes more effort lately. (D)

3. I've lost my sex drive. (D)

4. I've been eating all the time lately. (D)

5. I don't feel like being with anyone. (D)

6. I don't look forward to much of anything. (D)

7. I find it impossible to make decisions. (D)

8. I worry about my health all the time. (A)

9. I feel shaky all over. (A)

10. Sometimes I can't make myself get out of bed. (D)

Worksheet 1-11   Tyler's Reflections

I can see that I do have signs of depression. I didn't realize that
before. And I see that depression particularly shows up in my body.
It's affecting my energy, sex drive, and appetite. It's also making
me withdraw from my girlfriend, which I can see from my loss of
sex drive and lack of desire to be with her. Apparently, I also have a
few symptoms of anxiety, and I think I always have. It's time to do
something about this.

PRACTICE

Complete your own Personal Problems Profile in Worksheet 1-12. Look back at the quizzes earlier in this chapter and underline the most problematic thoughts, feelings, behaviors, and relationship issues you have. Then choose up to ten of the most significant items you've underlined and write them in the My Personal Problems Profile space that's provided.

In addition, put an *A* by the symptoms that are most indicative of anxiety (even-numbered items in the preceding quizzes) and a *D* by symptoms that are most consistent with depression (odd-numbered items).

Do your symptoms mostly involve anxiety, depression, or a mix of the two? And do they seem to mostly affect your thoughts, feelings, behaviors, or relationships? Take some time to reflect on your profile. What conclusions can you draw? Record them in Worksheet 1-13.

Worksheet 1-12   My Personal Problems Profile

1. _____
2. _____
3. _____
4. _____
5. _____
6. _____
7. _____
8. _____
9. _____
10. _____

Worksheet 1-13   My Reflections

_____
_____
_____
_____
_____

Choosing Your Challenge

The next four parts of this workbook cover the areas of thoughts, feelings, behaviors, and relationships. One obvious way of deciding which area to begin with is to choose the one that causes you the most problems. Or you can work through them in order. Sometimes it makes sense to start with a relatively minor problem and achieve quick success. Wherever you choose to start, you should know that all these areas interact with each other. For example, if you have anxious *thoughts* about being judged, you're likely to avoid *(behavior)* the spotlight. And you could very well experience butterflies *(feelings)*. Furthermore, you may be overly sensitive to criticism from others *(relationships)*.

PRACTICE

Nevertheless, we find that many people like to start out by tackling the problem area that best fits their personal styles. In other words, some folks are doers and others are thinkers; still others are feelers, and some are relaters. Use the Personal Style Questionnaire in Worksheet 1-14 to pinpoint and understand your preferred style.

Are you predominately a thinker, doer, feeler, or relater? If you checked considerably more items in one area than the others, you may want to start your work in the part of this workbook that corresponds to that style:

>> **Thinker:** Part II, "Thinking About Thinking: Thought Therapy"

>> **Doer:** Part III, "Actions Against Angst: Behavior Therapy"

>> **Feeler:** Part IV, "Focus on Physical Feelings"

>> **Relater:** Part V, "Relationship Therapy"

Worksheet 1-14   Personal Style Questionnaire

Thinkers

- ❑ I like facts and numbers.
- ❑ I tend to be a very logical person.
- ❑ I'm a planner.
- ❑ I like to think through problems.
- ❑ I carefully weigh costs and benefits before I act.

Doers

- ❑ I can't stand sitting around and thinking.
- ❑ I like to act on problems.
- ❑ I like accomplishing things each day.
- ❑ I like plowing through obstacles.
- ❑ I act first and think later.

Feelers

- ❑ I'm a very sensuous person.
- ❑ I pay a lot of attention to how I feel.
- ❑ I love massages and hot baths.
- ❑ Music and art are very important to me.
- ❑ I'm very in touch with my feelings.

Relaters

- ❑ I'm a people person.
- ❑ I'd rather be with people than anything else.
- ❑ I care deeply about other people's feelings.
- ❑ I'm very empathetic.
- ❑ Relationships are more important to me than accomplishments.

When and Where to Get More Help

Self-help tools benefit almost everyone who puts in the effort. Many people find they can overcome minor to moderate emotional problems by working with books like this one. Nevertheless, some difficulties require professional help, perhaps because your anxiety or depression is especially serious or because your problems are simply too complex to be addressed by self-help methods.

Work through The Serious Symptom Checklist in Worksheet 1-15 to find out if you should seriously consider seeking treatment from a mental health professional.

PRACTICE

Worksheet 1-15   The Serious Symptom Checklist

- ☐ I have thoughts about killing myself.
- ☐ I feel hopeless.
- ☐ My sleep has been seriously disturbed for more than two weeks (including sleeping too little or too much).
- ☐ I have unbearable pain.
- ☐ I'm a horrible burden to my family.
- ☐ My partner left me for another, and I can't take the humiliation anymore.
- ☐ I feel out-of-control anger toward someone and want to seek violent revenge.
- ☐ My life is worthless, and I have no reason to live.
- ☐ I've gained or lost more than a few pounds without trying to do so.
- ☐ I'm ignoring major responsibilities in my life, such as going to work or paying bills.
- ☐ I'm hearing voices.
- ☐ I'm seeing things that aren't there.
- ☐ My drug use or drinking are interfering with my life.
- ☐ My thoughts race, and I can't slow them down.
- ☐ Someone I trust and care about has said I need help.
- ☐ I've been getting into numerous fights or arguments.
- ☐ I've been making really poor decisions lately (such as making outlandish purchases or getting involved in questionable business schemes).
- ☐ Lately I've felt that people are out to get me.
- ☐ I haven't been able to get myself to leave the house except for absolute essentials.
- ☐ I'm taking risks that I never did before.
- ☐ Suddenly I feel like I'm a special person who's capable of extraordinary things.
- ☐ I'm spending considerably more time every day than I should repeating actions such as hand washing, arranging things, and checking and rechecking things (appliances, locks, and so on).
- ☐ I have highly disturbing flashbacks or nightmares about past trauma that I can't seem to forget about.

WARNING

Checking off any one item from the list means that you should strongly consider a professional consultation. Furthermore, please realize that no such list can be all-inclusive. If you're really not sure if you need help, see a mental health professional for an assessment.

WARNING

If you feel like ending your life, the suicide hotline is a quick and anonymous way to get immediate help. In the United States, the number is 800-273-8255 or 800-273-TALK. Trained counselors will talk to you 24/7. You can call the number even if you feel helpless or hopeless or not suicidal. Staff will offer support and local information. If you prefer, text 741741 and text **hello** or **help**. You will get an immediate response. Launching in July 2022, the suicide hotline can be reached by dialing 988.

If you checked one or more of the statements above and you're not suicidal but are beginning to think that perhaps you need help, where should you go? Many people start with their primary care provider, which is a pretty good idea because your provider can also determine if your problems have a physical cause. If physical problems have been ruled out or treated and you still need help, you can:

>> Ask your primary care provider for a recommendation.

>> Check with your state's psychology, counseling, social work, or psychiatric association.

>> Call your insurance company for recommendations.

>> Ask trusted friends or family for recommendations.

>> Contact your local university department of psychology, social work, counseling, or psychiatry for a referral.

WARNING

Either before or during your first session, talk to the mental health professional and ask if you'll receive a scientifically validated treatment for anxiety or depression, such as Cognitive Behavioral Therapy, Acceptance and Commitment Therapy (ACT), Emotion Focused Therapy, or Interpersonal Therapy. Unfortunately, some practitioners lack necessary training in therapies that have shown effectiveness in scientific studies. Also, make sure whoever you see is a licensed mental health practitioner.

REMEMBER

Understanding and accepting that you need more help is a sign of strength, not weakness. It takes bravery to admit that you might have a problem with your emotions, and it takes courage to seek a resolution.

At this point, you should pat yourself on the back. Whether this is the first chapter you've read or not, you've made a good start. Every minute you spend with this workbook is likely to improve your mood. Just give it a little time.

Chapter 2

Discovering the Beginnings

I f you're reading this book, you probably feel a little anxious or depressed, but you may not know where those feelings come from. It's valuable to understand the origins of your feelings, whether it's biology, genetics, personal history, or stress. This chapter helps you gain insight into the source of your problem and connect the dots. Knowing the origins of your emotions allows you to discard the baggage of guilt and self-blame, and what's not to like about that?

This chapter reviews the major causes of depression and anxiety: biological, genetic, personal history, and stress. Many therapy clients believe that they're to blame for having succumbed to emotional distress. They think that personal weakness is responsible for troubling emotions. However, when they discover the factors that have contributed to the origins of their problems, they usually feel less guilty. Getting rid of that guilt frees up energy that can be used for making important changes.

 Figuring out why you have anxiety or depression may help you stop blaming yourself. However, dwelling in the past doesn't move you forward. Once you understand your history, it's time to look to the future. Gently close the door on your grievances and look to the future to find solutions so you're not stuck in remaining a victim of your past.

REMEMBER

Biological and Genetic Influences

The debate over nature versus nurture is complicated. Are you who you are primarily because of the genetic code you've inherited? Or did you emerge from the many interactions with people and places over the course of your life? Of course, the answer is both. Genes interact with experiences to produce the person you are today.

Nevertheless, genetic makeup does influence certain tendencies. Does your Uncle Paul seem down in the dumps? Was Cousin Jack a neat freak? Was your grandmother a recluse? What was your great-grandmother like? Why are these questions important? Because depression and anxiety tend to run in families. And genes could be responsible for a portion of your emotional distress.

If you have access to family members, ask if they'd be willing to talk with you about your family's history. Ask them if any relatives, from either side of the family, suffered from symptoms of anxiety or depression. You may want to review the symptoms covered in Chapter 1 first. There's no exact number of relatives required for determining if genetics are responsible for your symptoms. However, the more family members sharing similar problems, the more likely you've inherited a tendency for symptoms of depression or anxiety. Fill in the in blanks with notes about what you learn (Worksheet 2-1).

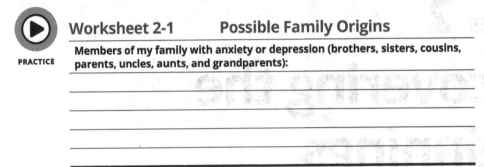

PRACTICE

Worksheet 2-1   Possible Family Origins

Members of my family with anxiety or depression (brothers, sisters, cousins, parents, uncles, aunts, and grandparents):

_____

_____

_____

_____

_____

REMEMBER

Before you go blaming your grandmother for your anxiety, consider the possibility that anxiety was learned and passed on from generation to generation. For example, imagine your great-grandmother grew up in the Great Depression. She always worried about money and food. Her worries were real: She didn't have enough money or food. She repeatedly told your grandmother that the world was unsafe. Your grandmother passed that tendency down to your mother, who also worried all the time. Now you, too, are a worrier. Is that trait genetic or learned? Probably both.

In addition to genetics, depression and anxiety can have biological underpinnings in the drugs you take (legal or illegal) or as the result of physical illness or injury. Drugs, whether over-the-counter, prescription, or illegal, have many side effects. Sometimes solving your problem is as simple as checking your medicine cabinet for possible culprits.

WARNING

Almost any medication you're taking can influence your emotions negatively. Check with your pharmacist or primary care physician to see if your medication may be causing part of your problem. Just don't stop taking the medication without medical consultation.

In addition, alcohol is widely known to contribute to depression or anxiety when it's abused. Some people find that even moderate amounts of alcohol exacerbate their problems with mood. Alcohol also interacts with a variety of prescribed and over-the-counter drugs to produce harmful and even deadly results.

Finally, illegal drugs such as cocaine, heroin, methamphetamine, ecstasy, and so on are sometimes taken to alter moods. In the short run, they accomplish that goal; but in the long run, they almost inevitably worsen mood problems.

Marijuana, legal in many states, has strong psychoactive qualities. Some people use marijuana to alleviate emotional distress and anecdotally report success. A few early studies suggest that for depressed and anxious people, cannabis may improve moods and decrease anxiety. However, empirical research studies have not been widely conducted to verify its usefulness for this purpose.

Physical illnesses or injuries (especially head trauma) can also produce symptoms of anxiety or depression. Not only can the illness itself cause mood problems, but worry and grief about illness or injury can contribute to your distress. If you've been diagnosed with a medical condition, check with your doctor to see if your depression or anxiety is related to that condition. Jot down any possible physical reasons for your anxiety or depression in Worksheet 2-2.

Worksheet 2-2   Physical Possibilities

_____
_____
_____
_____
_____
_____

Plotting Out a Lifeline

The sadness and angst you feel today may have sprouted from seeds planted in your past. Therefore, exploring your personal history provides clues about the possible origins of your problems. The exercise in this section, called the Emotional Origins form, takes a little time.

The Emotional Origins exercise makes you revisit your childhood by asking questions about your parents or other caregivers and your childhood experiences. Some of the memories involved may evoke powerful emotions; if you start to feel overwhelmed, you may want to stop the exercise and consult a mental health professional for guidance and support.

Filling out this form is a lot easier after you look over an example. Here's an example of how Tyler filled out his Emotional Origins form.

EXAMPLE

Tyler suffers from many physical signs of depression, such as lack of energy and increased appetite. He has little insight as to the origins of his depression. His physician refers him to a social worker, who suggests he fill out an Emotional Origins form (see Worksheet 2-3) to examine his childhood experiences.

Worksheet 2-3   Tyler's Emotional Origins

Questions About Your Caregivers

1. Who were the primary caregivers in my childhood, and what were they like? Describe their personalities.

My mother was self-centered and rarely thought much about what my sister and I needed. When things didn't go her way, she exploded. She was domineering and incredibly uptight. She was a perfectionist who talked about the "right way" or the "wrong way" to do things. I also remember that she always acted like a martyr.

(continued)

Everyone liked my dad because he was funny and friendly. But I don't really remember him joking that much with me. He mainly criticized me because I was clumsy and didn't like to go hunting with him.

My parents divorced when I was 11 years old. When I was in high school, my mother had a boyfriend who lived with us. He was nice, but we really didn't hit it off. I think I was sort of jealous of the attention my mother gave him.

2. How was love and affection expressed by each caregiver?

Neither of my parents ever said, "I love you," and I can't remember getting hugs from them. I always saw other families hug each other, and that made me feel awkward. As an adult, I still feel weird in social situations when people greet each other with hugs. My mother would tell other people how much she loved her kids, but it seemed like she was talking about some other kids, not my sister and me. She wanted everyone to think that she was the perfect mother, wife, and homemaker. It was all about her.

Like I said before, my father was friendlier to other people than to me. He seemed to care about himself more than his family. I never said "I love you" to either of my parents. Now they've both passed away, and I feel guilty that I never said those words to them. I do realize why it was so hard for me to tell them when they never told me either.

3. How was conflict expressed and resolved?

My parents fought a lot. We could hear them at night — my sister and I would be scared. They used horrible words that we'd never hear them say to us or anyone else. When they were in public, though, it was as if everything was perfect. My father just stayed away from the house. He said he was working, but now I know he was cheating on my mother. They divorced when I was in 6th grade.

There were never any arguments between my parents and me. I just shut up and let them talk. We didn't talk about politics or current events. It wasn't until I was in college that I realized how little I knew about the world.

4. What did I get in trouble for?

I was quiet and mostly stayed out of trouble. A few times I remember my mother screaming at me about something small, like when I forgot to pick up a wet towel in the bathroom. My father would make fun of my clumsiness. He'd blow up and call me stupid when I couldn't do a household project. I still get nervous when I try to fix something at home.

As long as I wasn't getting bad grades or getting caught doing something I shouldn't, no one at home seemed to notice me. My best friend and I started stealing alcohol from the liquor cabinet when I was in high school. My mom and her boyfriend never asked me about it. As soon as I went away to college, I was completely on my own.

5. How was I disciplined?

Other than occasionally getting screamed at, I don't think there was much discipline. Like I said, I was a pretty quiet kid who didn't make waves.

6. Were my caregivers critical or supportive?

I was really a good student, but I don't remember my parents being very supportive of that. Other than getting yelled at by my dad for not being good at fixing stuff, it's like I didn't exist.

7. Does anything else important about my caregivers come to mind, whether positive or negative?

My mother never seemed happy or satisfied. She never got over her divorce and complained about her cheating husband until the day she died. My father married a woman who was only a few years older than I am. I rarely saw him or his new wife after that. Looking back, my whole family was kind of sad.

Questions About Your Household

1. What were my earliest memories?

I don't remember much from when I was a little kid. My grandfather used to take us horseback riding. That was fun. I remember my father and my grandparents having a big fight over money. That was scary.

2. What were my best memories of childhood?

Riding my bike with my friend during summer vacation. We used to pack a lunch and take off in the morning and explore the neighborhood. We'd stop at a drug store and pick up sodas and sit in some park to eat. I don't really remember what we talked about, but it was great to feel free and independent.

3. What were my worst memories of childhood?

Definitely listening to my parents fighting. I felt so afraid and helpless. My parents also had fights with my grandparents. I realize now that my grandparents financed a part of my parents' lifestyle. When my grandparents didn't approve of some purchase, there were huge arguments. My sister and I were told to disappear, but we always stayed close by.

4. What adults spent time with me, and what did we do?

I grew up in a household where children were to be seen but not heard. I know that sounds like a cliché, but it's the truth. Everything revolved around my parents. We did take a vacation for two weeks every summer to the same cabin on a lake. Often my mother would be there during the week, and my dad would come out on the weekends. My parents had friends who rented cabins close by. So basically, all the kids would hang out together, and the parents would sit around talking or playing cards. I can't recall doing anything with an adult for fun. Oh, except for the two times my dad took me hunting and I was scared to death. I couldn't shoot straight and hated the thought of killing animals, so he never took me again.

5. Were there others in the household (siblings, relatives, or others) who influenced me?

I looked up to my older sister, but she didn't want anything to do with me after she went to junior high school. I think my parents favored her — at least my dad did. I never felt like I measured up to her. Over the years, my sister and I didn't have much of a relationship. We saw each other when my parents died. I went to her kids' weddings, but we didn't really connect.

My mom's boyfriend never paid attention to me at all. They broke up when I was in college, and I haven't heard from him since. He didn't influence me at all.

6. Were there special circumstances (for example, illness, trauma, death, divorce, military service, etc.)?

Nothing really. To the outside world, we seemed like a pretty typical family with no particular problems until the divorce. My mother talked constantly about how awful my father was. When I was in college, she'd call me to tell me how lonely she was and how she couldn't stand being alive. That was a horrible, frightening burden on me. I was terrified she was going to kill herself.

(continued)

Worksheet 2-3 *(continued)*

7. Does anything else important come to mind, whether positive or negative?

I don't think I knew how to be a good father or husband in part because I had no role model for what that looked like. During my marriage, I worked long hours, and after the first couple of years I didn't really pay attention to my wife or the kids. It took me years to understand why my wife divorced me.

Questions About School and the Neighborhood

1. Where did I live, and what was my house like? Did I have my own room? What were the conditions like?

I grew up in a small suburban house. I had my own room, but there was only one bathroom. It seemed fine at the time. When I was about 9, we moved to a bigger house, and I realized how small the first house was. Looking back, I think my grandparents helped my parents buy the new house. There was a lot more fighting after we moved, and a lot of times, I heard my mother yelling about my father needing to pay my grandparents back.

2. What was my neighborhood like? Was it safe? Were there places I could go outside and play? Were there things to do close by?

It was ordinary, but I now realize it was also completely composed of white families. I had no idea what diversity was about. I never heard about crime and didn't know what to think about occasional racist comments I'd hear from others. There was a small shopping center within walking distance, and the school had an open playground we could use any time on the weekends.

3. Did I participate in any extracurricular activities, such as sports or clubs? Was that a positive experience?

I started in boy scouts when I was little and got all the way through to Eagle Scout. I was proud of that. My mother came to the ceremony, but my dad didn't. He said he had to work. I was a long-distance runner in high school. I couldn't play basketball or baseball because I was so clumsy.

4. What do I remember about grade school? (Was I happy; what did I think about myself; how did I do in school; what were my friendships like; were there any important events?)

I remember being really shy. I had a few good friends, but they were sort of nerds like me. I was a good student.

5. What do I remember about middle school or junior high school? (Was I happy; what did I think about myself; how did I do in school; what were my friendships like; were there any important events?)

I was even shyer then. I felt clumsy and awkward all the time. I was also taller than all my friends by the seventh grade. I didn't get invited to parties much. I wasn't very happy. If I got upset, my mother sometimes would do some of my homework for me. Then she'd make me feel guilty about it.

6. What do I remember about high school? (Was I happy; what did I think about myself; how did I do in school; what were my friendships like; were there any important events?)

I had a few more friends then and started dating some. I got pretty down when a girl jilted me. I remember staying in my room for hours at a time. I realize now that I didn't know how to handle my emotions very well — when I didn't know what else to do, I'd just withdraw. I worked just hard enough to get Bs, but I know I could have done much better in school.

7. What did I do after high school?

I went to college because all my friends planned to do the same. It wasn't something my parents cared about, but I always assumed it was something I should do. I didn't have any particular goals or interests at first. I got good grades in chemistry, and that is what started my interest in chemical engineering.

8. **Were there any historical or cultural events during my childhood that had an impact on my development?**

I remained on the sidelines about politics at first when I went to college, but I had strong feelings about the issues. I was too shy to assert my thoughts for quite a while. During my college years I learned quite a bit about the world that my limited experiences as a kid in the suburbs did not prepare me for.

9. **What are the major events of my adulthood, such as trauma or winning the lottery?**

I graduated from college, got married, and had a couple of kids. My divorce after 14 years of marriage came as a shock, but I got through it okay.

10. **What did this exercise teach me about the origins of my anxiety or depression?**

When I think back on my childhood, I realize it wasn't very happy. My dad didn't seem to care much about me. My mother cared more, but she was like an emotional roller coaster. I just shut down, and I think I've had that tendency my whole life. Maybe I'm shutting down now, too; it's what I do when I'm unhappy. I guess I realize that I'm not totally to blame for my problems. It sort of makes sense that I shut down whenever I face possible rejection or criticism or when someone gets angry with me.

After completing the Emotional Origins form, Tyler has a better understanding of why he copes with stress the way he does. He sees that there's a reason he shuts down when facing certain types of situations. The exercise isn't about blame and faultfinding; rather, it helps Tyler forgive himself for being the way he is. These insights start him on the path toward a new beginning.

PRACTICE

Complete your Emotional Origins form in Worksheet 2-4. This is an important exercise, so take as much time as you need. If you happen to be receiving counseling or psychotherapy, your therapist will no doubt find this information useful and informative.

Start by reflecting on your childhood. You may jump-start your memory by talking with relatives or by looking through old photo albums. Then move on to answer the questions about your parents or caregivers as well as the questions about your childhood and adolescence. Don't worry about getting all the details right — just do the best you can. Memories aren't always completely accurate, but in a powerful way, they affect the way you feel today.

REMEMBER

Please realize that the intent of this exercise is not to place blame on your parents or other important people in your life. These people indeed may have made significant contributions to your problems, and that's useful to know. But they came by their own problems as honestly as you did. Understanding helps; blame and faultfinding do not.

Worksheet 2-4   My Emotional Origins

Questions About Your Caregivers

1. **Who were the primary caregivers in my childhood, and what were they like? Describe their personalities.**

_____

_____

_____

(continued)

Worksheet 2-4 *(continued)*

_____

_____

_____

_____

2. **How was love and affection expressed by each caregiver?**

_____

_____

_____

3. **How was conflict expressed and resolved?**

_____

_____

_____

4. **What did I get in trouble for?**

_____

_____

_____

5. **How was I disciplined?**

_____

_____

_____

6. **Were my caregivers critical or supportive?**

_____

_____

_____

7. **Does anything else important about my caregivers come to mind, whether positive or negative?**

_____

_____

_____

_____

1. What were my earliest memories?

_____

_____

_____

_____

2. What were my best memories of childhood?

_____

_____

_____

_____

3. What were my worst memories of childhood?

_____

_____

_____

_____

4. What adults spent time with me, and what did we do?

_____

_____

_____

_____

5. Were there others in the household (siblings, relatives, or others) who influenced me?

_____

_____

_____

_____

6. Were there special circumstances (for example, illness, death, trauma, divorce, military service, etc.)?

_____

_____

_____

_____

7. Does anything else important come to mind, whether positive or negative?

_____

_____

_____

_____

(continued)

Worksheet 2-4 *(continued)*

1. Where did I live, and what was my home like? Did I have my own room? What were the conditions like?

_____

_____

_____

_____

2. What was my neighborhood like? Was it safe? Were there places I could go outside and play? Were there things close by to do?

_____

_____

_____

_____

3. Did I participate in any extracurricular activities, such as sports or clubs? Was that a positive experience?

_____

_____

_____

_____

4. What do I remember about grade school? (Was I happy; what did I think about myself; how did I do in school; what were my friendships like; were there any important events?)

_____

_____

_____

_____

5. What do I remember about middle school or junior high school? (Was I happy; what did I think about myself; how did I do in school; what were my friendships like; were there any important events?)

_____

_____

_____

_____

6. What do I remember about high school? (Was I happy; what did I think about myself; how did I do in school; what were my friendships like; were there any important events?)

_____

_____

_____

_____

7. What did I do after high school?

_____

_____

_____

_____

8. Where there any historical or cultural events during my childhood that had an impact on my development?

_____

_____

_____

_____

9. What are the major events of my adulthood, such as trauma or winning the lottery?

_____

_____

_____

_____

10. What did this exercise teach me about the origins of my anxiety or depression?

_____

_____

_____

_____

Surveying Current Stress

PRACTICE

In the search for causes of your anxiety or depression, you need to include a review of your world. Open your eyes and observe. What's going on in your life that aggravates your distress? From daily traffic hassles to major losses, stressful events deplete your coping resources and even harm your health. Complete The Current Culprits Survey in Worksheet 2-5 to uncover the sources of your stress. You can't make your world less stressful unless you first identify the stress-causing culprits.

You may notice that a few of these items have positive aspects to them. For example, retirement or the purchase of a new home may be exciting. However, all major changes, whether positive or negative, carry significant stress that tags along for the ride.

Worksheet 2-5   The Current Culprits Survey

1. In the past year or so, have I lost anyone I care about through death, divorce, or prolonged separation?

_____

_____

_____

_____

2. Have I suffered from any serious physical injury or illness?

_____

_____

_____

_____

3. Have finances caused me any difficulty recently? Or have I made any major purchases such as a new house or car?

_____

_____

_____

_____

4. Am I having arguments or conflicts with anyone?

_____

_____

_____

_____

5. Are there problems at work, such as new responsibilities, longer hours, or poor management?

_____

_____

_____

_____

6. Have I made any major changes in my life, such as retirement, a new job, or a new relationship?

_____

_____

_____

_____

7. Do I have major responsibility for the care of a parent or child?

_____

_____

_____

_____

8. Do I have daily hassles, such as a long commute, disturbing noises, or poor living conditions?

_____

_____

_____

_____

9. Do I suffer from discrimination based on race, ethnicity, religion, appearance, or sexual identity?

_____

_____

_____

_____

10. What are my coping skills for dealing with disasters, such as the isolation of the COVID pandemic, floods, hurricanes, and fires?

_____

_____

_____

_____

Drawing Conclusions

PRACTICE

You didn't ask for depression or anxiety. Your distress is understandable if you examine the three major contributors: biology/genetics, your personal history, and the stressors in your world. Take a moment to summarize in Worksheet 2-6 what you believe are the most important origins and contributors to your symptoms of depression or anxiety.

REMEMBER

As you review your summary, realize that countless circumstances have influenced you throughout your life. Anxiety and depression can result from several factors; some happen during childhood, arise from your biological history, or are a result of current stressors. Many causes of emotional difficulties are completely out of your control.

You shouldn't feel guilty or ashamed for having acquired your emotional burdens. At the same time, you're responsible for doing something about your distress. Although no one can do the work for you, you can get yourself moving toward a better tomorrow by working through these exercises with or without professional help. Just remember that working on decreasing your emotional distress rewards you with lifelong benefits. Be patient and keep at it. The effort is worth it.

Worksheet 2-6　　　My Most Important Contributors

1. Physical contributors (genetics, drugs, illness, injury):

_____

_____

_____

_____

2. My personal history:

_____

_____

_____

_____

3. The current stressors in my world:

_____

_____

_____

_____

Chapter **3**

Overcoming Obstacles to Change

You don't *want* to feel depressed or anxious. No one does. Yet, at times it probably seems as if you have no choice but to feel that way. You want to do something about your distress, but you may feel overwhelmed and incapable. The truth is, you *can* do something about your predicament. But first, you have to understand and overcome the obstacles in your mind that prevent you from acting and moving forward. Realize that these obstacles may feel larger than they are and may seem impossible to overcome. Just know that you can make changes gradually, as you're able. Take your time.

This chapter helps you uncover assumptions or beliefs you may have that make it hard to tackle your problems. After you identify the beliefs that stand in your way, you can use a tool to remove these obstacles from your path. You also find out whether you're unconsciously sabotaging your own progress. If you discover that you're getting in your own way, you can rewrite your self-defeating scripts. Understand that everyone has these scripts. You're not unique in struggling with them.

Change-Blocking Beliefs

People hold many beliefs or assumptions about change, but a few beliefs are especially unhelpful. For example, some believe that change is frightening. Others think they don't deserve to be happy and therefore don't attempt to change their lives to improve their situations. By stealing your motivation to change, assumptions such as these can keep you stuck in a depressed or anxious state. Most people aren't aware of when and how these underlying assumptions derail sincere efforts for making changes.

The quizzes in this section are designed to help you discover whether any change-blocking beliefs create obstacles on your road to renewal. After the quizzes, you can find an exercise that assists you in ridding yourself of these beliefs through careful, honest analysis of whether each belief helps or hurts you.

Detecting beliefs standing in your way

People resist change because they're afraid, feel they don't deserve something better, or view themselves as helpless to do anything about their circumstances. Unknowingly holding any of these beliefs will inevitably impede your progress toward change. So, take the following three quizzes to see which, if any, of these barriers exist in your mind. Put a check mark next to each statement in Worksheets 3-1, 3-2, and 3-3 that applies to you.

PRACTICE

Worksheet 3-1   The Fear of Change Quiz

☐   1.   If I take a risk, I'm likely to fail.

☐   2.   If I reach out to others, they'll reject me.

☐   3.   Whenever I try something new, I manage to screw it up.

☐   4.   Every time I get my hopes up, I'm disappointed.

☐   5.   If I work on my problems, I'll fail.

☐   6.   I'd rather not try than fail.

☐   7.   I can't see myself as a success.

☐   8.   I'm too anxious and depressed to succeed.

PRACTICE

Worksheet 3-2   The Underlying Undeserving Belief Quiz

☐   1.   I don't deserve to be happy.

☐   2.   I don't expect much out of my life.

☐   3.   I feel less worthy than other people.

☐   4.   I feel guilty asking anyone for help, so I'd rather not ask.

☐   5.   There's something fundamentally wrong with me; that's why I'm distressed.

☐   6.   I don't feel I'm as good as other people.

☐   7.   I'm uncomfortable when people are nice to me.

☐   8.   I feel like other people deserve a lot more than I do.

Worksheet 3-3   The Unfair, Unjust Belief Quiz

PRACTICE

- ☐ 1. It's easy for me to dwell on how unfair life has been to me.

- ☐ 2. I feel helpless in dealing with my plight.

- ☐ 3. I can't stop thinking about how I've been mistreated.

- ☐ 4. I feel angry about all the bad things that have happened to me.

- ☐ 5. Other people don't understand how difficult my life has been.

- ☐ 6. Anyone with my life couldn't help but complain.

- ☐ 7. Hardly anyone could appreciate how much I've suffered.

- ☐ 8. Doing something about my problems would somehow discount the importance of the trauma that has happened in my life.

Now that you've taken the quizzes, you can probably see if any of these beliefs dwell in your mind.

> » If you checked two or more items in The Fear of Change Quiz, you probably get scared at the thought of changing.

> » If you checked two or more items from The Underlying Undeserving Belief Quiz, you may feel that you don't deserve the good things that could come to you if you were to change.

> » If you checked two or more items from The Unfair, Unjust Belief Quiz, you may dwell so much on how you're suffering that you have trouble marshalling the resources for making changes.

> » If, by chance, you checked two or more items in two or more quizzes, well, you have a little work cut out for you.

REMEMBER

It's not your fault if you hold any of these change-blocking beliefs. People pick up on these ideas as children or through traumatic events at any time in their lives. And some change-blocking beliefs have a touch of truth to them, such as these:

> » Life is often unfair.

> » It's reasonable sometimes to feel angry.

> » You can't always succeed.

However, people deserve to feel happy, including you. You can succeed in the things you do, and you can move past the bad things that have happened to you. Even if you've experienced horrific trauma, moving on doesn't diminish the significance of what you've experienced. Getting better simply makes you more powerful and allows you to live again.

EXAMPLE

Jasmine, a mother of two, worries all the time. Her drug-abusing parents neglected her as a child. Now she tends to be overly protective of her own children. Lately, she's been sleeping poorly; her youngest child has asthma, and Jasmine finds herself listening to her child's breathing throughout the night. She panics when her older child is late from school. Jasmine's doctor is concerned about her rising blood pressure, so Jasmine decides to work on her anxiety and stress. She takes the three change-blocking beliefs quizzes (presented earlier in this section) and discovers a variety of change-blocking beliefs, although the fear and undeserving beliefs predominate. She then fills in her Top Three Change-Blocking Beliefs Summary, which you can see in Worksheet 3-4.

Worksheet 3-4   Jasmine's Top Three Change-Blocking Beliefs Summary

1. Whenever I try something new, I manage to screw it up.

2. Every time I get my hopes up, I'm disappointed.

3. I feel guilty asking anyone for help, so I'd rather not.

Next, Jasmine jots down her reflections on both this exercise and the change-blocking beliefs she's identified in the summary (see Worksheet 3-5).

Worksheet 3-5   Jasmine's Reflections

I can see that I do have some of these change-blocking beliefs. I guess I've always thought that this is just the way my life is. But now that I reflect on it, I can see how these beliefs could get in the way of doing something about my problems. Nothing is going to change if I hold on tightly to these assumptions. But what can I do about them?

In the next section, Jasmine sees what she can do about her problematic beliefs. But before jumping to her resolution, try filling out My Top Three Change-Blocking Beliefs Summary in Worksheet 3-6. Go back to the three change-blocking belief quizzes and look at the items you checked. Then write down the three beliefs that seem to be the most troubling and the most likely to get in the way of your ability to make changes.

PRACTICE

Worksheet 3-6   My Top Three Change-Blocking Beliefs Summary

1.

2.

3.

In Worksheet 3-7, jot down your reflections about these beliefs. What have you learned? Do you think these beliefs are helping you or getting in your way? Write down anything that comes to mind.

Worksheet 3-7   My Reflections

Blasting through beliefs blocking your path

After completing the exercises in the last section, you should have an idea of which change-blocking beliefs may be holding up your progress. If you've tried to make changes in the past and failed, it's likely that one or more of these beliefs are responsible. *Unfortunately*, ridding yourself of such problematic beliefs isn't as easy as sweeping them out the door; it's more than a matter of knowing what they are and declaring that you no longer believe in them. *Fortunately*, there are some tools to help you revise your way of thinking.

Changing beliefs requires that you appreciate and understand the extent to which your assumptions cause trouble for you. If you've only just now discovered what your beliefs are, you can't fully understand their pros and cons. Analyzing advantages and disadvantages can help with that.

EXAMPLE

Jasmine fills out an Analyzing Advantages and Disadvantages Form (see Worksheet 3-8) so she can more fully comprehend how her change-blocking beliefs affect her. She starts by writing down the reasons her change-blocking beliefs feel good and advantageous to her. Then she writes about how each belief gives her problems — in other words, how it stands in her way. Finally, she reviews both lists carefully and writes down her conclusions. She fills out this form for each belief in her Top Three Change-Blocking Beliefs Summary. (This example only includes analysis of two of Jasmine's beliefs.)

Worksheet 3-8   Jasmine's Analyzing Advantages and Disadvantages Form

Change-Blocking Belief #1: Whenever I try something new, I manage to screw it up.	
Advantages of This Belief	Disadvantages of This Belief
If I don't try, I don't have to risk failing.	Of course, this means I can never succeed either.
I don't have to go through the effort. Change is a lot of work.	This belief keeps me feeling miserable.
I don't know why, but change is scary, and this belief keeps me from dealing with that fear.	I miss out on opportunities by clinging to this belief.
	It's possible that even if I do fail, I could end up learning something useful for my life.
	This view simply keeps me stuck.

Change-Blocking Belief #2: I feel guilty asking anyone for help, so I'd rather not.	
Advantages of This Belief	Disadvantages of This Belief
I don't expect anyone to help me, so I don't end up disappointed.	I don't get the chance to share my worries with anyone.

(continued)

Worksheet 3-8 (continued)

Change-Blocking Belief #1: Whenever I try something new, I manage to screw it up.	
Advantages of This Belief	Disadvantages of This Belief
People don't have to worry about me leaning on them.	I don't get as close to people as I could.
I don't worry anyone because they never know when I'm upset.	When I'm really upset, I get quiet, and people sometimes think I'm angry when I'm not.
	Sometimes, everyone needs a little help from others, and I'm at a disadvantage when I don't seek it.

After completing her Analyzing Advantages and Disadvantages Form, Jasmine takes some time to reflect. She considers whether the advantages she listed are truly advantages and concludes that her original change-blocking beliefs are causing her more harm than good. She then writes down her reflections in Worksheet 3-9.

Worksheet 3-9   Jasmine's Reflections

EXAMPLE

I realize that when I don't try, I still end up failing, so not trying isn't really an advantage. And even though change may be a lot of work and seem overwhelming, I'm utterly miserable. When I think about it, I get satisfaction from helping others. So logically, they wouldn't mind helping me from time to time. I could use some help, and it might feel really nice to get close to people. On balance, these change-blocking beliefs are keeping me stuck.

Clearly, Jasmine can see that her assumptions about change are causing her to remain in limbo. Now that she's completed the exercises and disputed those assumptions, she can start moving forward. Because she's aware of these beliefs, she can be on the lookout for them to pop up again and remind herself of their considerable disadvantages.

Now it's your turn.

PRACTICE

1. In Worksheet 3-10, write down each of your change-blocking beliefs (see Work-sheet 3-6).

2. Jot down all the reasons that each belief feels right, true, and useful to you.

3. For each belief, write down the other side of the argument; in other words, make a list of all the ways in which your belief may actually be causing you harm.

Worksheet 3-10　My Analyzing Advantages and Disadvantages Form

Change-Blocking Belief #1:	
Advantages of This Belief	Disadvantages of This Belief

Change-Blocking Belief #2:	
Advantages of This Belief	Disadvantages of This Belief

Change-Blocking Belief #3:	
Advantages of This Belief	Disadvantages of This Belief

Now read over the advantages and disadvantages you've listed for each change-blocking belief. Reflect on the advantages, and you're likely to see that they actually aren't all that advantageous. Weigh the pros and the cons of holding onto your beliefs, and write all your reflections in Worksheet 3-11.

Worksheet 3-11　My Reflections

If you get stuck on any of these exercises, or if you see more advantages than disadvantages to your change-blocking beliefs, consider talking with your therapist or a close friend for further help and advice.

Searching for Self-Sabotage

Overcoming anxiety or depression is tough, and sometimes even frightening. (Even positive change evokes fear in most people!) As a result, people tend to resist, avoid, or procrastinate working on their problems. This means you have to be on the lookout for *self-sabotage*.

Self-sabotage describes the things you do to keep from addressing and correcting your problems, and it appears in various forms and disguises.

Some people self-sabotage by telling themselves that change is impossible. Others defeat themselves by finding reasons to put off working on their issues. What are your reasons for avoiding change?

Complete the checklist in Worksheet 3-12 to see if you're falling into the self-sabotage trap. Check off any statements you hear running through your mind.

PRACTICE

Worksheet 3-12   The Hindering Change Checklist

❑   1.   My situation is hopeless.

❑   2.   I'll never be okay because of my past.

❑   3.   I want to wait to make changes until just the right time, but that time never comes.

❑   4.   I want a guarantee that I'll get better before I'm willing to risk change.

❑   5.   I use a lot of excuses for not dealing with my problems.

❑   6.   It's hard for me to stick with something if it doesn't help right away.

❑   7.   Sometimes I get confused or feel out of it when I try to tackle my issues.

❑   8.   If I don't succeed 100%, I get very critical of myself.

❑   9.   If I do something well, it's hard for me to give myself credit for it.

❑   10.   I want fast results, or I just can't get motivated to try.

❑   11.   I dwell so much on my past failures that it's hard to try something new.

❑   12.   My depression or anxiety is biological, so I can't do anything about it.

It isn't hard to see how thoughts like these could bog you down and prevent active efforts to change. Yet almost everyone engages in at least a little self-sabotage, whether consciously or not.

WARNING

Don't make your problems worse by beating yourself up when you see that you're self-sabotaging. Self-criticism merely piles on more self-sabotage. Instead, monitor your self-sabotaging thoughts. When you feel them getting in your way, fight back and argue against them using the Self-Sabotage Diary presented in the next section.

Stopping self-sabotage

Throughout this book, I suggest you write out your thoughts, feelings, beliefs, and life events. That's because writing is an invaluable tool for battling problematic emotions, sorting out issues, achieving important insight, and solving problems. In this section, I invite you to track and record your inevitable acts and thoughts of self-sabotage in a diary. But first, see how Molly fills out her Self-Sabotage Diary.

EXAMPLE

Molly is a successful IT manager. Her colleagues are unaware that she suffers from anxiety and depression. She worries that others will discover that she doesn't deserve her success. She realizes that, for the past decade, she has neglected friends and family in pursuit of her career. Now she feels lonely and despondent; success hasn't brought her the happiness she expected, and her anxiety and depression have only increased. Molly sees a psychologist, and together they identify her self-sabotaging ways. She keeps a diary in which she records her acts of self-sabotage and responses to them. Worksheet 3-13 contains five days' worth of Molly's diary.

Worksheet 3-13   Molly's Self-Sabotage Diary

Day	Self-Sabotage	Response to Self-Sabotage
Sunday	It was raining today, so I didn't feel like going to the gym like my psychologist suggested.	Obviously, that's not a helpful thing to do. I'm using an excuse. Everyone does that sometimes, but I want to try to push through excuses the next time.
Monday	I scraped my car on a pole in the parking lot. I was so upset — it ruined my day. I hate myself when I mess up.	I guess dumping on myself isn't particularly useful. I need to accept my flaws and imperfections if I'm going to get somewhere in life.
Tuesday	I was supposed to complete an exercise for my therapist, but I got too busy.	Wow, I guess that's just another excuse. The exercise only takes ten minutes. I'll be on the lookout for that excuse the next time.
Wednesday	One of my clients complimented me on my work, and I couldn't accept the compliment. I gave credit to someone else.	That didn't help me. I tend to discount positive things that happen to me. No wonder my self-esteem suffers sometimes.
Thursday	My assignment today was to ask a friend out for coffee. When I started thinking about calling, I felt confused and disoriented, so I didn't do it.	When I try to do something difficult, I become so anxious I can't think clearly. I need to slow down, give it some time, and relax — then go back to it.

Now it's time for you to make a Self-Sabotage Diary. Remember to take your time.

PRACTICE

1. **In the middle column of Worksheet 3-14, write down any thought or action from that day that you feel limits your efforts at overcoming your anxiety or depression.** If you get stuck, review Worksheet 3-12, The Hindering Change Checklist, for examples.

2. **In the right column, write down how helpful (if at all) you think the self- sabotage may have been as well as any arguments you can find against it.**

3. **Maintain this diary for at least a week; keep it up much longer if you continue to see lots of self-sabotage.**

Worksheet 3-14   My Self-Sabotage Diary

Day	Self-Sabotage	Response to Self-Sabotage
Sunday		
Monday		
Tuesday		
Wednesday		
Thursday		
Friday		
Saturday		

Criticizing yourself for the sabotage you notice yourself committing only leads to more sabotage. Stop the cycle!

WARNING

You can download extra copies of this form at www.dummies.com/go/anxiety&depressionwork bookfd2e.

Rewriting your self-sabotaging scripts

Your mind creates stories — about yourself, your life, and your world. If you feel stuck, your stories are probably cloaked in themes of failure. You may have a long-running play in your mind that has you as its central character. That character has a series of mishaps, failures, and missed opportunities. If this sounds familiar, it's time to rewrite the script. Try creating a new story about you and your life that allows you to succeed. But remember, in addition to success, the new story needs to contain realistic struggle and difficulty. After all, life isn't a fairy tale.

To the outside world, **Molly** is successful. On the inside, she feels like a fraud. Worksheet 3-15 illustrates her personal story.

EXAMPLE

Molly struggles to rewrite her script. When she finishes, she reads her new story every day for a month. Although it takes her a while to start believing it, gradually she begins to see her life in a new light. Worksheet 3-16 contains her revised story.

Worksheet 3-15   Molly's Current Life-Script

I might have money and a little prestige, but I deserve none of it. I don't believe I'm as talented as I should be for the position I have. No one likes me because I'm irritable. I have no friends or close family. I'm different from other people. I'll never really fit in. I'm going to die lonely and forgotten.
My life means nothing.

Worksheet 3-16   Molly's New Life-Script

I have a good job, and I worked hard to get it. I don't need to discount my accomplishments. Yes, I do get irritable sometimes, but who doesn't? Besides, I'm capable of learning new behaviors, and I'm working on my irritability. I don't have many friends because I'm a workaholic. This will be a struggle for me, but I see myself cutting back a little on my work and making new friends. I'm going to put more meaning in my life. For starters, I plan to do some volunteer work.

Now it's your turn. Follow these instructions:

PRACTICE

1. **In Worksheet 3-17, write your current life-script, including how you see yourself today and in the future. How do you view your accomplishments, relationships, and failures?**

2. **In Worksheet 3-18, write a new life-script. Be sure to include your thoughts on hope, change, possibilities, and struggle.**

3. **Read your new life-script daily for a month. Feel free to make changes to it as you see fit.**

Worksheet 3-17   My Current Life-Script

_____
_____
_____
_____

Worksheet 3-18   My New Life-Script

_____
_____
_____
_____

Chapter **4**

Minding Your Moods

Autopilot is not the right setting to overcome your symptoms of anxiety or depression. You have to do some of the driving yourself. Learning to feel better starts with self-observation. This chapter provides instructions for observing the relationships among your feelings, thoughts, and the happenings in your life.

Begin by monitoring your body's response to events. This information helps you become more aware of the physical components of depression and anxiety. Next, keep track of your feelings. Some people aren't very good at identifying their feelings, so this chapter gives you a comprehensive list of feeling words. Then observe how events, feelings, and bodily sensations go hand in hand. Finally, you find yourself becoming more aware of how thoughts link up with feelings, events, and bodily sensations. The road to feeling better starts with understanding these connections.

Deciphering Body Signals

Your heart may race or your hands may sweat when you feel anxious. Changes in appetite and sleep may accompany feelings of sadness and depression. These physical reactions signal that something important is going on internally. Monitoring your bodily sensations gives you an early warning that a storm of emotional distress is brewing.

Tyler is surprised when his doctor diagnoses him with depression. He hasn't handled working from home during the pandemic very well. He finds it hard to finish his work, feels isolated, and has trouble staying focused. His friends say he's out of touch with his feelings. Tyler begins to understand his body's signals by monitoring physical sensations on a daily basis. He fills out the Body Responses Tracking Sheet shown in Worksheet 4-1. He jots down any time that he feels something uncomfortable in his body and includes information about what was going on at the time.

EXAMPLE

Worksheet 4-1   Tyler's Body Responses Tracking Sheet

Body Response	How did my body feel?	When did this happen? What was I doing?
Muscle tightness	I felt pain in my shoulders and back.	Monday morning. I was going over the new project with my boss.
Breathing/Increased heart rate	I could tell my breathing was rapid and shallow.	Tuesday evening while talking with my ex-wife.
GI symptoms such as upset stomach, constipation, or diarrhea	None	
Teeth grinding	My jaws hurt, and I kept biting my cheek when I slept.	My dentist fit me with a night guard. He said he's seen lots of people need them during the pandemic.
Feeling constriction in the throat or chest	Oh, yes. Whenever I feel like someone is judging me.	Pretty much every day at work or with my ex-wife.
Fatigue	My body feels heavy. It feels like I'm walking through mud.	Lately, I've felt this way every day.
Problems going to sleep, staying asleep, waking early, or sleeping too much	I wake up early and can't get back to sleep.	Most days, especially when I'm worried about something.
Feeling hot and flushed or cold and shaky	None	
Headaches	None this week.	
Posture	I noticed I'm walking around stooped over. And I've been slumped at my desk.	I notice this mostly after sitting for long periods of time at my desk.

Body Response	How did my body feel?	When did this happen? What was I doing?
Dizziness, spaciness, disorientation, and trouble concentrating	Spacey and light-headed.	Saturday morning before paying bills. Almost every day trying to stay focused on work.
Changes in appetite or weight unrelated to dieting	I'm not enjoying my favorite foods like I used to.	Went out to eat with a friend for the first time in a year and didn't even finish my fries!

After filling out his Body Responses Tracking Sheet, Tyler takes some time to reflect on the exercise (see Worksheet 4-2).

Worksheet 4-2   Tyler's Reflections

I noticed that my body seems to react to what's going on in my life. I really wasn't aware of that before. These sensations aren't very pleasant, and maybe the doc is right that I'm depressed. I realize that talking with my ex-wife and my boss make me feel pretty weird and stressed. I also think I'm worried about finances, although I haven't wanted to admit it. And, like many people, this crazy pandemic has made everything in my life worse. Now that I know all this, I really want to do something to get myself to a better place.

Now fill out your own Body Responses Tracking Sheet (see Worksheet 4-3) and record your reflections on the exercise (see Worksheet 4-4).

PRACTICE

1. Once or twice a day, review each of the body responses in the left column.

2. If you experienced a reaction in a given category, elaborate and specify in the middle column how your body reacted.

3. Record when the body response happened and what was going on at the time. This information should help you connect the dots between events and responses.

4. After completing the tracking sheet, take some time to think about what you see. Write a few reflections.

Visit www.dummies.com/go/anxiety&depressionworkbookfd2e to obtain extra copies of this form. Stash a couple of them in your purse or briefcase, or take a picture on your phone so they're handy whenever you experience unpleasant physical sensations.

Worksheet 4-3   My Body Responses Tracking Sheet

Body Response	How did my body feel?	When did this happen? What was I doing?
Muscle tightness		
Breathing/Increased heart rate		
GI symptoms such as upset stomach, constipation, or diarrhea		
Teeth grinding		
Feeling constriction in the throat or chest		
Fatigue		
Problems going to sleep, staying asleep, waking early, or sleeping too much		
Feeling hot and flushed or cold and shaky		
Headaches		
Posture		
Dizziness, spaciness, disorientation, and trouble concentrating		
Changes in appetite or weight unrelated to dieting		

Worksheet 4-4   My Reflections

_____

_____

_____

_____

Connecting the Mind and Body

After you become more observant of your body's signals, it's time to connect your mental and physical states. _Feeling words_ connect and label these combined states. If you're unaccustomed to describing your feelings, spend some time looking over the list of words in the following chart and ponder whether they apply to you. Take your time, and don't rush the process.

PRACTICE

Track your feelings every day for a week using the Daily Unpleasant Emotions Checklist in Worksheet 4-5. See Chapter 18 for exercises relevant to positive emotions.

1. **Read over the lists of feeling words at the top of the chart. If the word for what you're feeling isn't in the list, be sure to add it.**

2. **Each day, write down all the feeling words that describe your emotions. Expect to experience more than a few emotions every day.**

3. **At the end of the week, look back over your checklist and tally the most prevalent feelings. Use Worksheet 4-6 to reflect on the exercise. What did you find out about your feelings?**

Worksheet 4-5   Daily Unpleasant Emotions Checklist

Possible Emotions:

- **Sadness:** despondent, miserable, hopeless, gloomy, grieving, joyless, dispirited, dejected, sad, morose, melancholy, empty, worthless

- **Fear:** panicky, nervous, tense, afraid, timid, terrified, apprehensive, worried, disturbed, insecure, agitated, intimidated, jittery

- **Shame:** guilty, regretful, remorseful, embarrassed, disgraced, dishonored, inadequate

- **Anger:** outraged, bitter, furious, resentful, mad, annoyed, irritable, indignant, frustrated

Day	Emotions
Sunday	
Monday	
Tuesday	
Wednesday	
Thursday	
Friday	
Saturday	

Worksheet 4-6   My Reflections

_____

_____

_____

_____

Putting Events, Feelings, and Sensations Together

As you work through this chapter, you should become more aware of how your body reacts to events in your life. Thanks to the Daily Unpleasant Emotions Checklist in the previous section, you have feeling words to label your mental and physical states. It's time to connect these body sensations and feeling words to the events that trigger them.

EXAMPLE

Jasmine suffers from constant worry and anxiety. She thinks that her worries mainly center on her children, but at times she has no idea where her anxiety comes from. She fills out a Mood Diary to help. She pays special attention to her body's signals and writes them down whenever she feels something unpleasant. She then searches for a feeling word that captures her emotion. She rates the emotions and sensations on a scale of 1 (almost undetectable) to 100 (maximal). She then asks herself what was going on when she detected her distress. Worksheet 4-7 is a sample of Jasmine's Mood Diary; specifically, it's a record of four days on which Jasmine noticed undesirable moods.

Worksheet 4-7   Jasmine's Mood Diary

Day	Feelings and Sensations (Rated 1–100)	Corresponding Events
Sunday	Apprehension, tightness in my chest (70)	I was thinking about going to work tomorrow morning.
Tuesday	Anger, trembling (85)	My secretary messed up my schedule.
Thursday	Worry, tightness in my chest (60)	My child has a cold, and I'm worried she'll have an asthma attack.
Saturday	Nervousness, tension in my shoulders (55)	I have a party to go to, and I won't know many people there.

Jasmine keeps track of her moods over the course of a couple of weeks. After studying her complete Mood Diary, she comes to a few conclusions (see Worksheet 4-8).

Worksheet 4-8   Jasmine's Reflections

Well, I'm surprised. I thought that all I worried about was the kids. Truth is, my job really gets me stirred up. Conflict isn't easy for me either. I'd better do something about that. My shyness gets in my way, too. I didn't realize how often I have these feelings.

PRACTICE

Now it's your turn to fill out a Mood Diary (see Worksheet 4-9). This exercise can provide you with invaluable information about patterns and issues that consistently cause you distress. This knowledge helps you see what needs to change in your life. The exercise also lays a foundation for changing your thinking, which is covered in Part 2 of this book.

1. **For at least one week, pay attention to your body's signals, and write them down whenever you feel something unpleasant.**

2. **Search for a feeling word that captures your emotion, and jot it down.** Refer to the Daily Unpleasant Emotions Checklist earlier in this chapter for help finding the right feeling words.

3. **Rate your feeling on a scale of intensity from 1 (almost undetectable) to 100 (maximal).**

4. **Ask yourself what was going on when you started noticing your emotions and body's signals.** The corresponding event can be something happening in your world, but an event can also be in the form of a thought or image that runs through your mind. Be concrete and specific; don't write something overly general, such as, "I hate my work." Instead, ask yourself what happened at work that you didn't like.

5. Look over your Mood Diary to see if you can draw any conclusions or come up with any new insights into where your body signals come from. Write a few sentences of reflection in Worksheet 4-10.

Worksheet 4-9   My Mood Diary

Day	Feelings and Sensations (Rated 1–100)	Corresponding Events
Sunday		
Monday		
Tuesday		
Wednesday		
Thursday		
Friday		
Saturday		

Worksheet 4-10   My Reflections

_____

_____

_____

_____

Visit www.dummies.com/go/anxiety&depressionworkbookfd2e for extra copies of the Mood Diary. Continue filling out the forms for several weeks for maximum benefit.

Becoming a Thought Detective

Imagine yourself in a parking lot at night. You're tired and back your car into a cement pole. Crunch. What's your reaction? Do you have angry thoughts like, "Who the bleep put that post there!?" Do you feel anxious and worried about the costs of repair? Or do you feel distraught and upset with yourself because you believe you were careless?

Anyone is likely to feel upset for a little while after banging up their car. However, if your thoughts are intense or persistent, they provide clues about your *negative thinking habits*. These habits dictate how you interpret the accident and thus the way you feel about it. If you feel terribly worried, it's probably because you tend to have lots of anxious thoughts. If the accident leaves you overly down on yourself, you may be prone to depressive thoughts.

Thought Trackers show you how feelings, events, and thoughts connect — they lay it all out for you. What are you saying to yourself when you feel upset? See how Molly, Tyler, and Jasmine complete their Thought Trackers before you try a few for yourself.

EXAMPLE

Molly runs her car into a pole one night. Her psychologist has been having her fill out Thought Trackers for the past week whenever she notices upsetting feelings. So later that night she completes a Thought Tracker on the incident (see Worksheet 4-11).

Worksheet 4-11   Molly's Thought Tracker

Feelings and Sensations (Rated 1–100)	Corresponding Events	Thoughts/Interpretations
Despair (70); nauseous	Crunched my car fender.	I can't believe I did that. I'm such an idiot. Everyone at work will notice.
Tense (90); tightness though my back and shoulders		I don't have time to deal with this. I'll have to call the insurance company, get estimates on the repair, and arrange alternative transportation. I'm already feeling way behind on work. I'll never get it done on time now.

EXAMPLE

Strange as it may seem, **Tyler** slams his car into that same pole, although not until the next night. He also fills out a Thought Tracker on the incident (see Worksheet 4-12).

Worksheet 4-12   Tyler's Thought Tracker

Feelings and Sensations (Rated 1–100)	Corresponding Events	Thoughts/Interpretations
Rage (80); flushed face and rapid breathing	I hit that stupid pole with my new sports car.	There's not a single good reason that anyone would have a pole there! I should sue whoever owns this parking lot.
Sad (65); tired		This is terrible. I've only had that car for three months. Cars are never the same after you wreck them. Bad things are always happening to me.

Now, you're going to find this *really* hard to believe, but **Jasmine** happens to be in that same parking lot a week later. Cars seem drawn to that pole. Like Molly and Tyler, Jasmine completes a Thought Tracker (see Worksheet 4-13) following her run-in with that pesky pole.

Worksheet 4-13   Jasmine's Thought Tracker

Feelings and Sensations (Rated 1–100)	Corresponding Events	Thoughts/Interpretations
Panic (95); terrified, sweaty, rapid shallow breathing, dizzy	I slammed my car into a pole.	At first, I thought I might have run into someone's car and could have hurt somebody. I never know how to handle things like this. I'll probably lose my driver's license, or my insurance will drop me. My husband will be furious with me. I can't stand it when he's mad at me.

Three people, same event. You can see how their thoughts contribute to the way they feel. All three of them look at this event in unique ways, and they feel differently as a result. Molly worries about the consequences of the accident and puts herself down. Because of the way she interprets the event, Molly's at risk for anxiety and depression. Tyler gets mad and catastrophizes the fender-bender. He tends to have problems with anger and depression. On the other hand, Jasmine panics about the bash into the pole; her reaction is the product of her frequent struggles with anxiety and panic.

Sometimes people say they really don't know what's going on in their heads when they feel distressed. They know how they feel and they know what happened, but they simply have no idea what they're thinking. You may experience this problem. If so, ask yourself the questions in Worksheet 4-14 about an event that accompanied your difficult feelings.

Thought Trackers give you important information about the way your mind interprets events and your related feelings. That's why we recommend that you do them often. See Part 2 for ways of changing your thinking habits and improving your moods.

The Thought Tracker demonstrates how the way you think about occurrences influences the way you feel. Sad feelings inevitably accompany thoughts about loss, low self-worth, or rejection. Anxious or worried feelings go along with thoughts about danger, vulnerability, or horrible outcomes. To complete your Thought Tracker in Worksheet 4-15, follow these instructions:

1. **Pay attention to your body's signals, and write them down whenever you feel something unpleasant.**

2. **Search for a feeling word that captures your emotion, and jot that down, too.** Refer to the Daily Unpleasant Emotions Checklist earlier in this chapter for help.

3. **Rate your feeling on a scale of intensity from 1 (almost undetectable) to 100 (maximal).**

4. **Ask yourself what was going on when you started noticing your emotions and body's signals.** The corresponding event can be something happening in your world, but an event can also come in the form of a thought or image that runs through your mind. Be concrete and specific; don't write something overly general, such as, "I hate my job." Instead, ask yourself what happened at work that you didn't like.

5. **Record your thoughts in the Thoughts/Interpretation column.** Describe how you perceive, interpret, or think about the event. Refer to the preceding Thought Query Quiz if you experience any difficulty figuring out your thoughts about the event.

Do you notice any patterns to the types of thoughts you have? Are these thoughts associated with certain types of feelings? Take the time to reflect on this exercise using Worksheet 4-16.

Worksheet 4-14   The Thought Query Quiz

1. What meaning does the event have for me in my life?

_____

_____

_____

_____

2. Will this event affect my future in any way?

_____

_____

_____

3. What bothers me about the event?

_____

_____

_____

_____

4. Does the event say something about me as a person?

_____

_____

_____

5. What passed through my mind as I noticed the event?

_____

_____

_____

_____

Worksheet 4-15   My Thought Tracker

Feelings and Sensations (Rated 1–100)	Corresponding Events	Thoughts/Interpretations

Worksheet 4-16   My Reflections

2

Thinking About Thinking: Thought Therapy

Chapter **5**

Untangling Twisted Thinking

This chapter helps you apply the principles of *cognitive therapy* to your challenging emotions. Cognitive therapy is based on the premise that the way you interpret or think about events largely determines the way you feel. The great thing about cognitive therapy is that changing the way you think changes the way you feel.

All human beings have some thoughts that don't match reality, or what cognitive therapists call distorted thinking. Distorted means that your thinking doesn't accurately reflect, predict, or describe what's going on. Have you ever heard a noise in the night that woke you up and scared you? Perhaps your mind filled with thoughts of dread and images of someone breaking into your house. Only rarely are such thoughts accurate. More often than not, the noise results from wind or creaking floorboards. But when you hear a bump in the night, your fear is very real. Your thoughts, while understandable, are distorted.

Perhaps you send a text with a new idea to a colleague and after a couple of days your colleague doesn't reply. You might come to a distorted conclusion that the colleague:

» Thinks you and your idea are idiotic and not worth considering

» Doesn't pay attention to texts

» Is rude and inconsiderate

You decide to confront your colleague and discover that your text never went through. So all your previous hypotheses were distortions, and your conclusions were inaccurate.

Distorted thinking can be overly positive as well as negative. For example, isolation and loneliness during the pandemic have caused a tidal wave of human suffering. It's not helpful to tell people who suffer from emotional distress to stop being weak and cheer up, that at least they're not dead from COVID or in the ICU, or broke and homeless. Depression and anxiety symptoms cannot be willed away with overly positive thinking.

Distorted thinking is a problem when it leads to depression and anxiety. Although there are probably infinite ways the human brain can distort reality, the following three types of distortions are particularly common:

>> Reality scramblers

>> Judging errors

>> Blaming the wrong source

REMEMBER

Although this chapter makes distinctions among various types of cognitive distortions, in reality, they often overlap or exist in groups. To put it another way, a single thought can involve several reality scramblers, misjudgments, and misguided blame.

Introducing the Reality Scramblers

Reality scramblers warp your perceptions of your world and events occurring around you; they distort how you think about what's actually happening. You may not know that reality scramblers affect your thinking, but if you give it a little thought, you're likely to see that they do.

Reality scramblers consist of the various ways in which the mind distorts the information coming into it. For example, suppose a depressed man receives a satisfactory but not outstanding performance review at work. He's likely to enlarge this event and turn it into a complete catastrophe by assuming that he's worthless as a person. People with depression tend to exaggerate negative information. That reality scrambler is called *catastrophizing*. Without the scrambler, the reality is simply that his performance was considered average even though he would have preferred a better rating.

PRACTICE

This exercise shows you all the ways that reality scramblers can affect your thinking and ultimately the way you feel.

1. **Read the description of each type of reality scrambler and the accompanying examples in Worksheet 5-1.**

2. **Think about when your thoughts might have been influenced by the reality scrambler.**

3. **Reflect and write down any examples of specific thoughts you've had that might be distorted by a reality scrambler.** If you can't think of an example for each type of thought distortion, that's okay. There are more exercises for seeing how reality scramblers do their work later in this chapter.

Worksheet 5-1   Reality Scramblers Exercise

1. **Catastrophizing:** Your mind magnifies the awfulness of unpleasant events and minimizes the value and importance of anything positive about yourself, your world, or your future. For example, you have saved up enough money for a down payment on a car. You arrive at the dealer, and the car you want is not available because of the shortage of computer chips. You are stunned and start a quick online search for other places to purchase the car. But not a single model is for sale, even out of state. You're furious at the world as well as the poor salesperson. How can this happen? However, instead of catastrophizing, you begin to realize you can order the car, save your money, and maybe even have a bit of extra cash in the meantime.

_____

_____

_____

_____

2. **Filtering:** Your mind searches for dismal, dark, or frightening data while screening out more positive information. The not-too-surprising result? The world (or yourself) looks bleak or more frightening than it is. For example, you are sent home by your boss because you've been exposed to someone with a positive COVID test. You assume that you're likely to get sick, possibly be hospitalized, and perhaps die. You call your brother to say your goodbyes, and he reminds you that you've been vaccinated, you were wearing a mask, and your workplace has increased ventilation. Filtering took you to the darkest outcome instead of a more reasonable conclusion.

_____

_____

_____

_____

3. **Seeing in black-or-white, all-or-none terms:** Your mind views events and your character as either black or white, with no shades of gray. People who see in those terms may end long-term relationships over a single argument. They conclude that a person who was once loved and cared for is now an enemy. Or an adolescent notices a blemish on their face and often concludes that they look horrible. The problem with such polarized thinking is that it's the perfect setup for inevitable failure, disappointment, and self-abuse.

_____

_____

_____

_____

4. **Dismissing evidence:** Your mind discards evidence that may contradict its negative thoughts. For example, suppose you're preparing a speech and have the thought that when it comes time to give the speech, you'll be so scared you won't be able to talk. Your mind automatically dismisses the fact that you've given numerous speeches before and never been so afraid you couldn't talk.

_____

_____

_____

_____

(continued)

5. **Overgeneralizing:** You look at a single, unpleasant occurrence and decide that this event represents a general, unrelenting trend. For example, a wife tells her husband that she's furious because he's *always* late, but in reality, he's late only about 10 percent of the time. Words like *always* and *never* are clues to overgeneralization.

_____

_____

_____

_____

6. **Mind reading:** You assume that you know what others are thinking without checking it out. Thus, when your boss walks by you without saying hello, you automatically think, "She's really angry with me; I must have messed something up." In reality, she's merely distracted.

_____

_____

_____

_____

7. **Emotional reasoning:** You treat feelings as facts. For example, if you feel guilty, you conclude that you must have done something wrong. Or if you don't feel like working on your depression, you assume that means you're unable to. And if you're afraid of something, it must be dangerous merely because you fear it.

_____

_____

_____

_____

8. **Unreliable forecasting:** You presume a negative outcome without any real evidence. For example, you have an argument with your partner and believe that he or she will certainly leave you. Or you avoid driving on the freeway because you're convinced you'll get in an accident.

_____

_____

_____

_____

Recording Reality Scramblers on Thought Trackers

Tracking your thoughts and looking for distortions in them helps clear your thinking, which in turn starts improving your mood. Before you get to work on your own Thought Tracker, see what Bradford (see Worksheet 5-2) and Sheila (see Worksheet 5-3) discover when they track their thoughts and analyze them for reality scramblers.

EXAMPLE

Worksheet 5-2   Bradford's Thought Tracker

Corresponding Events	Thoughts/Interpretations/Feelings	Reality Scramblers
My boss said we had to increase our productivity.	I hate this job. The boss must hate me. It will never get better. I can't possibly meet this standard; what then? I feel despondent and anxious. My chest feels tight.	Catastrophizing, mind reading, seeing in black-and-white terms, overgeneralizing, unreliable forecasting
My bid on that house fell through. The real estate agent said we could get just as good of a deal on another house.	I'll never find a deal that good. Things like this never work out for me. I'm overwhelmed, tired of all of this, and feel so sad.	Overgeneralizing, seeing in black-and-white terms, dismissing evidence

EXAMPLE

Worksheet 5-3   Sheila's Thought Tracker

Corresponding Events	Thoughts/Interpretations/Feelings	Reality Scramblers
Jason's 20 minutes late coming home from school.	He's never this late; something horrible must have happened. I just feel it in my gut. I'm nauseous, panicked, and shaky.	Emotional reasoning, unreliable forecasting
Getting the house ready for a party.	No one is going to show up. I know people came to the last party, but they felt they had to come. Even though they said they had a good time, I know they were just being polite. I'm so nervous I feel sick to my stomach.	Unreliable forecasting, mind reading, dismissing evidence

Now that you've seen a couple examples of reality scramblers at work, it's time to take a challenge and see if you can pick out reality scramblers in different situations. Worksheet 5-4 presents an incomplete Thought Tracker with samples from an assortment of people and events. Review the events, thoughts, and interpretations of those events provided, and then fill in the reality scramblers that you believe apply. The answers are later in this section, but don't peek!

PRACTICE

Worksheet 5-4   Thought Tracker Reality Scrambler Practice

Corresponding Events	Thoughts/Interpretations/Feelings	Reality Scramblers
Scenario #1 My wife said I've gained a little weight.	It's true. I've let myself go completely. I'll probably die of a heart attack. I feel out of control, so I must have no willpower at all. I feel miserable, embarrassed, and tired of all of this.	
Scenario #2 I was appointed department chair.	The dean is setting me up for failure; he wants to get rid of me. I'll get more money, but the only reason I got the job is because no one else wanted it. I'm tense, spacey, and apprehensive.	
Scenario #3 Some jerk keyed my car.	This kind of thing always happens to me. This is going to cost a fortune to fix. I'm just bitter, my back and neck hurt, and I feel like nothing works for me.	

Here are the answers to the Thought Tracker Reality Scrambler Practice exercise. Don't worry if your answers don't perfectly match — the point is simply learning to observe distortions at work. And sometimes the precise distortions involved are debatable.

>> **Scenario 1:** Catastrophizing, unreliable forecasting, seeing in black-and-white terms, emotional reasoning

>> **Scenario 2:** Dismissing the evidence, mind reading, filtering

>> **Scenario 3:** Catastrophizing, overgeneralizing, unreliable forecasting

It's time to start tracking your own thoughts and looking for possible reality scramblers. This process helps you see that some of your unpleasant feelings actually come from the way your mind misinterprets events in your world. The following instructions guide you in building your own Thought Tracker in Worksheet 5-5, but for more complete information about Thought Trackers, see Chapter 4.

Worksheet 5-5   Thought Tracker Reality Scrambler Practice

Corresponding Events	Thoughts/Interpretations/Feelings	Reality Scrambler

PRACTICE

1. **Ask yourself what was going on when you started noticing your emotions changing and becoming more negative. Briefly summarize that event.** The event can be something happening in your world right now, or it can come in the form of a thought or image that runs through your mind. Be concrete and specific when recording events. Don't write something overly general, such as, "I hate my work;" instead, ask yourself what happened at work that you didn't like. After you've recorded the event, notice and write down your feelings and emotions.

2. **Record your thoughts in the appropriate column by describing how you perceive, interpret, or think about the event.** Refer to The Thought Query Quiz in Chapter 4 if you experience any difficulty figuring out your thoughts about the event.

3. **Using the list of reality scramblers earlier in this chapter, record the distortions you believe are at work.**

For extra copies of this form, visit www.dummies.com/go/anxiety&depressionworkbookfd2e.

In working through the exercise in Worksheet 5-5, were you able to find the reality scramblers in your thinking? If so, you'll likely begin questioning whether or not your thoughts about events are always accurate. With that doubt comes the possibility of seeing things a little differently — more realistically, actually. Record your reflections in Worksheet 5-6. These strategies should begin to shake up your thinking. (See Chapter 6 for a variety of strategies for replacing distorted thinking with more accurate perceptions.)

Worksheet 5-6   My Reflections

_____

_____

_____

_____

Making the Wrong Judgment

You can also have distortions in the way you judge yourself and your behaviors. Depressed and anxious minds tend to be harshly critical, judgmental, and self-abusive. Why is that a problem? Because self-judging is another form of self-sabotage. Although you may think otherwise, self-criticism doesn't motivate you to do anything positive or productive; rather, it only makes you feel worse and leaves you with less energy for changing.

Distorted self-judging comes in three different forms:

>> Shoulds

>> Critical comparisons

>> Loathsome labels

Shoulding on yourself

One of my favorite quotes comes from psychologist Dr. Albert Ellis (1913–2007), who said, "Stop shoulding on yourself." That phrase is good advice for the majority of clients I've seen in my practice as a psychologist, as well as friends and family members. And I must admit, in my humanness, I occasionally fall victim to the tyranny of the should. *Shoulding* involves putting yourself down by telling yourself that you *should* be or act different in some way. It can refer to past, present, or future actions. Shoulding scrambles accurate self-views and turns them into self-criticisms.

PRACTICE

To identify your own shoulds, take the quiz in Worksheet 5-7, putting a check mark next to each thought that has run through your mind.

Worksheet 5-7   The Shoulding-on-Yourself Quiz

❑ I should have known better.

❑ I shouldn't eat that much.

❑ I should be a better person.

❑ I shouldn't avoid people so much.

❑ I should have been more careful.

❑ I shouldn't have distorted thoughts!

❑ I shouldn't be so crabby.

❑ I shouldn't make so many mistakes.

❑ I should be able to take more risks in my life.

❑ I should exercise more.

❑ I should be nicer to people.

❑ I shouldn't get so upset about things.

So what's wrong with these thoughts? (I can almost hear you thinking, "But I *SHOULD* eat less, be a better person, or not get so upset about things!") Well, there's no rule chiseled in granite stating that you should or must act or think in certain ways. Shoulding is a form of criticism that makes you feel bad because guilt and shame don't motivate positive behavior. The bottom line is that shoulding doesn't help. You *shouldn't* should on yourself — just kidding, sort of.

The alternative to shoulding on yourself is recognizing that it may be a good idea to do things differently but refusing to engage in harsh self-judgment. Before you get to your own should alternatives, in Worksheet 5-8, you can read **Zara's** should statements and see how she develops alternatives to shoulding on herself.

PRACTICE

Review any items you endorsed from The Shoulding-on-Yourself Quiz (see Worksheet 5-7), and listen to your self-dialogue. Then fill out My Should Alternative Exercise in Worksheet 5-9 by following these instructions:

1. Tune into what you're telling yourself when you feel upset.

2. Listen for any time that you tell yourself, "I should" or "I shouldn't."

3. Record those statements in the left column.

4. Come up with alternative perspectives for each should statement, and write them in the column on the right. Words like *prefer*, *would like to*, *wish*, and *would be better if* make good alternatives to *should*.

EXAMPLE

Worksheet 5-8   Zara's Should Alternative Exercise

Should Statement	Should Alternative Statement
I shouldn't get upset so often.	I wish I didn't get upset so often, but I do. And I'm trying to master relaxation as an alternative.
I shouldn't get in bad moods so often.	I don't like bad moods, but they're tough to change. I do want to work on them, but I don't need to pummel myself when they happen.
I shouldn't let myself get out of shape.	I would prefer to get into better shape. It's difficult to find the time to exercise. I'll try to make more time for taking care of myself.
I should spend more time on the exercises in this workbook.	I do want to spend more time on these exercises, but every bit that I do is worth something.
I shouldn't make mistakes.	I prefer not to make mistakes, but I'm human, after all.

Worksheet 5-9   My Should Alternative Exercise

Should Statement	Should Alternative Statement

Making critical comparisons

Are you the richest, best-looking, or smartest person in the world? Who is? There's always someone who has more of something than you do. Even if you're the best at one thing, that doesn't mean you're the best at everything. People have strengths and weaknesses, and if you do think you're the best at everything, you have a problem that's quite different from anxiety or depression.

REMEMBER

Everyone engages in comparing themselves to others sometimes. But anxious and depressed folks tend to rate themselves more negatively and place more value on those comparisons.

To identify your negative personal comparisons, put a check mark next to each item in Worksheet 5-10 that you sometimes examine in yourself and then compare to others.

PRACTICE

Worksheet 5-10   The Critical Comparison Quiz

❑ Finances or wealth

❑ Looks and appearance

❑ Intelligence

❑ Popularity

❑ Fame

❑ Gadgets

❑ House

❑ Car

❑ Clothes

❑ Status

❑ Age

❑ Knowledge

Essentially, the less comparing you do, the better off you are. However, the seduction of comparisons lies in the fact that they contain a kernel of truth. The reality is that there's always someone richer, younger, smarter, or higher on the ladder than you. Comparisons may be unavoidable, but they become problematic when you conclude that you're not good enough because you're not the top or the best.

What's the alternative to making critical comparisons that scramble the way you see yourself? Like should alternative statements (see "Shoulding on yourself"), comparison alternatives are all about looking at an issue from a different, less harsh perspective. Before creating your own alternative statements, take a look at Worksheet 5-11 for an example.

Review the items you checked on your Critical Comparison Quiz (see Worksheet 5-10) and listen to your self-dialogue. Then fill out the Comparison Alternative Exercise in Worksheet 5-12 by following these instructions:

PRACTICE

1. **Tune into what you're telling yourself when you feel upset, and listen for any time that you critically compare yourself to others.**

2. **List those statements in the left column.**

3. **Come up with alternative perspectives, and record them in the right column.** Because only one person in the world is at the top on any given issue or activity, try to accept that you'll be average, normal, or even occasionally less than average at many things. Comparing yourself to the very top only leaves you disappointed, so appreciate your own strengths, weaknesses, and chosen priorities.

Worksheet 5-11   Scott's Comparison Alternative Exercise

Critical Comparison	Comparison Alternative
My friend Jose has done a lot better than I have in his career.	Well, he has. But I've done fine. I spend a lot of time with my family, and that's my real priority.
When we went to that Super Bowl party, I was really jealous of that 75-inch TV. Our TV is pitiful in comparison.	There was nothing wrong with my TV before that party. I don't even watch that much TV.
I went to the gym and noticed that everyone was more fit than I am.	Of course, most of the really unfit people don't even go to the gym. I'm in better shape than I was a month ago; that's progress, and that's what matters.
I read an article on retirement and got anxious when I realized that I don't have as much put away as a lot of people do.	Having kids was more expensive than I thought it would be, but I wouldn't trade them for the world. Once Eli's college is paid for, we'll prioritize saving.

Worksheet 5-12   My Comparison Alternative Exercise

Critical Comparison	Comparison Alternative

Tagging yourself with loathsome labels

Sticks and stones can break your bones, and words *can* really hurt you. The final self-judging reality scrambler amounts to calling yourself bad names. It's so easy to tag yourself with demeaning labels, and when you do, you inevitably feel worse.

To pinpoint the loathsome labels you give yourself, take the quiz in Worksheet 5-13. Check off the words that you use to describe yourself when things go wrong.

This list is a small sample of the horrible things that people label themselves or others. Feel free to add other words if those are the ones you use on yourself.

Worksheet 5-13   The Loathsome Label Quiz

- ❑ Loser
- ❑ Pathetic
- ❑ Misfit
- ❑ Freak
- ❑ Clod
- ❑ Klutz
- ❑ Fat pig
- ❑ Failure
- ❑ Nerd
- ❑ Pitiful
- ❑ Stupid
- ❑ Monster
- ❑ Disturbed
- ❑ Crazy
- ❑ Idiot
- ❑ Jerk
- ❑ Imbecile
- ❑ Fool
- ❑ Moron
- ❑ Dummy (well . . . not really!)

Negative labels erode your self-worth. They always involve overgeneralization and black-and-white thinking. (See the section "Introducing the Reality Scramblers" earlier in this chapter.) Labels represent concepts that hold no redeeming value; they don't help you, and they often lead to increased emotional distress. So what should you do when you hear these labels floating through your mind? See Worksheet 5-14 for examples of self-labels and new ways of looking at them.

PRACTICE

If you stop calling yourself useless, hurtful names and replace the labels with more reasonable perspectives, you'll feel better. Therefore, complete the Label Replacement Exercise in Worksheet 5-15 each time you hear those destructive labels in your mind:

1. **Tune into what you're telling yourself when you feel upset, and listen for any time that you tag yourself with a hurtful label.**

2. **Write the triggering event in the left column.**

3. **Write the label you're putting on yourself in the middle column.**

4. **Come up with alternative perspectives to the labels, and record them in the right column.** In creating label replacements, try to accept any portion of the event that has truth in it, such as having gained some weight, but look at the issue more realistically. Try to be self-forgiving. Because labels tend to be overarching ratings (that is, they imply a bigger problem than the event that triggered them), your replacement thoughts should be specific and look for positive possibilities.

EXAMPLE

Worksheet 5-14   Label Replacement Exercise

Event	Corresponding Label	Label Replacement Thought
I spilled a drink at a restaurant.	I'm a total klutz!	I've seen other people spill drinks. Good grief, it's not a big deal.
I started to tear up when I was talking about my mother's illness.	I'm pathetic and pitiful.	There's nothing wrong with showing some emotion.
My voice started to shake during a meeting at work.	I'm a loser.	I was talking about something very important to me. At times like that I do get a little tense. I wish I didn't, but that doesn't make me a loser.
I didn't get into the graduate school I wanted.	I'm a failure.	It was very competitive. I did get my third choice. Sure, I wish I'd gotten my preference, but I can still succeed in my chosen career.
I can't seem to lose weight.	I'm a fat pig!	The doc said that after 50, metabolic changes make it harder to lose weight. I do have extra weight, and I don't like it, but it doesn't help to call myself a pig.

Worksheet 5-15   My Label Replacement Exercise

Event	Corresponding Label	Label Replacement Thought

TIP

If you have trouble coming up with Label Replacement Thoughts, don't worry. Jump to Chapter 6 for lots of ideas for challenging negative self-talk.

Now that you've completed the label replacement exercise, take a few minutes to reflect on what self-labels have been doing to you and how it feels to change them (see Worksheet 5-16).

Worksheet 5-16   My Reflections

_____

_____

_____

_____

_____

The Blame Game

When sadness or anxiety clouds your thinking, you're likely to add to your distress by assuming full responsibility for your misery. You may accuse yourself of being inept, incapable, or inadequate and therefore fully culpable for all your suffering. When this cognitive distortion is at work, you attribute all fault and blame to yourself. Doing so leads you to wallow in shame and self-loathing.

This section gives you a tool for figuring out if you tend to overly blame yourself. After you begin to understand that your problem isn't completely your fault, you can act on the portion for which you own responsibility. The Rating Responsibility Exercise helps you see that most problems have many causes and that you only own a portion of the responsibility. Accepting these facts can help you lessen the guilt and shame you feel. After you understand the causes of the problem, you'll be more ready to do something productive about it.

EXAMPLE

Robin blames herself for her recent divorce and believes that she is almost entirely responsible for her husband leaving the marriage for another woman. Robin considers herself boring and unattractive, and she berates herself for not seeing the signs early enough to prevent what happened. Robin decides to take the Rating Responsibility Exercise (see Worksheet 5-17), focusing on the blame she places on herself for her divorce.

As you can see, Robin initially assigns 95 percent of the blame for the divorce on herself. At the end of the quiz, Robin reassesses her level of responsibility because she's able to see things a bit more objectively. She rerates the level of blame she puts on herself and identifies that 20 percent seems more appropriate — she's only partly responsible. This knowledge helps her feel less guilty and self-disparaging.

PRACTICE

Now that you've seen the Rating Responsibility Exercise in action, it's time to evaluate the level of responsibility you feel you carry. In other words, you're figuring out how much of the problem is you. Complete your Rating Responsibility Exercise in Worksheet 5-18 by following these steps:

1. Name the problem you're blaming yourself for. Write this at the top of the worksheet.

2. Using a percentage from 1 to 100, rate how much blame you put on yourself for this problem. At the top of the worksheet, write this percentage under the problem you've identified.

3. In the left column, list all imaginable causes of your problem.

4. In the right column, using a number from 1 to 100, estimate the percentage of actual responsibility for this problem that each cause in the left column owns. Also record your contributions to the problem.

5. Rerate the percentage of responsibility you have for the problem you identified.

My rerated level of responsibility is:_____

Worksheet 5-17   Robin's Rating Responsibility Exercise

I blame myself for: My recent divorce

I rate the blame at: 95%

All Possible Causes of Your Problem	Percentage of Responsibility
My husband's roving eye.	10%: He does have a roving eye!
My husband's hostility.	15%: He's a difficult man.
Diana's conniving, manipulative plan to steal him.	20%: She was after him for months, no doubt about it.
The strain of our financial problems.	10%: This didn't help.
My husband's grief over losing his mother, father, and brother over the past year and a half.	10%: He could never talk about these losses, and I know they got to him.
The stress of our daughter's bout with cancer. She's recovered now, but my husband still worries.	10%: Again, he couldn't talk about it.
I gained ten pounds during our marriage.	5%: I know I'm not that overweight.
My husband can easily find women more attractive than me.	5%: Yeah, but I do look better than many women my age.
We had stopped talking about our days.	10%: I probably should have paid more attention to that issue.
Random events.	5%: I'm sure there are things I'm not factoring into this equation.

Worksheet 5-18   My Rating Responsibility Exercise

I blame myself for: _____

I rate the blame at: _____

All Possible Causes of Your Problem	Percentage of Responsibility

WARNING

Some people deny any and all responsibility for problems they encounter. These folks usually find a convenient scapegoat such as a mother, father, significant other, society, or event to blame for all their woes. Failing to accept any responsibility for your troubles makes you see yourself as helpless and the world as unfair and unjust. (Check out Chapter 3 for more information about such self-sabotaging beliefs.) Realize that you don't want to fall into that trap. Read the next section to see how to avoid it.

Doing What You Can to Solve the Problem

In this section, you face your problem and take action to change it. By assessing your responsibility and determining what you can do about your problem, you avoid immersing yourself in self-loathing and harsh self-blame. This approach allows you to take responsibility for an appropriate portion of the problem and do what you can with it. If your responsibility involves something that's over and done with, no action is possible. But you can still try to let go of the shame that leads nowhere and does nothing to help you. And you may be able to do some things to prevent a similar problem in the future.

EXAMPLE

Robin reviews her Rating Responsibility Exercise (see Worksheet 5-17) and notices that she owns partial responsibility for some of the problems that led to her divorce. She lists those contributions and then plans steps for productive action on the Action Strategy Worksheet shown in Worksheet 5-19.

PRACTICE

After completing your Rating Responsibility Exercise in Worksheet 5-18, the next step is to create an action strategy to determine how you can begin solving your problem. By identifying productive actions to address the problem, you're able to move forward and stop berating yourself. Follow these steps to create an action strategy in Worksheet 5-20:

1. **Name the problem you're blaming yourself for, and write it at the top of the worksheet.**

2. **In the left column, list the specific contributions you've identified that you have some control over.** In other words, record anything you did that may have led to the problem or made it worse.

3. **In the right column, list any steps you can take now or in the future that may be useful in solving this problem.**

Worksheet 5-19   Robin's Action Strategy Worksheet

The problem: My divorce.

My Specific Contributions to the Problem	Specific Actions I Can Take
I am ten pounds overweight.	I can lose ten pounds by increasing my exercise and watching my diet. It won't help this divorce, but my counselor said exercise will lift my spirits and I'll be healthier.
I'm not the most attractive woman in the world.	I can't do a lot about my appearance other than realize it's not that important. I don't want a man who wants me just for the way I look anyway.
I ignored our lack of communication in the marriage.	If I find another relationship, I need to pay attention to how we talk and any other problems that crop up. I don't want to bury my head in the sand.

Worksheet 5-20   My Action Strategy Worksheet

The problem: _____

My Specific Contributions to the Problem	Specific Actions I Can Take
_____	_____
_____	_____
_____	_____
_____	_____

As you finish this chapter, take the time to reflect on what you've discovered about your patterns of thinking and how they affect your view of yourself. Write down your feelings, thoughts, and insights in Worksheet 5-21.

Worksheet 5-21   My Reflections

_____

_____

_____

_____

Chapter **6**

Indicting and Rehabilitating Thoughts

ost people simply assume that thoughts they have about themselves and the world are true. But thoughts don't always reflect reality, just as funhouse mirrors don't reflect the way you really look. Chapter 5 helps you uncover the common distortions in your thoughts.

In this chapter, you become a thought detective. No, you don't need a magnifying glass or sharp-looking hat and trench coat. All you need are the tools and instructions in this chapter and an open mind. The following sections show you how to take your distorted thoughts to court and charge them with the crime of inflicting misery on you. If you find them guilty as charged, you see how to rehabilitate those criminal thoughts so that they can contribute to your well-being.

From Arraignment to Conviction: Thought Court

This technique, called Thought Court, is based on the principles of *cognitive therapy*. Cognitive therapy was founded in the late 1950s by Dr. Aaron T. Beck, who discovered that changing the way people think changes the way they feel. Many studies attest to the fact that cognitive therapy works very well to alleviate anxiety and depression. Therefore, I recommend that you regularly work on the exercises in this section. Do this work until you find yourself starting to think and feel differently, and then go ahead and do it for a little while longer.

Thought Court begins with a Thought Tracker. Thought Trackers show you how feelings, events, and thoughts connect. You can find examples of Thought Trackers in this section, but for more information, flip to Chapter 4.

Thought Court is the process of indicting the accused thought (the one you pinpoint in your Thought Tracker) and then bringing it to trial. You play the roles of defense attorney, prosecutor, and judge. As the defense attorney, you present the evidence that supports the validity or accuracy of the thought. In other words, the defense claims that your thought is true and isn't culpable for your anguish. On the other side, you, as the prosecutor, lay out a case demonstrating that the thought is actually guilty of distortion and has caused you unnecessary emotional distress. In Thought Court, you're also the judge. If you find the thought guilty, there are ways to replace or rehabilitate your thought in the later section titled "After the Verdict: Replacing and Rehabilitating Your Thoughts."

TIP

Frankly, you're unlikely to find the thought innocent, but if you manage to consistently find your thought justified or innocent of causing you unnecessary harm, you should seek consultation with a mental health professional. You may need a fresh perspective to help sort out your troubles.

Most people learn better through stories and examples than through laborious explanations. With that in mind, the following section presents an example to help you master the process of Thought Court. Then there is an opportunity to put *your* thoughts on trial, and in case you need more help, there is a follow-up to your practice in the form of more case examples.

Examining a sample case in Thought Court

EXAMPLE

Jeremy is a good looking 23-year-old personal trainer who takes pride in his healthy lifestyle. People admire his strength and athleticism. He's known at the gym for the colorful, long-sleeved T-shirts that he always wears. Jeremy gets more than his share of attention from women, but he never becomes involved with them because he has a secret: He was seriously burned as a child, and his chest and arms are deeply scarred.

Jeremy has never had a serious relationship; he believes any woman seeing his body would recoil in disgust. Rather than face rejection and ridicule, he locks himself away in solitary confinement. His embarrassment and fear of detection have led Jeremy to feel lonely, depressed, and anxious.

Jeremy finds himself very attracted to a young woman he meets at the gym. She's obviously drawn to him as well. When she asks him out for coffee, he panics and puts her off. His combination of fear and yearning motivates him to see a therapist, and he manages to tell his therapist about his lifelong secret. Jeremy's therapist suggests that he start examining his thoughts with a Thought Tracker (see Worksheet 6-1) and then take his thoughts to Thought Court.

After he completes his Thought Tracker, Jeremy and his therapist pull out his most troubling thoughts — what I call the *most malicious thoughts*.

Jeremy's most malicious thoughts:

I couldn't stand to see the look of repulsion on her face.

It's not fair that I was burned and have to go through life this way.

Worksheet 6-1   Jeremy's Thought Tracker

Feelings & Sensations (Rated 1–100)	Corresponding Events	Thoughts/Interpretations
Anxiety (85), fear (95); shaking hands, flushed face	Chelsea asks me out for coffee.	I can't possibly go out with her. If she ever saw my scars, she'd freak out. I couldn't stand to see the look of repulsion on her face.
Anxiety (75), shame (85), bitterness (85); sweaty, sinking feeling in the pit of my stomach	The guys asked me to go into the hot tub with them after work.	The shame would overwhelm me. I look like a monster. It's not fair that I was burned and have to go through life this way. This will never end.

Jeremy finds the Thought Tracker exercise interesting. He realizes that two thoughts create the most emotional pain for him. Next, his therapist suggests that Jeremy put the first of these thoughts on trial using a worksheet. (Later on, the therapist addresses his other malicious thoughts.) As you can see in Worksheet 6-2, Jeremy writes down the malicious thought first. Then in one column he defends the thought by listing all the reasons, logic, and evidence he can muster to support the case that the thought is true. In the other column, Jeremy attempts to prosecute the thought by demonstrating that it's false.

Worksheet 6-2   Jeremy's Thought on Trial Worksheet

<u>Accused thought</u>: I couldn't stand to see the look of repulsion on her face.

Defense: Evidence in Support of the Thought	Prosecution: Evidence Refuting the Thought
People are repulsed by burn scars.	The medical team is the only group that doesn't seem shocked.
I've seen the look of shock on people's faces before.	My family seems to have gotten used to my scars.
I can remember my mother crying when she saw how badly I was burned.	
After one surgery, a physical therapist made a comment that my burns were permanently deforming and I'd just have to learn to live with them.	
Sometimes when I go for a checkup, I hear people talking about me.	

So far, this case is going very well for the defense and very poorly for the prosecution. Thus, Jeremy remains quite convinced that his thought is a true reflection of reality; it's just the way things are. He can't imagine being persuaded to change his thought. The therapist tells him he's made a good start but asks him to consider the Prosecutor's Investigative Questions in Worksheet 6-3 and write down his reflections on those questions (see Worksheet 6-4).

Worksheet 6-3   Prosecutor's Investigative Questions

- Is this thought illogical or distorted in any way? (See Chapter 5 for a list of reality scramblers that indicate distortions in thoughts.)
- Is this event as horrible as I'm letting myself believe it is?
- Were there any times in my life when this thought wouldn't have held true?
- Do I know of friends or acquaintances who have experienced similar events but for whom this thought wouldn't apply?
- Am I ignoring any evidence that may dispute this thought?
- Is this thought really helping me?
- Have I ever coped with something like this before and gotten through it okay?
- What would happen if I just started acting as though the thought weren't true?

Worksheet 6-4   Jeremy's Reflections

These questions are a little difficult to contemplate. But let's see. Are there any distortions in my accused thought? Well, I guess I would really dislike seeing repulsion on her face, but I could probably "stand it." So I might be catastrophizing somewhat. And I suppose I've seen attractive women who are with guys who have substantial disabilities, like morbid obesity, missing limbs, and so on. I was in that burn support group, and I admit there were some people who had nice relationships after they'd been burned. So I guess it's possible Chelsea may not be repulsed. And I guess the thought is doing me more harm than good because it keeps me from ever considering a relationship. Maybe it's worth testing out if it's true or not.

After Jeremy reflects on the list of Prosecutor Investigative Questions, his therapist advises him to take another look at his Thoughts on Trial Worksheet and try to add more evidence and logic to his case (see Worksheet 6-5).

At this point, Jeremy carefully reviews the case presented in his Thought on Trial Worksheet. He finds his accused thought guilty of inflicting unnecessary misery. He and his therapist agree to work on a replacement thought for his most malicious thought. (See the section "After the Verdict: Replacing and Rehabilitating Your Thoughts" later in this chapter.) After Jeremy creates the first replacement thought, he continues putting his other malicious thoughts on trial and replacing them, one at a time.

Worksheet 6-5   Jeremy's Revised Thought on Trial Worksheet

<u>Accused thought</u>: I couldn't stand to see the look of repulsion on her face.

Defense: Evidence in Support of the Thought	Prosecution: Evidence Refuting the Thought
People are repulsed by burn scars.	Actually, there are a few people I know who haven't been shocked or repulsed by my scars. That thought is overgeneralizing.
I've seen the look of shock on people's faces before.	My family seems to have gotten used to my scars. If they can, it's certainly possible that others could do the same — especially if they cared about me.
I can remember my mother crying when she saw how badly I was burned.	Just because my mother cried doesn't mean that she can't stand looking at me.
After one surgery, a physical therapist made a comment that my burns were permanently deforming and I'd just have to learn to live with them.	The physical therapist was right in that I do have to live with this. But that doesn't mean I can't have a relationship. This thought involves catastrophizing and overgeneralizing.
Sometimes when I go for a checkup, I hear people talking about me.	My burns are noticeable; it doesn't mean people don't like me when they talk about me. Here, I'm mind reading.
	Lots of people with disfiguring disabilities have partners. In many cases, they found those partners after the disfigurement occurred.
	If Chelsea really likes and cares about me, she ought to be able to look past my scars.
	If I don't try, I'll never have a relationship. This thought isn't helping me.
	If Chelsea does reject me, it doesn't mean that everyone will. I've handled the pain of burns; rejection can't be that much worse.

Putting your thoughts on trial

PRACTICE

You guessed it; it's your turn to visit Thought Court. Don't be concerned if you struggle in your initial attempts; this important exercise takes practice. (And if you're still confused after examining your own thoughts, you can find several more examples to illustrate further how this process works.) The first step is to complete a Thought Tracker (see Worksheet 6-6) by following these instructions:

1. **Pay attention to your body's signals, and write them down whenever you feel something unpleasant.**

2. **Search for a feeling word that captures your emotion, and jot it down.** Refer to the Daily Unpleasant Emotions Checklist in Chapter 4 for help finding the right feeling words.

3. **Rate your feeling on a scale of intensity from 1 (almost undetectable) to 100 (maximal).**

4. **Ask yourself what was going on when you started noticing your emotions and your body's signals.** The corresponding event can be something happening in your world, but an event can also be in the form of a thought or image that runs through your mind. Be concrete and specific; don't write something overly general, such as, "I hate my work." Instead, ask yourself what happened at work that you didn't like.

5. **Record your thoughts in the Thoughts/Interpretations column of the worksheet. Describe how you perceive, interpret, or think about the event.** Refer to The Thought Query Quiz in Chapter 4 if you experience any difficulty figuring out your thoughts about the event.

6. **Review your thoughts and write down the thought or thoughts that evoke the greatest amount of emotion — your most malicious thoughts.**

Worksheet 6-6   My Thought Tracker

Feelings & Sensations (Rated 1–100)	Corresponding Events	Thoughts/Interpretations

My most malicious thoughts:

1. _____

2. _____

You can find this worksheet on the Web at www.dummies.com/go/anxiety&depressionworkbookfd2e. Download as many copies as you need, and be sure to practice this technique often. In time, you're likely to start changing the way you think and, therefore, the way you feel. Just give the changes some time.

The Thought Tracker prepares you for the next step: Thought Court. Thought Court takes some planning and preparation. Take a malicious thought and consider the Prosecutor's Investigative Questions in Worksheet 6-3. Reflect on your answers in Worksheet 6-7.

PRACTICE

Worksheet 6-7   My Reflections

_____
_____
_____
_____
_____

Now you're ready to put a malicious thought on trial. After you put one thought on trial using the instructions that follow, proceed to put other malicious thoughts through the same process.

PRACTICE

1. **In Worksheet 6-8, designate one of your most malicious thoughts as the accused thought and write it down.**

2. **In the left column, write all the reasons, evidence, and logic that support the truth of your accused thought.** In other words, defend your thought as best you can.

3. **In the right column, write refutations of all the reasons, evidence, and logic presented by the defense. Then write down any additional points that help prosecute the thought.**

Worksheet 6-8   My Thought on Trial Worksheet

Accused thought: _____

Defense: Evidence in Support of the Thought	Prosecution: Evidence Refuting the Thought

You can download extra copies of this form at www.dummies.com/go/anxiety&depressionwork bookfd2e. After all, you need to use the Thought Court method numerous times to feel the full benefit.

After you complete the Thought Court process, decide for yourself whether or not your thought is guilty of causing you unneeded emotional distress, such as anxiety, depression, or other difficult feelings. Even if you conclude that your thought has some grain of truth, you're likely to discover that it's highly suspect of causing you more harm than good. In Thought Court, you don't judge your thought guilty only on the basis of "beyond a reasonable doubt." Rather, judge your thoughts on the "preponderance of evidence;" in plain English, convict your thought if the evidence weighs heaviest on the guilty side.

Reviewing more Thought Court cases

To help you understand Thought Court better, this section contains a few more examples. Because the Thought Tracker also appears in Chapters 4 and 5, I begin with the accused thought here, which comes from the most malicious thoughts at the end of a Thought Tracker (see the earlier section, "Putting your thoughts on trial").

Connor: Doomed to unhappiness

EXAMPLE

Over the years, **Connor**, a 58-year-old high school teacher, has become an avid lover of the outdoors, spending his summer vacations camping, fishing, and hiking. Although his arthritis has been getting progressively worse, Connor has tried to ignore the pain. In fact, he only consults his doctor when the pain becomes overwhelming. His doctor refers him to an orthopedic specialist, who tells Connor he needs a hip replacement. Connor slips into depression at the news. He fills out some Thought Trackers and zeroes in on a malicious thought: "I'll never be happy again. Life will just be a downhill slide from here." He accuses this thought of increasing his misery and puts it on trial (see Worksheet 6-9).

Worksheet 6-9 Connor's Thought on Trial Worksheet

Accused thought: I'll never be happy again. Life will just be a downhill slide from here.

Defense: Evidence in Support of the Thought	Prosecution: Evidence Refuting the Thought
This hip replacement is just the beginning of the end.	Many people get hip replacements without experiencing a series of health problems. This thought is catastrophizing and using unreliable forecasting.
I get my greatest pleasure from the outdoors. If I can't do that anymore, I can't imagine being happy.	That's hogwash. I do get pleasure from other things, such as going to movies, reading novels, and going out to dinner. I'm filtering out these other pleasures.
I'll be suffering from chronic pain the rest of my life. Pain will rob me of all joy.	That's unreliable forecasting and catastrophizing. I need to check with the doctor before I come to this conclusion. And there are many ways to manage pain. Other people have arthritis and manage to have a good quality of life.
No one wants to be around someone who's sick and feeble.	That's probably true if I act like a whining victim. But I don't have to do that. I'm mind reading.

I won't even be able to climb the stairs to my classroom.	Here I go again with unreliable forecasting. I just read that most people with hip replacements return to active lives.
I should have exercised more and kept my weight down; if I had, I never would have needed this hip replacement.	Now I'm shoulding on myself. That doesn't help me at all.
I'm sure I'll be confined to a wheelchair soon.	That's distorted logic; it's using unreliable forecasting. I realize I do that a lot! And even if it turns out to be the case, people in wheelchairs can lead productive lives.
	Most likely, I'll have some discomfort after the surgery, and it will take some time to get better. But, odds are, I'll be almost back to normal if I go to physical therapy.
	Good grief. One of the other teachers at school had a hip replacement last summer, and he looks good as new.

Connor carefully considers the evidence. His verdict: Guilty as charged. He now realizes the thought, "I'll never be happy again — life will just be a downhill slide from here," is far from the truth and certainly doesn't help him cope with his reality.

Emma: Filled with anxiety

EXAMPLE

Emma, a 37-year-old loan officer, regularly puts in a 50-hour workweek. A divorced mom, she juggles the responsibilities of work and parenting. She's also a perfectionist and expects to be able to handle everything. Understandably, Emma is often plagued with anxiety. She worries about keeping up with her job and being a good mother to her two children. So when Emma's son brings home a mediocre report card, she crashes into a terrible depression. She loses her temper and screams at her son, and then she berates herself for being a terrible mother. Emma completes a Thought Tracker and then puts her most malicious thought on trial (see Worksheet 6-10).

REMEMBER

Thought Court is one of the most effective tools for combating anxiety, depression, and other unpleasant emotions. If you have trouble with the exercise, spend more time going over the Prosecutor's Investigative Questions in Worksheet 6-3. It also doesn't hurt to review Chapter 5 and reread the examples in this chapter. If you still struggle, it's a good idea for you to consult a mental health professional who's proficient in cognitive therapy.

Worksheet 6-10   Emma's Thought on Trial Worksheet

Accused thought: I'm a complete failure as a mother; my son is falling apart.

Defense: Evidence in Support of the Thought	Prosecution: Evidence Refuting the Thought
My son is doing horrible in school.	He had one bad report card. It wasn't even all that bad, just worse than his usual. Overall, he has done okay. I'm enlarging here.
I screamed at him. I shouldn't have done that.	I'm not the only mother to lose it. Usually, I'm pretty calm. I'm shoulding on myself; I don't need to do that.
If I were a good mother, I would have known that he needed more help in school.	I wonder why the teacher didn't contact me before report card time.
My son started to cry when I yelled at him.	That's pretty normal; after all, he's a child. It doesn't mean he's falling apart. I'm mind reading here.
I haven't gone on a field trip with my son's class because of work.	Out of 30 kids, only a few parents were able to drive on field trips.
Other mothers even volunteer in the classroom. That's what good moms do.	I wish I could spend more time with my son, but I also need to support the family. I'm engaging in critical comparisons of myself to others.
I've been putting my job ahead of my children.	That's not really true. When my kids really need me, I take the time off. I'm overgeneralizing.
I don't know what to do to help him.	I guess I'll do what the teacher suggests and put him on a weekly grade check.
	If my son were falling apart, he certainly wouldn't have so many friends.
	Up until this last report, he's carried a B+/A- grade average. I just need to see what's going on lately.
	Clearly, I do a lot of things with my son. I can't be Supermom.

After the Verdict: Replacing and Rehabilitating Your Thoughts

Hopefully, the prosecution presents a convincing case against a variety of your malicious thoughts, and you begin to see that many of your thoughts are guilty of scrambling reality and causing excessive emotional distress. When criminals are convicted, society usually tries to rehabilitate them and give them a second chance. The same thing goes for guilty thoughts.

In this section, you see how to rehabilitate your guilty thoughts, one at a time. Rehabilitating your thoughts decreases feelings of depression and anxiety because rehabilitated thoughts are less distorted, judgmental, and critical. Rehabilitated thoughts are actually *replacement thoughts* because they replace your old malicious thoughts.

REMEMBER

A replacement thought is a balanced, *realistic* appraisal of your problem. The reason for forming a *single* replacement thought is that you can use that new thought repeatedly whenever the old, malicious thoughts start rumbling through your mind. The new thought is a quick and easy comeback to negative, distorted, reality-scrambled thinking.

You can use a number of different techniques to develop effective replacement thoughts. The strategies outlined in the following sections help you discard distortions and straighten out your thinking. With these strategies, you discover how to replace your twisted thoughts with more helpful, realistic replacement thoughts. Four different strategies help you develop replacement thoughts. If one doesn't work for you, be sure to try the others.

Getting a little help from a friend

This rehabilitation strategy is pretty simple. You start by imagining that a good friend of yours is going through the same kind of problem as you are. Your friend has the same kind of thoughts as you do about the problem. Now imagine your friend sitting across from you. You feel empathy for your friend, and you want to help.

What would you say? How would you suggest your friend think about this situation? It's important that you look at your friend's problem from an honest viewpoint. Don't simply try to make your friend feel better by sugarcoating the issue; rather, tell your friend about a reasonable way to think about the problem.

The essence of this powerful, yet surprisingly simple, technique is that the advice you would give a friend is advice you can give to yourself. The strategy works by helping you get a little distance from your problem. Viewing thoughts and feelings from a distance helps you be more objective. The following example shows you how to use Getting Help from a Friend to your advantage.

EXAMPLE

Emma (see "Emma: Filled with anxiety" earlier in this chapter) has taken her most malicious thought to Thought Court and found it guilty. Now she turns to Getting Help from a Friend to rehabilitate that thought. She thinks about her best friend, Louise. She imagines Louise coming to her with the same problem and concerns about her son. In other words, Louise is thinking Emma's most malicious thought and seeking advice (see Worksheet 6-11).

Emma's/Louise's most malicious thought:

I'm a complete failure as a mother; my son is falling apart.

Emma reviews her imaginary discussion with Louise. She sees that her perspective changes when she gives Louise advice rather than listens to the negative automatic dialogue in her own head. Next, she distills this perspective into a single replacement thought (see Worksheet 6-12).

Worksheet 6-11   Emma's Getting Help from a Friend (Louise)

Well, Louise, I know you feel like a failure, but your son only came home with two Cs and three Bs. That's not exactly catastrophic. Sure, you haven't spent as much time with him lately, but you've been pretty tied up at work. That happens. You don't need to beat up on yourself. Talk with his teacher and see what you can do to help. Quit sounding like a helpless victim. Besides, your son is 16 now; don't you think he has something to do with his own success and failure? It isn't all about you.

Worksheet 6-12   Emma's Replacement Thought

My son isn't falling apart, and I'm not a failure. All I can do is see what I can do to help. The rest is up to him.

PRACTICE

Take one of your most malicious thoughts and use the Getting Help from a Friend strategy to devise an effective response to that thought. Of course, it helps to take the malicious thought to Thought Court first, which you've done, right? This is a workbook after all. That means you need to do the work for this book to help you. So if you haven't worked on these exercises yet, it's okay, but start now!

1. **Write down one of your most malicious thoughts from your Thought Tracker (see Worksheet 6-6).**

2. **Think of someone you know and respect.**

3. **Imagine that the friend has a problem similar to your own and has similar thoughts about the problem.**

4. **Imagine you're talking with your friend about a better way to think about and deal with the problem.**

5. **Write down the advice you would give your friend in Worksheet 6-13.**

6. **Look over that advice and try to rehabilitate your most malicious thought into a more balanced, summary replacement thought in Worksheet 6-14.**

My most malicious thought: _____

Worksheet 6-13   My Getting Help from a Friend

_____

_____

_____

Worksheet 6-14   My Replacement Thought

_____

_____

_____

_____

Traveling to the future

The events that disrupt your life today rarely have the same meaning after a few days, weeks, or months. For example, have you ever felt distraught about any of the following?

>> Being cut off in traffic

>> Being embarrassed

>> Locking yourself out of your car

>> Forgetting someone's name

>> Experiencing a minor illness or injury

>> Spilling something

>> Discovering a stain on your shirt after you get to work

>> Being late on a credit card payment by two days

>> Having a bad hair day

>> Being involved in a fender bender

>> Getting a traffic ticket

>> Running late

Events like these so often lead to very malicious thoughts and highly distressing feelings. If you think back on these events after some time has passed, however, rarely can you muster up the same intensity of emotion. That's because most upsetting events truly aren't all that important if you look at them in the context of your entire life. Check out the following example of the Traveling to the Future technique in action.

EXAMPLE

Joel owns a piece of land on a busy corner. He'd like to sell the property, but he knows it's worth far more if it can be zoned for commercial purposes first. In order to do that, Joel must present his case in front of the Planning and Zoning Commission. He expects some opposition and criticism from homeowners in the area, so he's been putting this task off for months because of the intense anxiety it arouses in him.

He fills out a Thought Tracker (see "From Arraignment to Conviction: Thought Court" earlier in this chapter) and identifies his most malicious thought: "I'll make a fool out of myself. I'll probably stumble all over my words and sound like an idiot." He travels to the future with this thought to help him gain a better perspective; Joel asks himself how he'll look at this issue at various times in the future (see Worksheet 6-15). He rates the emotional upset and effect on his life that he feels right now, and then he rerates the impact on his life at the conclusion of the exercise.

Worksheet 6-15　Joel's Traveling to the Future

If I do indeed make a fool out of myself, I'll probably feel pretty bad, and the impact on my life will feel like 30 or even 40 on a 100-point scale. I'll still feel embarrassed a week later. I suspect that images of the incident will go through my mind fairly often, but six months from now, I doubt I'll think about the incident much at all. I'm sure that a year later I'll have almost completely forgotten about it. So I guess the overall effect on my life will likely be about a 1 on a 100-point scale.

After pondering what his malicious thought will seem like in the future, Joel feels ready to develop a more realistic replacement thought (see Worksheet 6-16).

Worksheet 6-16　Joel's Replacement Thought

Even if I should happen to make a fool out of myself, it's hardly going to be a life-changing event. I may as well just go ahead and present the case.

REMEMBER The Traveling to the Future technique won't apply to all your thoughts and problems, but it works wonders with quite a few. In Joel's case, he could have analyzed his malicious thought for obvious distortions such as labeling and enlarging. He also could have taken the malicious thought to Thought Court. In other words, be sure to try out a variety of strategies for rehabilitating your thoughts to find the one that works best for you and for a particular thought or thoughts.

PRACTICE Take one of your most malicious thoughts and use the Traveling to the Future strategy to devise an effective response to it.

1. **Write down one of your most malicious thoughts from your Thought Tracker (see Worksheet 6-6).**

2. **In Worksheet 6-17, rate the overall upset and impact you feel at the moment (on a scale of 1 to 100, with 100 representing the highest imaginable impact).**

3. **Think about how your thoughts are likely to change in a week.**

4. **Think about how your thoughts are likely to change in six months.**

5. **Think about how your thoughts are likely to change in a year.**

6. **Rerate how much impact you'll feel as a whole.**

7. **In Worksheet 6-18, write down a balanced, summary replacement thought based on any new perspective you obtain with this strategy.**

My most malicious thought:

Worksheet 6-17   My Traveling to the Future

_____

_____

_____

_____

Worksheet 6-18   My Replacement Thought

_____

_____

_____

_____

Recalculating risks

When you're anxious, worried, or depressed, your mind frequently focuses on the future and makes dire predictions. People worry about things yet to happen to them, such as facing a plane crash, becoming infected with COVID, encountering heights, and experiencing embarrassment. They predict that whatever they undertake will result in horror, misery, or unhappiness. Yet, such worries typically far exceed the actual odds of unwanted outcomes. In other words, people tend to overestimate the risks of negative outcomes, and they do so more often when they're in emotional distress.

When you predict negative outcomes, you have malicious thoughts that paralyze you from taking action. To develop replacement thoughts for your malicious ones, you first need to rethink your negative predictions. Then recalculate your actual risks. After you analyze your predictions, you can rehabilitate your malicious thoughts. The following example illustrates this technique.

EXAMPLE

Melinda's boss, Allison, takes a month off work after the birth of her baby. Melinda takes on Allison's responsibilities in her absence and assumes the extra work without thinking about it. She performs flawlessly. After a month, Allison announces that she isn't returning to work. Melinda is offered Allison's job. Oddly, Melinda now finds herself racked with fear and anxiety. She predicts that she won't be able to handle the job, and she can't see herself as a boss. Her most malicious thoughts are, "I'm not cut out to handle supervising others. I'm a follower, not a leader. I can't do this."

Melinda takes the Rethinking Negative Predictions Quiz shown in Worksheet 6-19 so she can test out her negative predictions.

After filling out her answers to this quiz, Melinda decides to act on her recalculated risk by taking the job. She finds she actually enjoys the new challenges. She looks back over her most malicious thought and develops a replacement thought (see Worksheet 6-20).

Worksheet 6-19　Melinda's Rethinking Negative Predictions Quiz

1. How many times have I predicted this outcome, and how many times has it actually happened to me?

There are other challenges in my life that I thought I couldn't do. I didn't think I'd make it through college, and I did. I actually can't think of any times that I've failed at something important to me.

2. How often does this happen to people I know?

I can't recall a single instance in this company when someone has been promoted and then fired.

3. If someone else made this prediction, would I agree?

Not necessarily. I would base my prediction on past performance. I guess mine has been pretty good.

4. Am I assuming this will happen just because I fear that it will, or is there a reasonable chance that it will truly happen?

Of course, there's a small chance I won't be able to handle the job. But clearly, I'm making some unwarranted assumptions here. After all, I've done the job successfully for a month.

5. Do I have any experiences from my past that suggest my dire prediction is likely to occur?

Again, for the past month, I've done fine. I've never really failed at anything important, come to think of it.

Worksheet 6-20　Melinda's Replacement Thoughts

Although I don't "feel" like a leader, the evidence says otherwise. I'm capable, and I'm doing it!

PRACTICE

Take one of your most malicious thoughts and use the Testing Thoughts strategy to devise an effective response to that thought.

1. **When you find yourself making a negative prediction about some upcoming event or situation, write down your most malicious thought.**

2. **Take the Rethinking Negative Predictions Quiz in Worksheet 6-21.**

3. **Act on your recalculated risk by doing the thing you fear.**

4. **In Worksheet 6-22, write out a replacement thought for your original prediction and use it in similar future situations.**

Assuming your answers tell you that the odds are in your favor, go ahead and test out your negative predictions. Jump right in and do what you fear. Then jot down a replacement thought (in Worksheet 6-22) for your original malicious thought.

Worksheet 6-21   My Rethinking Negative Predictions Quiz

1. How many times have I predicted this outcome, and how many times has it actually happened to me?

_____

_____

_____

_____

2. How often does this happen to people I know?

_____

_____

_____

_____

3. If someone else made this prediction, would I agree?

_____

_____

_____

_____

4. Am I assuming this will happen just because I fear that it will, or is there a reasonable chance that it will truly happen?

_____

_____

_____

_____

5. Do I have any experiences from my past that suggest my dire prediction is likely to occur?

_____

_____

_____

_____

Worksheet 6-22   My Replacement Thoughts

_____

_____

_____

_____

If the odds of a bad outcome are high, go to the Worst-Case Scenario strategy in the next section of this chapter, where you can find techniques for coping with bad outcomes.

Imagining the worst

The preceding section shows you how to rethink risks because, in general, when people are depressed or anxious, they greatly overestimate the odds of bad things happening. *And* they grossly underestimate their abilities to cope.

But just in case you're starting to think otherwise, this section does not try to convince you that bad things never happen. They do. People get sick, accidents happen, and relationships end. Stuff happens. Sometimes really bad stuff. What then? Imagining yourself dealing with worst-case scenarios is a useful exercise because it helps you understand that you can get through whatever it is that you fear.

Millions of people worldwide have died during the global pandemic. That is truly a worst-case scenario. However, you can improve your odds by following health guidelines, such as masking, getting a vaccination, staying away from crowds, and washing your hands. Those at high risk because of age, preexisting conditions, or other factors should be more cautious. Most worst-case scenarios involve less actual risk.

For example, the following situation shows you how the Worst-Case Scenario Quiz helps Martha make a decision and develop a replacement thought for her malicious thought.

Martha has been single for the past 20 years. Since her painful divorce, she's had a number of casual dates, but work and raising her child have kept her attention away from developing a serious relationship. Now at age 50, Martha has fallen in love with someone special, and he feels the same way. However, she finds herself withdrawing out of fear that things won't work out. She predicts that if she commits to the relationship, her companion will ultimately reject her, and she couldn't stand that. Martha identifies her most malicious thought as, "I'd rather be alone forever than risk the pain of rejection again; I don't think I could deal with that."

Martha takes the Worst-Case Scenario Quiz shown in Worksheet 6-23 to identify and work through her greatest fear.

Now Martha's ready to devise a more realistic replacement thought (see Worksheet 6-24).

Take one of your most malicious thoughts and use the Worst-Case Scenario strategy to devise an effective response to that thought.

Worksheet 6-23   Martha's Worst-Case Scenario Quiz

1. Have I ever dealt with anything like this in the past?

   I was rejected by my ex-husband. It took me quite a while, but I got through it. Today, I'm actually fairly happy.

2. How much will this affect my life a year from now?

   If he rejects me, I'll be hurt and alone. I've been okay alone for a while now. A year from now, I suspect I'll be sad, but I think I'll be getting over the worst of the rejection.

3. Do I know people who have coped with something like this? How did they do it?

   I have lots of friends who've lost a relationship. They got through it by staying active and seeking support from others. A couple of my friends went to therapy, which they said helped.

4. Do I know anyone I could turn to for help or support?

   Over the years, I've developed a pretty good network of friends. I know I could get support from them. My family has always been there for me, too.

5. Can I think of a creative, new possibility that could result from this challenge?

   If this relationship doesn't work, I think I'll volunteer to work with Habitat for Humanity in another country. I've always wanted to do something like that. I love travel and meeting new people. I think that experience would be very meaningful to me.

Worksheet 6-24   Martha's Replacement Thoughts

If I do get rejected, I can handle it. I love this guy. Now I feel more like taking the risk, committing myself to this relationship, and seeing what happens.

1. **When you find yourself thinking of a worst-case scenario that you think you can't cope with, write down your most malicious thought.**

2. **Take the Worst-Case Scenario Quiz in Worksheet 6-25.**

3. **Rehabilitate your malicious thought with a replacement thought written in Worksheet 6-26.**

Use the techniques in this chapter to combat malicious thoughts. Take each of your malicious thoughts and develop a replacement, one at a time. The more thoughts you rehabilitate, the more you'll benefit.

Worksheet 6-25   My Worst-Case Scenario Quiz

1. Have I ever dealt with anything like this in the past?

_____

_____

_____

2. How much will this affect my life a year from now?

_____

_____

_____

3. Do I know people who have coped with something like this? How did they do it?

_____

_____

_____

4. Do I know anyone I could turn to for help or support?

_____

_____

_____

5. Can I think of a creative, new possibility that could result from this challenge?

_____

_____

_____

Worksheet 6-26   My Replacement Thought

_____

_____

_____

Reflections on Chapter 6

This chapter is full of exercises and ideas for overcoming anxious and depressed thinking. Work through it carefully — this isn't a timed test. After completing the exercises and looking at your thoughts in new and different ways, take time to reflect on your new insights using the space in Worksheet 6-27.

Worksheet 6-27   **My Reflections**

_____

_____

_____

_____

Chapter **7**

Looking at Problematic Assumptions

When people get out of bed every morning, they open their eyes and look at their world. Some folks grab glasses off the nightstand, while others need to get up and put in their contacts to see better. Some lucky people have 20/20 vision.

What most people don't know is that everyone's vision of reality is altered by special *assumptions*. Assumptions are strongly held beliefs or views that you have about yourself, your relationships with others, and your world. These views powerfully influence how you respond to, interpret, and feel about events, but you probably aren't aware that you hold them.

Perhaps you know of people who view the world through rose-colored glasses. As perpetual optimists, they see the best in everything and everyone. You could say these people have overly optimistic assumptions. On the other hand, you likely know a few folks who view the world through dark, gloomy shades. They expect the worst and rarely see the positive side of things. In other words, they have pessimistic assumptions.

Ever wonder why people respond to the same event with widely different emotions and actions? Why do some people get extremely mad when caught in traffic while others, Zen-like, wait patiently? Why do some react to adversity with severe anxiety, while others are angry or depressed. The way people look at the world, through their assumptions, determines the way they react and feel about everyday life.

TIP

An assumption can be thought of as a personal prescription for eyeglass lenses that causes your vision to be accurate, slightly out of focus, or grossly distorted. Throughout this chapter, lenses will be used as a metaphor explaining the nature of assumptions.

This chapter helps you understand the nature of assumptions. Your views of people, events, and even your self-image depend upon which lenses you look through. Appreciating how assumptions work helps you realize whether your lenses are dirty, cracked, smoky, colored, or clear. A quiz shows you which lenses you look through and how they may cause you emotional trouble. The exercises that follow in the section "Changing Your Assumptions" demonstrate how to change problematic assumptions.

Examining Unhelpful Beliefs

Everyone has certain unquestioned assumptions about life. Many assumptions are quite useful. For example, it's not a bad idea to assume that day follows night, taxes must be paid, food is located at grocery stores, most drivers stop at red lights, and hard work usually pays off. Not questioning these assumptions makes life more efficient. Think about how snarled traffic would be if no one assumed that red means stop and green means go. Or just consider how much time you'd waste if you searched for food in department stores, schools, and libraries rather than *assuming* that you'd find it in grocery stores.

Unquestioned assumptions can also involve views about how the world and people work. These assumptions or beliefs color the way you feel about yourself and the things that happen to you. For example, you may look through a *perfectionistic* lens and believe that you must be perfect all the time. Or perhaps you have a *vulnerable* view and thus assume that the world is a dangerous place. As you explore assumptions such as these, you can see that they form the foundation for your most distressing emotions, such as depression, anxiety, worry, irritability, apprehension, and even anger.

REMEMBER

Assumptions are the broad themes or expectations that you live by. These themes directly influence the kinds of thoughts you have and, in turn, how you feel about what happens to you. Each assumption can be activated by many types of events.

EXAMPLE

Shauna and **Diana** work as nurses at a local hospital. They both apply for one open management position. Although both Shauna and Diana are well qualified, a nurse from another hospital gets the job. Shauna reacts with anger and comments, "I deserved that job; the administration had no right to give that job away. I feel cheated and disrespected. I'm angry and bummed out."

Diana reacts quite differently. She feels gloomy and says, "I'm sure they made the right decision picking someone else. I shouldn't have let my supervisor talk me into applying. I'm not management material."

Shauna and Diana have different life assumptions. Shauna has the assumption of *entitlement*. She believes that she always deserves the best; she feels that the world owes her and that if she wants something, it should be hers. On the other hand, Diana sees through the lens of *inadequacy*. She thinks that she's not good enough and that others have more skill and talent than she does. She assumes that she couldn't do the job even though her supervisor told her she has the appropriate ability and background.

Same event. Different thoughts and different feelings. Shauna's *entitlement* assumption makes her prone to tension, anger, and despondency when her needs aren't met. Diana's *inadequacy* lens steers her in the direction of depression when her adequacy is called into question. Shauna and Diana apply their respective assumptions to many different events in their lives. For example, when they're both caught in an unexpected traffic jam, they view the event through their own lens and thus experience different thoughts and feelings. Shauna's *entitlement* leads her to feel rage and have thoughts like, "No one in this town knows how to drive. What idiots!" Diane, who looks through an *inadequacy* belief, scolds herself, "I should have left earlier. Why didn't I listen to the traffic report this morning? I'm an idiot!"

With some understanding of problematic assumptions, it's time to take a look at which ones may be affecting you and your life. After all, changing the way you feel starts with identifying your problematic beliefs. If you're unaware of your own assumptions, you're powerless to do anything about them.

Recognizing your problematic assumptions

There are, perhaps, an unlimited number of problematic assumptions. However, the following list emphasizes those that tend to cause the most emotional distress, such as anxiety and depression. Look these over, and then take the quiz in Worksheet 7-1 to see which lenses may distort your view of yourself, those around you, and the world.

>> **Approval Addiction:** This assumption leads a person to constantly seek the approval of others. Criticism causes instant feelings of distress — either anxiousness or depression.

>> **Control Seeking:** Control freaks need to be in charge of everything. No one else can be trusted. They rely on themselves until faced with exhaustion or despair.

>> **Dependent:** This assumption is held by people who don't feel able to manage life on their own. They need someone to direct every aspect of their lives. And when faced with abandonment, they're inconsolable.

>> **Entitled:** Those who have an entitlement assumption about themselves believe that they have a right to have whatever they want. They respond with sharp anger and shock when they don't get their own way.

>> **Inadequate:** People who feel inadequate see themselves as inferior. They believe that they can't measure up to others and tend to shy away from challenges.

>> **Perfectionist:** This problematic assumption tells a person they must do everything perfectly, or they'll be complete failures. Perfectionists who inevitably fail to meet their own impossible standards often become anxious or depressed.

>> **Unworthy:** People who feel unworthy believe that they're undeserving of having good things happen to them. They rarely ask for help and don't expect consideration from others.

>> **Vulnerable:** Those with a vulnerable lens believe that the world is a dangerous place, and they're not able to manage life's challenges, big or small.

PRACTICE

The questionnaire in Worksheet 7-1 is designed to clarify which lenses may be causing you trouble. After you identify your lenses, you discover a little more about how they work, where they come from, and most importantly, what you can do about them. Before you start marking the statements in the worksheet that apply to you, consider the following tips.

>> **Answer as honestly as possible.** Sometimes people respond how they think they should rather than responding with honest self-appraisals. Self-deception isn't useful.

>> **Take your time to reflect on various events and situations that have happened to you and that are relevant to each assumption.** You shouldn't rush this task.

>> **Base your answer on how you feel and react in situations that relate to each assumption.** For example, if you frequently feel inadequate but know in your head that you're actually not, answer on the basis of how you feel when your adequacy comes into question, such as when you're asked to make a speech.

>> **Don't worry about inconsistencies.** For example, if you're a perfectionist, you may also quite often feel inadequate when you make a mistake. Or if you normally feel unworthy and undeserving, you may find yourself feeling quite angry and entitled on occasions when your needs unexpectedly go unmet.

>> **Each assumption is followed by five statements that are consistent with the presence of the assumption. In Worksheet 7-1, answer true or false for each statement that applies to you.**

Worksheet 7-1 Problematic Assumptions Questionnaire

True	False	Problematic Assumption
		Approval
		It's extremely important that other people think highly of me.
		I get terribly upset if someone disagrees with me.
		I hate it when I'm criticized.
		I hardly ever say no to people even when it's inconvenient.
		I feel driven to be nice to everyone around me.
True	**False**	*Control Seeking*
		Nothing is worse than losing control of what I'm doing.
		I don't like to work for anyone but myself.
		I like everything to be predictable and go according to plan.
		I prefer to be in charge of everything and everyone.
		I don't delegate; I need to be involved in every decision.
True	**False**	*Dependent*
		I need lots of support and help from others.
		I lack the confidence to do things on my own.
		I need lots of reassurance that I'm doing okay.
		I like to work as a team; I don't like to take the lead.
		I feel insecure when I'm not with friends or family.

True	False	Problematic Assumption
True	**False**	*Entitled*
		I deserve to have what I want when I want.
		I get angry when I don't get my way.
		I feel like I'm better than most other people.
		People should go out of their way to pay attention to me.
		My needs come before others.
True	**False**	*Inadequate*
		I'm less capable than others in many ways.
		I avoid taking on tough challenges.
		I'm afraid of taking risks because I'll likely fail.
		I'd rather sit back and chill than try and screw up.
		I just don't measure up.
True	**False**	*Perfectionist*
		If I can't do something right, I won't do it at all.
		The slightest flaw is unacceptable.
		When I make a mistake, I feel horrible.
		There's a right way and a wrong way to do things.
		I dwell on any mistake I've ever made in my life.
True	**False**	*Unworthy*
		I put my needs last.
		I feel uncomfortable when someone compliments me.
		I never ask others for help or favors.
		I don't deserve success.
		I don't believe that I handle life's challenges very well.
True	**False**	*Vulnerable*
		I worry about bad things happening all the time.
		The world is a dangerous place.
		I think constantly about all the possible threats that are coming.
		I believe that every day is filled with peril.
		I believe that it's far too late to solve the world's problems.

REMEMBER Any problematic assumption in which you endorsed three or more items as true likely gives you trouble now and then. If you discover that you have many problematic assumptions, don't worry. Many people have a range of these beliefs. Change takes time, but you can do it — one lens at a time.

Take a few minutes now to reflect on the results of your Problematic Assumptions Questionnaire. In Worksheet 7-2, first list the assumptions on which you endorsed three or more statements. Then jot down thoughts about how these beliefs or lenses may be causing you to have troubling emotions. Don't worry if you're not quite sure of the connections; there will be more ways of seeing the assumptions' influence on your life in the next few sections of this chapter.

_____

_____

_____

_____

_____

How assumptions work

You may wonder just how much trouble these assumptions create and why they're the root cause of most emotional turmoil. The examples in this section give you an idea about how they work their mischief. The exercise in this section is likely to convince you of just how much distorted lenses affect your vision and your emotional life.

After you identify your problematic assumptions, it's a good idea to consider more examples of how the beliefs lead to problematic thoughts and feelings. Notice how the assumptions reflect a broad theme and the thoughts are specific to a given event.

EXAMPLE

Ayman, Paul, and **Wayne** are friends and neighbors. All three have teenage daughters who are the same age and also best friends. One evening, the girls are late coming home. All three men have very different reactions. See how problematic assumptions influence how the fathers interpret this identical event and respond to their daughters.

Ayman has an inadequate assumption. He feels like he's done something wrong, even when it's not his fault (see Worksheet 7-3).

Worksheet 7-3   Influence of Problematic Assumption on Ayman

Event: My daughter is 30 minutes late getting home.

Problematic Assumption	Thoughts	Feelings
Inadequate: I'm never able to do what's best for my family. I can hardly handle my own life.	I must be a terrible father; otherwise, my daughter would be home on time.	Sad and depressed

Paul has a _control seeking_ assumption. He likes to be in charge and feels uncomfortable when others challenge his authority (see Worksheet 7-4).

Wayne's major assumption is _vulnerable_. He worries that the people he cares about are in danger and he's unable to save them (see Worksheet 7-5).

Worksheet 7-4   Influence of Problematic Assumption on Paul

Event: My daughter is 30 minutes late getting home.

Problematic Assumption	Thoughts	Feelings
Control Seeking: I like to be in charge of everyone and everything.	How dare she be late? I'm her father; she'd better respect me and do what I say.	Anger and anxiety

Worksheet 7-5   Influence of Problematic Assumption on Wayne

Event: My daughter is 30 minutes late getting home.

Problematic Assumption	Thoughts	Feelings
Vulnerable: I worry about losing people I care about; the world is a dangerous place.	Oh no! She's probability had an accident. She might be hurt, and I couldn't go on if I lost her.	Fear and anxiety

PRACTICE

These three examples show you how these pervasive assumptions affect people's thoughts and feelings. Guess what? It's your turn to complete an Influence of Problematic Assumptions worksheet (see Worksheet 7-6). Filling out these exercises works a whole lot better than just reading about them, so don't forget to do the work.

1. **When events happen and you notice distressing feelings, write the event down.** The event can be something happening in your world or something that runs through your mind. Whatever it is, be specific.

2. **In the middle column, write down the thoughts or interpretations you have about the event.** In other words, describe how you perceive or think about the event. If you have difficulty with this step, flip to Chapter 6 for more information about events and thoughts.

3. **In the right column, write down any feelings you have about the event.** Check out the Daily Unpleasant Emotions Checklist in Chapter 4 for a list of feelings.

4. **Review your Problematic Assumptions Questionnaire in Worksheet 7-1. (You did do it, didn't you?) Think about which assumption fits your thoughts and feelings best, and write that in the left column.** You may discover that more than one assumption applies. Also, include a brief definition of the assumption based on the reflections you recorded in Worksheet 7-2. Feel free to shorten or tailor the definition so that it fits you better.

5. **In Worksheet 7-7, reflect on what this exercise tells you about your problematic emotions and where they come from.**

Worksheet 7-6   The Influence of My Problematic Assumptions

Event:

Problematic Assumption	Thoughts	Feelings

Event:

Problematic Assumption	Thoughts	Feelings

Event:

Problematic Assumption	Thoughts	Feelings

Worksheet 7-7   My Reflections

_____

_____

_____

_____

_____

For more copies of this form, visit www.dummies.com/go/anxiety&depressionworkbookfd2e. The more forms you fill out, the more you'll understand how these lenses impact your life.

Many people find that working with a therapist to complete these exercises helps them sort out different feelings, thoughts, and assumptions. This work is especially important for long-lasting improvements in mood.

The origins of assumptions

Usually, the prescription for your lenses is established in your childhood. People don't come into the world seeing themselves as *inadequate, unworthy, entitled,* or *perfectionistic.* Rather, they learn these patterns through repeated experiences. Assumptions emerge from abuse, abandonment, betrayal, excessive praise, harsh criticism, natural disasters, loss, rejection, and other emotionally powerful events.

Some problematic assumptions even develop from well-meaning parents who unwittingly go overboard (probably because of their own life experiences). For example, some parents worry so much that they overprotect their children, who subsequently feel vulnerable. Other parents overindulge their children in the name of love and caring, and their kids may end up feeling entitled.

TIP

On the road to understanding and changing your assumptions, it helps to reflect on what caused you to acquire the lenses you look through in the first place. When you understand these origins, you can release the notion that you're crazy, weird, or messed up. Self-forgiveness releases energy that you can use for grinding new lenses for better vision. Spend a few minutes thinking about what experiences in your childhood may have led to your problematic assumptions. Reflect on those on Worksheet 7-8.

Worksheet 7-8   My Reflections

_____

_____

_____

_____

Changing Your Assumptions

After you complete the exercises in the preceding sections, you should know which lenses or assumptions cause you problems. This section gives you three techniques for regrinding your lenses. It would be nice if you could toss the old lenses in the trash or throw them on the ground and stomp on them. But these lenses consist of almost shatterproof material — after all, they're cast from intense emotional turmoil. Thus, you need to proceed slowly and cautiously.

WARNING

You may find the task of changing your assumptions more challenging than you expected. Even if you put a lot of time and work into it, when you're tired or stressed, you may find yourself looking through your outdated prescription. That's okay. Your new prescription takes a while to break in. You're bound to use the old one out of habit. Your goal is simply to use the new lenses more often than the old ones (until you can't even find the old ones). If you find the task too difficult, please consult a mental health professional.

Distinguishing the past from the present

Assumptions most often develop from emotionally significant events in childhood, and they make sense when viewed in conjunction with those events. Your world has no doubt changed a great deal over the years, but you probably still look through many of the same old lenses. And those lenses don't give you a clear vision of present-day reality.

EXAMPLE

Hannah developed the problematic assumption of *perfectionistic.* As a kid, she was harshly criticized when she wasn't perfect, so the lens helped her avoid some of that criticism. The lens was a healthy adaptation to her life at the time. But today, as an adult, her *perfectionistic* lens causes her anxiety, stress, and even depression when she fails. Furthermore, no one in her life is nearly as critical as her father was. So, she doesn't need to be perfect to avoid harsh criticism today. Her *perfectionistic* lens distorts her vision. Hannah completes the Then and Now Exercise in Worksheet 7-9 to help her understand how her past experiences cause her to overreact to current triggers. Seeing this connection will help her change her problematic assumption.

Worksheet 7-9   Hannah's Then and Now Exercise

Problematic Assumption	Childhood Image(s)	Current Triggers
Perfectionistic: I feel like I must do everything perfectly. And if I don't, it's awful.	My mother would scream at me if I got my clothes dirty.	If I get a blemish, I freak. And a stain on my blouse drives me insane.
	My father was never satisfied with anything but straight As. Even when I got them, he was unimpressed.	I can't stand being evaluated at work. I lose sleep for days. Even a single rating just one notch below Outstanding sends me into a depression.
	Both of my parents talked about other people critically. They put people down for just about anything.	I judge everything I do — my hair, my housecleaning, my job, everything. And sometimes I judge other people too harshly over trivial things.

EXAMPLE

Eleven-year-old **Adam** had a warm and caring family. He lived in a nice neighborhood and attended a reputable public middle school. He was bright, but not brilliant. He played sports well enough and had many friends. In short, he was an unlikely candidate for developing problematic assumptions.

Tragically, one beautiful fall day a highly disturbed classmate brought a gun to school and shot three students. Adam witnessed the event and was slightly injured. Subsequently, Adam suffered from nightmares, experienced intrusive images of the event, and was easily startled. Understandably, Adam developed a *vulnerable* assumption or view of life.

Now an adult, anxiety often overwhelms Adam. His *vulnerable* assumption is activated by events only superficially similar to the original trauma. Adam completes the Then and Now Exercise in Worksheet 7-10 to help him understand how his past experiences contribute to his current responses. This connection helps him begin to change his original assumption.

WARNING

Some people who experience trauma develop post-traumatic stress disorder, which is a chronic and serious condition. If you have symptoms such as nightmares, flashbacks, avoidance, or high levels of arousal when triggered by past memories, please seek a mental health consultation.

Worksheet 7-10   Adam's Then and Now Exercise

Problematic Assumption	Childhood Image(s)	Current Triggers
Vulnerable: I'm scared. The world feels very dangerous.	The image of a gun pointing at me is burned deeply into my brain. I hear the screams of the kids. I see blood and feel searing pain. I thought I was going to die.	When someone suddenly cuts me off in traffic, I feel the same surge of adrenaline and fear.
		Crowds make me feel nervous. I find myself watching my back.
		Whenever I meet someone new, I get anxious and have trouble trusting them. I wonder about the motives of even the nicest people.

PRACTICE

You know the routine. Take some time to fill out the Then and Now Exercise (see Worksheet 7-11) for each problematic assumption that you identified in Worksheet 7-1 earlier in this chapter. Whenever one of your problematic assumptions is activated, refer back to this form to remind yourself that your feelings and reactions today have more to do with yesteryear than with your current reality.

1. **In the left column, write down one of the problematic assumptions that you endorsed three or more items on your Problematic Assumptions Questionnaire (see Worksheet 7-1).** Also include a brief definition of the lens based on your reflections from Worksheet 7-2. Feel free to shorten or tailor the definition so that it fits you better.

2. **Reflect on your childhood and, in the middle column, record any memories or images that probably had something to do with the development of your problematic assumption.** Review Worksheet 7-10 for ideas.

3. **Be on the lookout for events that trigger your assumption, and write those events in the right column as they occur.**

Worksheet 7-11   My Then and Now Exercise

Problematic Assumption	Childhood Image(s)	Current Triggers

TIP

Because each lens often has multiple associated images and a variety of triggers, you should fill out a separate form for each problematic lens. And whenever your problematic lens is triggered, review this Then and Now Exercise as a reminder of what your reaction is actually all about.

WARNING

For almost any problematic assumption, you need to employ an array of strategies to feel significant benefit. Don't expect a single exercise to "cure" you, and always consider professional help if your own efforts don't take you far enough.

After you complete the exercise, take some time to reflect on what you've learned about yourself and your feelings, and record your reflections in Worksheet 7-12.

Worksheet 7-12   My Reflections

_____

_____

_____

_____

_____

_____

Tallying up costs and benefits

The process of changing long-held assumptions stirs up anxiety in most people. That's because they believe (whether consciously or unconsciously) that these strongly held beliefs either protect or benefit them in some important ways. For example, if you have a *vulnerable* assumption, you probably think that seeing the world as dangerous helps you avoid harm. Or if you possess a *dependent* belief, you likely think that it guides you to find the help from others you truly need.

But you may not have as much awareness of the *costs* of your beliefs. This section helps reveal the hidden costs of problematic assumptions. Only when you fully believe that your assumptions cause you more harm than good do you have the motivation to change them.

EXAMPLE

Cameron, a 22-year-old college student, loves to have a good time. He looks at his world through the *entitled* assumption. He rarely sets limits on himself or others and doesn't think he should have to. He says what he thinks and does what he wants. His high intelligence and easy-going personality have enabled him to get by — until recently.

Lately, Cameron's drinking, which has never been under great control, escalates. He hangs out at bars until they close. Hangovers cause him to miss classes, and his grades, previously hovering just above passing, sink into the failure zone. Cameron gets picked up for a DWI and is put on academic probation in the same week. He reels from the impact of these events and becomes angry, then depressed. Alarmed, his parents encourage him to see someone at the Student Mental Health Center.

After discovering that Cameron looks through an *entitled* lens, his therapist suggests that he fill out a Cost/Benefit Analysis of his assumption that he should always get what he wants. Because patients often downplay the benefits of their assumptions when they're in therapy, his therapist suggests that he first ponder the advantages of his assumption (see Worksheet 7-13).

Worksheet 7-13   Cameron's Cost/Benefit Analysis (Part I)

<u>Assumption:</u> Entitled. I believe that I deserve to be happy and get what I want. I should be able to do what I feel like. It's good to express feelings and do what feels good.

Benefits	Costs
It feels good to do what I want.	
I know how to have a good time.	
I don't have to be a slave to rules and to what people tell me to do.	
My friends know that I say what I think and that I'm honest.	
I like showing how I feel no matter what others think.	
I don't have to deny my needs.	

Cameron doesn't have much trouble figuring out benefits for his problematic assumption. In fact, at this point, he's not even sure the lens is problematic at all. However, his therapist urges him to carefully consider any negative consequences, or *costs*, of his *entitled* assumption. Worksheet 7-14 shows Cameron's completed Cost/Benefit Analysis.

Worksheet 7-14   Cameron's Cost/Benefit Analysis (Part II)

<u>Assumption:</u> Entitled. I believe that I deserve to be happy and get what I want. I should be able to do what I feel like. It's good to express feelings and do what feels good.

Benefits	Costs
It feels good to do what I want.	It feels good at the moment, but later I get hangovers.
I know how to have a good time.	I have a good time for a while, but my grades have suffered.
I don't have to be a slave to rules and to what people tell me to do.	When I didn't follow the rules about drinking and driving, I got a DWI and spent a night in jail. I never want that to happen again.
My friends know that I say what I think and that I'm honest.	I know I've hurt some good friends by what I've said. I don't like doing that.
I like showing how I feel no matter what.	It's not always smart to express everything I feel. I'm a lousy poker player. And my anger gets me in trouble sometimes.

(continued)

Worksheet 7-14 *(continued)*

I don't have to deny my needs.	Eventually, this is all going to catch up with me.
	My life is spinning out of control this way.
	I want to succeed in life, and that's not where I'm headed at all.
	A lot of my friends seem more mature than I am. I used to think they were just boring, but I see that, in some ways, they seem happier than I am.

As Cameron wraps up his Cost/Benefit Analysis, he comes to a realization: "My *entitled* belief is ruining my life!" He feels an increased desire to do something about what he now sees as a real problem.

PRACTICE

A Cost/Benefit Analysis helps you boost your motivation to regrind problematic lenses or beliefs. Take the time to carefully complete this exercise in Worksheet 7-15.

1. **Write down one of the problematic assumptions that you identified in Worksheet 7-1.** Also, include a brief definition of the belief based on your reflections in Worksheet 7-2. Feel free to shorten or tailor the definition so that it fits you better.

2. **Think about any and all of the conceivable benefits for your problematic assumption, and record them in the left column.** Sometimes these may come readily; other times, you may need to reflect a while. Write down everything you come up with.

3. **In the right column, record any and all conceivable costs of your problematic assumption.** It's a good idea to start by looking at the presumed benefits and responding with a counterargument. Then, add any additional costs that you come up with.

4. **Review your Cost/Benefit Analysis carefully. Decide whether the disadvantages or costs outweigh the advantages or benefits. Write down your conclusions in Worksheet 7-16.**

Worksheet 7-15   My Cost/Benefit Analysis

Assumption:

Benefits	**Costs**

Go to www.dummies.com/go/anxiety&depressionworkbookfd2e to print out extra copies of this form. You need to fill one out for each problematic assumption you identify.

Worksheet 7-16   My Reflections

_____

_____

_____

_____

_____

Taking direct action against problematic assumptions

The exercises in the previous two sections were designed to increase your motivation and set the stage for altering your assumptions. In this section, guidelines for developing an action plan show you how to prepare for an all-out assault on those unhelpful beliefs. Ready . . . set . . . go!

To tackle the action steps, you start by figuring out the effect your assumption has had on you, your emotions, and your life. For example, if you have the _perfectionistic_ lens, you may realize that this belief causes inordinate tension and worry; basically, you obsess over every little error.

The next step in taking action is to devise a plan that tests the assumptions. For example, an action step for the _perfectionistic_ lens tests out the assumption that you must never make mistakes. The test is an experiment in which you intentionally make small mistakes and see what happens.

To help you devise your own action steps, Worksheet 7-17 contains some examples for each problematic assumption. But don't let the list stifle your own creativity. Be adventurous and take risks.

TIP

These sample action steps are just ideas, but if one or more of them fit your situation, great! However, your action steps need to specifically address the ways in which your problematic assumptions are affecting your life. Make your steps _small, doable, and personalized._ After you develop your action steps, don't forget to actually do them! And if you have trouble carrying out some action steps, try breaking them into smaller steps.

PRACTICE

Fill out Worksheet 7-18 with your Problematic Assumption Action Steps for at least three of your assumptions. If you need to review your assumptions, look back at Worksheet 7-1 and 7-2.

Worksheet 7-17   Sample Problematic Assumptions Action Steps

Assumption	Action Steps
Approval Addict:	I'll wear sweats to the supermarket without make-up.
	I'll quit trying to please others and do something for myself.
	I'll stop trying to do twice as much as others on my team at work.
Control Seeking:	I'll allow my roommate to make decisions about meal planning.
	I'll refrain from advising my adult son about finances.
	I'll start listening to my partner about childrearing.
Dependent:	I'll go out to a restaurant by myself.
	I'll solve some household tasks by looking up how to do them online instead of getting a handyperson.
	I'll stop calling my mother for advice every day.
Entitled:	I'll stop demanding that other people meet my needs immediately.
	I'll try to compromise more.
	I'll give back to my community by volunteering.
Inadequate:	I'll learn a new skill at the community college.
	I'll look for a more demanding and rewarding job.
	I'll stop putting myself down all the time.
Perfectionistic:	I'll try to make a bunch of trivial mistakes in one day to show I can live through it.
	I won't go over my work product more than twice before turning it in.
	I'll try something new that I probably won't be great at.
Unworthy:	I'll ask someone for a favor.
	I'll remind myself that I deserve good things.
	I'm going to ask for a raise that I'm entitled to.
Vulnerable:	I'll fly in an airplane even though it scares me.
	I'm vaccinated, so I'm going to go and enjoy lunch outside with friends even though I'm still scared about COVID.
	I'm going to allow my daughter to take driver's education despite my fear of her eventually driving alone.

Worksheet 7-18   My Problematic Assumptions Action Steps

Assumption	Action Steps
1.	1.
	2.
	3.
2.	1.
	2.
	3.
3.	1.
	2.
	3.
4.	1.
	2.
	3.

REMEMBER

The assumptions or lenses you see through were largely ground by circumstances and events rooted in your childhood, events over which you had little control. Thus, you don't deserve blame for carrying your lenses around. However, you do own the responsibility for doing something about regrinding your lenses. Regrinding lenses is slow, arduous work that takes patience, but the new, clear vision that results from your efforts is worth the wait.

Squeeze your eyes shut. Now open them. How is your vision? Any clearer? Jot down a few of your thoughts and feelings in Worksheet 7-19.

Worksheet 7-19   My Reflections

_____
_____
_____
_____
_____

Chapter **8**

Managing Mindfulness and Achieving Acceptance

S it quietly for a few moments and pay attention to your breathing. Feel the air as it passes through your nostrils and slowly fills your lungs. Experience the sensation of your lungs deflating as you exhale. If thoughts come into your mind, notice them as an observer and allow them to pass through. Go back to focusing on your breathing.

This breathing exercise introduces you to *mindfulness*. Mindfulness is a state of awareness of the present in the absence of judgment, analysis, and reasoning. In other words, it's awareness without dwelling on *thinking*. (That's why the term mindfulness really ought to be "mindless-ness," but alas, the world has adopted the term "mindfulness.") You can't achieve mindfulness without *acceptance*, which involves patience and tolerance as well as the willingness to feel and experience "what is," without resistance. This chapter guides you through the acceptance of your thoughts and feelings so that you can achieve mindfulness.

TIP

Focusing on the present moment usually decreases symptoms of depression and anxiety. That's because most of what makes people miserable involves regret, guilt, grief, trauma, or disappointment from the past or predictions of future unhappiness or danger. Research studies across many years and disciplines have validated the usefulness of mindfulness to cope with difficult emotions.

Making Space for Meditation

Meditation is one way to mindfully experience the present moment. Meditation involves a set period of time, focused attention, and an open mind. There are many types of meditation, such as breathing meditation, walking meditation, sitting meditation, Yoga, Tai Chi, mantra-focused meditation, and loving-kindness meditation. Rather than explain each type, this section provides you with a few general tips about meditation and an example of a breathing and mantra-focused meditation that you can easily work into your day. For more information, check out *Meditation For Dummies,* by Stephen Bodian (Wiley).

Thoughts are just thoughts

A common myth about meditation is that the main goal of the practice is to achieve a blank, totally focused mind. The first dozen or so times I tried to meditate, my mind raced with unwanted, unrelated thoughts that I worked hard to banish. Not possible. The harder I worked to think about nothing, the more I thought about everything. The laundry list of things to do, the buzzing of the air conditioner in the room, someone coughing in the background, and everyday worries flooded my mind.

Over time and with additional guidance and practice, I learned to accept the thoughts without undue concern. The more I allowed for thoughts to come and go, the less disturbing they became. Now, after many years of practice, I still have thoughts most times I meditate, but they are less attention grabbing and don't disturb my practice.

Be aware of your thoughts, but don't attach importance to them. They'll arrive, but let them be. Return your focus to your breath, your position, your body, or a mantra. Thoughts are merely thoughts.

Practicing meditation

Like any skill, meditation requires practice over time. Frequency is probably more important than length of time meditating. In other words, a short daily practice of ten minutes will give you more benefit than an hour or two a few times a month. If you decide to commit to a meditation practice, find a time of day that works for you. Avoid distractions and interruptions to the extent possible. However, if interrupted, just resume.

You can learn meditation from reading articles, taking a class, or using an app. Whatever you choose, again, the main focus should be repetition and consistency. Don't give up after a few sessions. If you give meditation a chance, you'll likely be surprised at the calmness you can achieve with patience and persistence.

The following meditation strategy may be helpful for dealing with a variety of symptoms of anxiety, depression, or other difficult emotions. It combines breathing and mantra-based meditation techniques. Take the following steps:

1. Pick a pair of words from the list in Table 8-1. The left column has positive words, and the right has negative words. You can choose any word pair that has meaning to you. Feel free to use other meaningful words. You can limit your choice to one pair of words or add more. It's up to you.

2. Sit in a comfortable position. Set a timer for about 10 minutes (more or less depending on your own needs).

3. Take a couple of deep breaths. Hold each one for a few seconds, and slowly let it go. Close your eyes.

4. Next, as you breathe in, repeat, "I breathe in. . ." a positive word such as *serenity*, *tranquility*, or *peace*. Then "I breathe out. . ." a negative word such as *worry*, *fear*, or *sadness*.

Table 8-1   Mantra-Based Breathing Meditation

I breathe in. . .	I breathe out. . .
Acceptance	Judgment
Stillness	Tightness
Serenity	Agitation
Tranquility	Turmoil
Love	Hate
Possibilities	Hopelessness
Relaxation	Rigidity
Calmness	Tension
Peace	Anger
Hope	Despair

TIP

You can also play with using a single-word mantra such as *Omm* or simply concentrate on breathing in and out. Some who teach meditation believe in a rigid, structured approach, but I've found a more permissive, open strategy seems to work best for many people.

Start by Losing Your Mind!

You aren't the same as your mind. What's that? You may be thinking, "This author sounds like she's losing her mind. She's speaking flakey hogwash!" It's perfectly okay if you want to think that, but how about playing along for a few moments more and working through the next few sections?

Distinguishing between observing and evaluating

Sit back and wait for a thought to enter your mind. Don't rush it; one will come along pretty soon. When it does, ask yourself this question: Who noticed that thought? The obvious answer is *you*. The you who observes, breathes, and experiences isn't the same as your thoughts or your mind.

The following exercise helps you connect with the mindful, observant you by first demonstrating the ease with which you can slip into thoughts that come from an overly evaluative, judgmental state of mind.

EXAMPLE

As I sit in my office working on this chapter, I'm connecting with my evaluative, judgmental mind. In this exercise, my job is to criticize everything I see. Therefore, I make the following critical thoughts and judgments about my surroundings:

>> Papers are piled and stacked everywhere. What a disastrous mess!

>> Who could ever work around this place?

>> How could anyone type endlessly on a keyboard crammed into this small space?

>> How many glasses and cups am I going to accumulate before I finally break down and take them to the kitchen?

>> That picture on the wall is crooked.

>> Look at this mess of computer wires under the desk. It looks like a snake pit.

>> There are way too many books on the shelves — and just look at all that dust on them!

>> See that basket full of paper clips, highlighters, pens, and sticky pads? What a mess!

>> With all this chaos, I'll never be able to finish this ^*!&*%#^@! book!

I found this exercise quite simple to do because I, like everyone else, easily slip into a judgmental, critical state of mind. The more challenging task is to access the observing, nonevaluative mind — in other words, to merely look at and experience what's around you. Here's what I experience when I'm being mindful:

> *Right now, I can hear birds chirping outside, and in the background, the sound of the dryer warning me that the laundry is ready. I see papers piled in stacks of varying heights, the flat computer screen, smooth-finished wood desks and shelves, a phone, and the dog napping on the floor. I see black and white wires entangled underneath the desk in patterns. I feel the plastic keys of the keyboard, the textured leather of the chair, slick paper lying on the desk, and a cold glass of iced tea. I also notice my breath as it gently goes in and out.*

After the first, judgmental look at my present moment, I felt a little irritable, overwhelmed, and discouraged. When I simply allowed myself to experience what was in front of me without evaluation, I relaxed. The tasks at hand seemed less daunting. I pulled back from self-disparagement and soon found myself absorbed by writing.

PRACTICE

Do this three-part exercise right now. Don't let a thought like, "This is stupid," "What can this do for me?," or "I'll do this when I have more time" get in your way. Follow these instructions to complete Worksheet 8-1. Then move on to Worksheets 8-2 and 8-3.

1. **Sit and look at everything around you.**

2. **Find something negative in everything you see.**

3. **Write down each and every critical thought that comes to mind.**

4. **Notice how you feel when you're finished, and write those feelings down.**

Worksheet 8-1   Your Critical State of Mind

Critical thoughts:

1. _____
2. _____
3. _____
4. _____
5. _____
6. _____
7. _____
8. _____
9. _____
10. _____

Feelings after writing critical thoughts:

_____
_____
_____

1. **Take a new look around you, but this time don't judge or evaluate. Connect with your senses. Describe what you experience as objectively as you can, and write these experiences as they come to you in Worksheet 8-2.** Don't worry about sentence structure, punctuation, or grammar.

2. **Notice how you feel now. Jot these feelings down in Worksheet 8-2.**

3. **Reflect on this exercise, and write your conclusions under My Reflections in Worksheet 8-3.**

Worksheet 8-2   Observing Your State of Mind

Observations, sensations, and experiences:

_____
_____
_____
_____

Feelings after writing observations and experiences:

_____
_____
_____

_____

_____

_____

_____

_____

Tuning in and tuning out mind chatter

Depressed and anxious minds chatter constantly. And the chatter usually predicts, judges, and evaluates in harsh or frightening ways. Think of part of your mind as a chatter machine that produces a stream of toxic verbiage, including:

» I'm not good enough.

» I'm a terrible person.

» I'll never make it.

» I don't deserve good things.

» I'm a screw-up.

» I'll fail if I try.

» I can't do this.

» No one will like me.

» If I ask them out, they'll reject me.

» Pretty soon, people will know I'm a phony.

» I'm going to fall apart.

» What if I get cancer?

» I might throw up.

» What if I cry?

Do you have thoughts like these? Tune into them using this exercise.

PRACTICE

1. **Listen to the chatter rumbling through your mind.**

2. **In the left column of Worksheet 8-4, write down the comments you hear over and over.**

3. **Think of a good friend of yours. Change your mind chatter to a statement about your friend, and write that statement in the right column.** For example, change, "Pretty soon, people will know I'm a phony" to "Pretty soon, people will know you're a phony, Richard." Or change, "I'm a terrible person" to "You're a terrible person, Richard."

Worksheet 8-4   Mind Chatter Turned on Its Head

Mind Chatter	Mind Chatter Said to a Friend

4. **Imagine what it would feel like to express this mind chatter to your friend, and record your reflections in Worksheet 8-5.** You'd *never* say such things to a good friend, would you?

Worksheet 8-5   My Reflections

_____

_____

_____

_____

_____

Consider treating yourself, as well as your friend, kindlier. Stop being so mean to yourself. When your mind chatters with negativity, remember that you want to be a friend to yourself.

TIP

Playing with your mind chatter

Chapters 5, 6, and 7 show you how thoughts and beliefs that run through your mind contribute to emotional distress. These thoughts are almost always distorted and built on a foundation of sand — based on flimsy evidence or outright distortions. Flip back to those chapters for a review of how you can wage war against unhelpful thoughts and beliefs.

You can certainly wage war on your unhelpful thoughts, but sometimes a warrior needs a break or a change in tactics. This section asks you to change tactics and put down your weapons. Instead of going to war, disarm damaging thoughts with humor. After all, it's hard to be upset when you're laughing. When you hear negative chatter, thank your mind for having those thoughts. Tell your mind how creative it's being. (Yes, this involves more than a hint of sarcasm.) Take a look at an example, and then have some fun taking on your own thoughts.

Joseph works as a correction officer during the day and attends college at night. He hates his job and hopes that getting a counseling degree will allow him to change careers. His schedule is grueling, and at times he gets discouraged. He tracks his mind chatter and notices three recurring thoughts. After reading about thanking his mind, he comes up with the responses shown in Worksheet 8-6.

EXAMPLE

Worksheet 8-6   Joseph's Thank-You Mind Exercise

Mind Chatter	Playful Response
I'll never be able to finish the degree.	Thanks, mind. That's such a useful way to look at things!
Even if I finish my degree, I'll make a lousy counselor.	Wow, mind. That's sooo helpful! Thanks!
I'm going to be stuck with this job for the rest of my life.	Good thinking! I really like it when you come up with such creative ways of helping me!

PRACTICE

Try thanking your mind when you hear unhelpful mind chatter. If you take such chatter seriously, it's sure to drag you under. But if you play with the thoughts, you can take away their power. Follow these instructions to complete the exercise in Worksheet 8-7, and then record your overall reflections in Worksheet 8-8.

1. **Pay attention to your negative mind chatter.**

2. **In the left column, write down upsetting thoughts that you hear repeatedly.**

3. **In the right column, write a playful response to your mind chatter machine. Consider complimenting or thanking your mind.**

TIP

Keep this exercise in mind when your mind starts to chatter. Thank your mind for those thoughts, and smile!

Worksheet 8-7   My Thank-You Mind Exercise

Mind Chatter	Playful Response

TIP

Just for fun, consider trying out some other ways of playing with your mind's chatter. Try singing the negative thoughts to the tune of "Happy Birthday to You" or "Row, Row, Row Your Boat." You can also speak the thoughts out loud in a different voice, such as a cartoon character, or in a high squeaky pitch. When you sing or say your self-downing thoughts in a humorous manner, it's much harder to take them seriously.

Worksheet 8-8   My Reflections

_____

_____

_____

_____

_____

Arriving at Acceptance

Once or twice each winter, my husband and I take a drive up to the crest of New Mexico's Sandia Mountains, elevation 10,000 feet. We like to tromp around in the snow and sometimes go cross-country skiing. We bring our dog, who loves the snow more than we do.

The parking lot at the crest is usually plowed, but one time we went, we managed to get stuck in a snowbank. I mean *really* stuck. As the wheels spun uselessly, my husband uttered a few choice words of frustration. I reminded him that you have to accept where you are to get where you want to go.

So, he took his foot off the accelerator and allowed the car to rock back. He gently applied the gas again until the tires started to spin, and once again, took his foot off the accelerator. He continued rocking the car until we finally escaped from the snow.

TIP

No, this isn't a lesson in how to extract your car from a snowbank. Rather, the message here is that to move forward, it's important to ease up and accept where you are for a moment. When the time is right, you can gently push ahead.

Are you wondering what acceptance has to do with anxiety and depression? Well, everyone feels anxious or sad now and then. Recognizing and accepting those feelings is important because if you absolutely can't stand to be worried or down, then you'll inevitably feel more upset when you experience these normal feelings. In other words, you'll get more upset and distressed about getting distressed. That's clearly not very helpful.

Don't get me wrong; I want you to feel good most of the time. But as far as I know, the only humans who don't feel some anxiety or sadness are, well . . . dead. Besides, if you don't know sadness, it's difficult to know what happiness is. Without worry, you wouldn't appreciate calm. Accept a certain degree of difficult emotions as part of your life.

One way to accept a few negative feelings is to view them objectively. Imagine that you're writing a report on the experience of anxiety or depression. To accurately express the experience, you need to acquire a dispassionate understanding of the essence of your emotions. In other words, observe and accept your feelings without judgment. As you do, you'll likely see that your distress lessens. Whether you're depressed or anxious, accepting the emotional angst dispassionately will help you handle your bad feelings without becoming more upset. Read the following example, and then try out the exercise when you're feeling troubled.

EXAMPLE

Kelsey needs to renew her driver's license, so she runs over to the Motor Vehicles Department on her lunch hour. Although there's only one clerk on duty, she's pleased to see only four people ahead of her. Then the man at the front of the line starts arguing with the clerk. The argument continues, and the supervisor is summoned. As the discussion at the front of the line drags on, Kelsey looks at her watch and starts to worry about getting back to work on time. She recalls the Accepting Angst Dispassionately exercise (see Worksheet 8-9) and runs through it in her mind.

Worksheet 8-9   Kelsey Accepting Angst Dispassionately

1. Write about your current physical feelings. Is your stomach upset? Are you sweating? Is your heart pounding? Do your shoulders feel tight? Describe everything going on in your body in objective terms.

I'm jiggling and rocking back and forth. I can feel the tension in my shoulders. My breathing is becoming fast and shallow. My heart is even starting to race. How interesting.

2. Notice fluctuations in these physical feelings. Over time, feelings vary in intensity. Are the waves long or short? How high do they go at their peaks and how low at their ebbs?

Now that I'm paying attention, I can see that these feelings go up and down every few minutes; they aren't constant. As I'm observing them, they actually seem to be lessening.

3. Predict how long you'll have these physical feelings. An hour, a minute, a day, a year?

They probably won't last more than however long I'm here.

4. Notice with dispassion the thoughts that go through your mind. Imagine those thoughts floating away on clouds. Write them down and say goodbye as they float away.

It's interesting to notice my thoughts. I'm thinking things like, "I'm going to be late, and that's horrible," "That stupid man; who does he think he is anyway?" It's funny, but as I listen to these thoughts objectively, they don't seem so important.

5. Predict how long you'll have these thoughts. An hour, a minute, a day, a year?

They're already floating away as I zero in on them.

PRACTICE The next time you notice unpleasant feelings, work through the exercise in Worksheet 8-10. If you miraculously have this book in front of you at the time, write your reactions down immediately. If you don't have your workbook on hand, recall as many of these questions as you can and answer them in your mind or record them on your phone. The main goal is simply to adopt an objective perspective that describes your feeling without judging it.

REMEMBER The point of this exercise is to accept the way you feel in the moment without jumping to evaluation or judgment. Think of yourself as a scientist interested in objective observation and description. This exercise is particularly useful when you find yourself in frustrating, unavoidable predicaments, such as

>> Being on hold for customer service

>> Waiting in long lines

>> Sitting through boring meetings

>> Moving through crowds

>> Suffering through travel delays

>> Waiting for someone who's late

>> Meeting a deadline

>> Getting rejected

>> Receiving criticism

Worksheet 8-10   Accepting Angst Dispassionately

1. Write about your current physical feelings. Is your stomach upset? Are you sweating? Is your heart pounding? Do your shoulders feel tight? Describe everything going on in your body in objective terms.

_____

_____

_____

_____

2. Notice fluctuations in these physical feelings. Over time, feelings vary in intensity. Are the waves long or short? How high do they go at their peaks and how low at their ebbs?

_____

_____

_____

_____

3. Predict how long you'll have these physical feelings. An hour, a minute, a day, a year?

_____

4. Notice with dispassion the thoughts that go through your mind. Imagine those thoughts floating away on clouds. Write them down, and say goodbye as they float away.

_____

_____

_____

_____

5. Predict how long you'll have these thoughts. An hour, a minute, a day, a year?

_____

>> Feeling afraid

>> Taking a risk such as giving a speech

>> Getting sick

Connecting with Now

People have the rather curious habit of allowing their thoughts to dwell on the past or the future. In the process, they make themselves miserable. If you really think about it, most of what you get unhappy or worried about has to do with events that happened in the past or are yet to occur. You feel guilty about past transgressions and worry about future calamities.

When you spend too much time in the past or future, you're bound to ruin your present. You lose the enjoyment and pleasure you may otherwise feel about the present. Rarely is the present as miserable as your memories or predictions.

For example, I had a great dog named Murphy who loved to ride in the car. What's odd is that most of the time she was in the car, she was going to the groomer. Murphy hated the groomer — as in *really* hated the groomer. Nevertheless, every time the car door opened at home, she eagerly bounded in and enthusiastically stuck her head out the window to enjoy the wind. When she arrived at the groomer's shop, she gleefully jumped out of the car, hoping to go for a walk. About 20 feet from the door, however, she saw where she was going and promptly plopped down on the parking lot pavement. She refused to move, so I'd end up carrying her in.

If Murphy were a person, she'd mark her calendar with her grooming dates and then worry and obsess about the appointment for days, if not weeks, ahead of time. She certainly would *not* enjoy the car ride. This example shows you how *you* miss your present because you're focusing on the past or future, all those enjoyable moments lost in apprehension.

PRACTICE

The exercise laid out in Worksheet 8-11 facilitates becoming more now or present focused. Practice it for four or five minutes during your day; you can do it almost anywhere. This exercise will refresh you. (Some people need to use a timer because the five-minute rule is hard to follow at first, but it'll become easier as your practice becomes routine.)

Worksheet 8-11   Embracing Present Moments

1. **Sit comfortably in a chair or on the floor.** (Location doesn't matter as long as you're comfortable.)

2. **Extend your legs and place your feet about shoulder width apart.**

3. **Put your hand on your abdomen and feel your breath go in and out.** Take your time breathing. Keep it low and slow.

4. **When you feel comfortable, close your eyes. Continue to think about your breathing.**

5. **When thoughts intrude, let them be.** Notice them and watch them float away. Just keep breathing — low and slow.

6. **Sit quietly.** When you start this practice, you may feel an urge to scratch some part of your body. When that sensation occurs, concentrate mentally on the area, and the desire is likely to pass.

7. **Remain for just five minutes of stillness.** If you feel a muscle tensing, send your mental effort to that area. Study the feeling, and it will pass.

Five quiet minutes is all it takes to become mindful of the present. Follow the steps above, and then take a few moments to reflect in Worksheet 8-12 on how you felt.

Almost any activity can be conducted mindfully, connecting only with the activity itself without judgment, evaluation, or analysis. For example, eating is an activity that occurs often and thus gives you numerous opportunities for practicing mindfulness. Few present moments elicit high distress, and mindfulness connects you with the present. Mindful connection with the present takes some practice, so don't rush the process or judge your success or failure. Instead, simply practice, practice, practice.

Worksheet 8-12   My Reflections

_____
_____
_____
_____
_____

Try this mindfulness exercise at any meal (see Worksheet 8-13). You'll find yourself slowing down and enjoying your food more than before. In fact, people who eat mindfully typically lose weight more easily (if that's what they're trying to do) because they're no longer eating to rid themselves of unpleasant feelings. After you work through the steps, record your reflections in Worksheet 8-14.

PRACTICE

Worksheet 8-13   Eating Mindfully

1. **Look at what you're about to eat.** What colors are in front of you? Are they shiny or dull? What does the texture look like? Is it smooth, rough, or varied?

2. **Smell the food.** Does it smell sweet, garlicky, fishy, pungent, or something else?

3. **Take a small piece of food and place it on your tongue.** What does it feel like?

4. **Gently, slowly, move the piece around your mouth.** Are you salivating? Does this food need to be chewed?

5. **As you chew, note the different tastes and textures that are released.**

6. **As the food begins to break down, feel it as it gets close to the back of your throat. Swallow.**

7. **Start again with the next piece of food.**

Worksheet 8-14   My Reflections

_____
_____
_____
_____
_____

3

Actions Against Angst: Behavior Therapy

Chapter 9

Facing Feelings: Avoiding Avoidance

This chapter is all about avoidance. People naturally attempt to avoid unpleasant emotions and situations. After all, who actually wants to feel bad?

For example, if you're dreadfully afraid of snakes, you probably don't hang out in swamps. Or if crowds make you nervous — really nervous, that is — you likely avoid the shopping mall during the holidays. Similarly, if standing up for yourself when you're wronged makes you uneasy, you may avoid conflict, even when it will benefit you overall. If you feel sad and a stiff drink makes you feel better, what's the harm in that?

Well, the problem is that avoidance, over time, increases or intensifies anxiety and depression. When you make the decision to avoid something unpleasant, you instantly feel relief, and relief feels pretty good. In a sense, you've rewarded yourself for avoidance. People tend to do things more often when they're rewarded; therefore, you're more likely to avoid again. In fact, you'll probably find yourself avoiding more frequently and in response to other, somewhat similar events.

For instance, if crowds make you nervous, you may start out avoiding only huge crowds. That avoidance feels good until smaller crowds start making you nervous, too. So, you avoid smaller and smaller crowds, and your avoidance continues to grow until you're barely able to get yourself out of your house, lest you run into even a few people.

Or, if you avoid significant depression or sadness by numbing yourself with drugs or alcohol, eventually the smallest discomfort will lead to more abuse of substances. It's easy to understand that substance abuse often begins with avoidance of feelings.

You may avoid emotional discomfort in more subtle ways, such as pretending that nothing is wrong. That pretense is often stated as "everything's fine," even though it's not. People may deny feeling sick, not wanting to seek uncomfortable treatment, and put their health at risk by doing so. They may describe troubled relationships as normal so they don't have to deal with the possible fallout of a confrontation. In fact, humans are masters at avoidance.

Avoidance is the opposite of acceptance (see Chapter 8). Acceptance comes with a willingness to experience all feelings, whether positive or negative. It involves the courage to come into contact with reality in the present moment.

This chapter gives you a list of common feelings and situations that people experience and avoid so that you can identify the ones that cause you the most distress and choose one or more to battle. Different methods of avoidance are explained, and you discover which ones you use. Then you decide which situation or feeling you want to face and follow strategies to challenge what you avoid with *exposure*.

REMEMBER

Many of the situations in this chapter cause fear and anxiety. You may wonder why the emphasis is on anxiety when the book is supposed to deal with both depression and anxiety. Fear is connected to anxiety, and anxiety (especially chronic anxiety) leads to depression. If you avoid all that troubles you, your life can become quite small. And a small life is usually a sad life.

What's Wrong with Avoidance?

Most people have at least a few minor worries or anxieties, and that's no big deal. A little anxiety prepares you for action. When the guy in the car in front of you slams on his brakes, the sudden spike in anxiety helps your body respond quickly — and that's a good thing.

Everyone alive feels sad and depressed from time to time. Depression can also be an adaptive reaction. A small amount of depression makes you withdraw and gives you time to regroup or heal, even to reflect on what's bothering you.

PRACTICE

But when fear and sadness start dominating your life, you might be reluctant to take action. However, action is necessary for improvement. The first step in taking action involves figuring out exactly what makes you depressed and anxious. Go through the Three Dozen Things People Avoid Checklist in Worksheet 9-1 and check off each item that causes you significant concern or that you avoid dealing with.

TIP

If you didn't recognize any fears, worries, or concerns in this list, you may be able to just skip this chapter and move on. However, it's possible that you have a few stressors or things you avoid that weren't listed. If that's the case, write down your causes of distress and subsequent avoidance on Worksheet 9-2 and keep reading.

Worksheet 9-1   Three Dozen Things People Avoid Checklist

- ☐ 1. Getting started on something difficult
- ☐ 2. Crowds
- ☐ 3. Airplanes, trains, elevators, or heights
- ☐ 4. Difficult relationship issues
- ☐ 5. Panic triggers
- ☐ 6. Leaving the house
- ☐ 7. Reminders of past trauma
- ☐ 8. Giving a speech
- ☐ 9. Rodents, bugs, snakes, and such
- ☐ 10. Being trapped in a small place
- ☐ 11. Dealing with sleep problems
- ☐ 12. Checking out health issues
- ☐ 13. Getting dirty or messy
- ☐ 14. Being alone
- ☐ 15. Spending time with an unsupportive family
- ☐ 16. Confronting stressful situations
- ☐ 17. Improving an unhealthy diet
- ☐ 18. Seeking pleasurable activities
- ☐ 19. Finding purpose and meaning in your life
- ☐ 20. Driving on the highway or busy roads
- ☐ 21. Getting help for sexual performance problems
- ☐ 22. Meeting and talking to new people
- ☐ 23. Indicating interest in someone
- ☐ 24. Acknowledging and dealing with financial problems
- ☐ 25. Making mistakes
- ☐ 26. Experiencing feelings like dizziness, queasiness, or rapid heartbeat
- ☐ 27. Going to the doctor or dentist
- ☐ 28. Dealing with a conflict
- ☐ 29. Traveling
- ☐ 30. Job interviews
- ☐ 31. Taking medication
- ☐ 32. Surgery, the sight of blood, needles, and injections
- ☐ 33. Open spaces, dark places
- ☐ 34. The possibility of being criticized
- ☐ 35. Using a public restroom
- ☐ 36. Eating in public

PRACTICE

List the top five things you avoid in Worksheet 9-2.

Worksheet 9-2   My Top Five Things I Avoid

1. _____
2. _____
3. _____
4. _____
5. _____

If what you avoid doesn't seriously interfere with your life, you may decide simply to live with your avoidance, and that's okay! For example, I really don't like bugs, and I have no intention of doing anything about that fear. It doesn't prevent me from enjoying the outdoors or life in general, and for the most part, I leave the bugs alone as long as they leave me alone. If I find a bug in the house, 15 tissues provide enough of a barrier between me and any bug to allow me to dispose of the bug (and my fear) without too much distress.

However, if one or more of your top five things you avoid interferes with your ability to function competently, then it's time to take charge and carry on. The following sections give you some strategies to challenge those issues that get in the way of living your life fully.

How do you avoid?

If you have an emotion that is unpleasant, it's not a surprise that you may want to avoid having that feeling. Emotional avoidance is a common response to negative emotions such as anxiety and depression. There are two strategies people use to avoid their feelings. The first is obvious; the second is more subtle.

People who are *obvious or overt avoiders* simply stay away from situations that make them feel bad. For example, they may:

>> Avoid parties or large groups because of fear of crowds

>> Not take risks because of fear of failure

>> Stay out of relationships to avoid conflict or rejection

>> Avoid regular medical appointments to escape bad news or unwanted procedures

>> Stay at home as much as possible to avoid traffic

Subtle or covert avoiders are probably more common than obvious avoiders. They have plausible deniability when confronted. Examples of subtle ways of avoiding difficult feelings include:

>> Becoming riveted to phones when in public to avoid conversations

>> Working long hours to avoid conflict with family members

>> Using drugs or alcohol to avoid feeling

>> Overeating to decrease anxiety or depression

>> Pretending that nothing is wrong when it is

>> Denying feeling sad or bad

>> Getting help from others so that it's possible to avoid being uncomfortable

>> Refusing to talk when there's a conflict or even denying there's a conflict at all

>> Finding ways to become distracted when feeling distress

>> Procrastinating to avoid something unappealing

Thinking back to the list of Three Dozen Things People Avoid, here are several examples of avoidance strategies:

>> Juan feels anxious in crowds, so he doesn't accept invitations to any activity that might include crowds.

>> Kendra hates being criticized, so she takes easy classes in community college instead of the more challenging engineering curriculum that she'd like to take.

>> Matthew's wife tells him they need marriage counseling. Matthew refuses to go, telling her that nothing's wrong with their marriage.

>> William is embarrassed to eat in front of others, so he eats lunch in his office and never goes out to a restaurant with friends or colleagues.

>> Tessa gets extremely anxious around new people, so she tends to drink too much at parties or other gatherings.

In each case, their avoidance results in an immediate sense of relief — in other words, *they're instantly gratified* by getting out of something uncomfortable. But you can see that, over time, these actions can lead to problems.

Now think about the items you picked for the My Top Five Things I Avoid. Then look back on the various ways you avoid either overtly or covertly. Write them down in Worksheet 9-3.

Worksheet 9-3   My Top Five Things I Avoid and My Avoidance Strategies

What distresses me	How I attempt to avoid (both overtly and covertly)
1.	
2.	
3.	
4.	
5.	

Do you find that you attempt to avoid unpleasant feelings or interactions? Don't be too hard on yourself if you do. Avoidance is one of the most common human responses to distress. Unfortunately, it just doesn't work in the long run, and it's likely to make distress more distressing.

Take a minute to jot down your thoughts on Worksheet 9-4 about avoidance.

Worksheet 9-4   My Reflections

_____
_____
_____
_____

Interrupting avoidance

As previously mentioned, avoidance can feel beneficial in the short term. For example, if you avoid an argument with your partner by ignoring inconsiderate behavior, you'll likely feel a sense of relief. Nobody got mad. However, your partner won't hear necessary feedback about the inconsiderate behavior, and the situation, in the long term, might become worse. You can easily understand why people tend to avoid conflict. Conflict, for most people, is a hard choice to make.

Fear is another emotion that often leads to avoidance. If you avoid what you fear, well, you don't have to feel afraid. People avoid driving during rush hour, and then they avoid freeways. The feelings of fear over driving increase, and life becomes more difficult. Avoidance of feared situations inevitably increases fear.

TIP

There are times when avoidance is a logical and safe option. For example, most police suggest that when you encounter a road rage situation, the best defense is to ignore it, find an exit or a well-lit place, and avoid direct confrontation.

More commonly, though, there's a cost to avoidance. Whether it's increased fear, anxiety, misbehavior, or depression, avoidance makes life more difficult over the long haul. Getting through and facing difficult emotions opens opportunities for growth, provides excitement, and improves relationships.

TIP

When faced with a distressing problem, take the time to approach (not avoid) it smartly. Use this simple strategy to accept a bit of discomfort and move forward rather than stagnate.

1. **Stop and feel.** What's happening in my body? What thoughts am I having? Notice feelings. Observe and take a few deep breaths.

2. **Assess the situation.** What's happening in the here and now? Why do I feel distress? What are my options? Should I approach or avoid? How do I change this situation into an opportunity?

3. **Take action.** Choose an option that you think will work best. If you choose to engage, take a few more breaths, remain calm, and talk in a quiet voice. Whatever you choose to do, remember that you can learn from both good and bad results. Accept your decision.

Exposure: Jumping in Feet First

Pick a fear, any distressing emotion, or situation that you usually avoid. Well, maybe not *any* one. It should be one that bothers you and that you'd like to do something about. (It's probably from your Top Five Things I Avoid list; see Worksheet 9-2.) The best way to overcome fear is to face it head-on. Not all at once, mind you, but one step at a time.

TIP

Don't push yourself to do the most feared and avoided situation first. For example, if you are terrified of public speaking, don't sign up to do the opening remarks at the next corporate meeting. Instead, start small by making yourself speak up at a team meeting.

The exposure technique for facing and overcoming anxiety involves breaking your avoidance into manageable activities and gradually confronting each one. You don't proceed until you've conquered the one you started with. You'll know you've mastered a given issue when you can repeat it without becoming overly anxious.

Identifying your fears

The first stage of the exposure technique involves zeroing in on your fear and where it comes from. Breaking down the exposure process into components is helped by delving deeply into the situation you're trying to overcome. The following example about Jason will help you see the type of information you need to consider before beginning exposure for yourself.

EXAMPLE

Jason is painfully shy, especially when it comes to women and dating. He has a number of good male friends but trembles at the thought of asking someone out. He tries online dating and finds that engaging in conversations via text is pretty easy. But he stops short of setting up a face-to-face meeting for fear of rejection. Jason vows to overcome this fear on his 30th birthday. His first step is to work through the Questions About What I Avoid (see Worksheet 9-5).

Now it's your turn. You've already identified the stress you tend to avoid. Now take some time to think more deeply about what you're actually attempting to escape. The following questions can help. Complete Worksheet 9-6 regarding one of the situations you avoid.

WARNING

After answering these questions, how do you feel? Are you more or less anxious? There's no right or wrong answer, but if this task overwhelms you with negative emotions, consider getting ting professional guidance before you go any further with these exercises.

Developing an exposure plan

Once you understand the nuances of what you avoid, it's time to act. But not all at once. If you avoid swimming because you're afraid of the water, it wouldn't be a great idea for you to jump off a boat in the middle of the ocean. The first step would be more likely to take beginning swim lessons at a local pool. Similarly, if you avoid dealing with conflict, I wouldn't recommend that you start by joining a debate club without a bit of training and practice, perhaps with a tutor.

Worksheet 9-5 Jason's Questions About What I Avoid

1. What stirs up my desire to avoid?

The mere image of asking someone out scares me to death. Even conversing with women can trigger my anxiety. Gosh, I get nervous when I talk to a good-looking clerk at the grocery store. Even writing about asking someone out makes me anxious!

2. What thoughts go through my mind about what might happen?

The whole relationship thing worries me. If I did get a date, I wouldn't know what to do or what to say. And I wouldn't know when to make an advance — that's really scary. The one brief relationship I had in college really hurt me, so I worry that if I were to find someone, she'd just reject me, too. Heck, I can hardly even ask for directions from a woman.

3. What activities do I avoid?

Obviously, I haven't had a date in a long time. I avoid going to parties. I avoid talking to available women. I even avoid the staff lunchroom with the excuse that I have too much work to do. My shyness seems to be getting worse, and lately I'm avoiding meeting and talking with new people, even guys.

4. Do I use overt or covert (like denial, medications, or drugs) strategies to avoid? Or do I use others as crutches to get me through difficult situations?

I have a prescription for a tranquilizer. I take one of those sometimes before I have to talk with a woman. At work, I avoid committees and meetings and let my coworkers cover for me.

5. What's the worst outcome if I face my struggle?

If I try to ask someone out, I imagine my voice shaking and not being able to speak. I would look like a fool. My stomach would churn, and I'd sweat like a pig. And if I did go out on a date, she'd probably laugh in my face or walk away before the evening was over. If someone was dumb enough to go out with me more than once, she'd no doubt break my heart.

Worksheet 9-6 Questions about What I Avoid

Questions	Answers
What stirs up my desire to avoid?	
What thoughts go through my mind about what might happen?	
What specific activities do I avoid?	
Do I use overt or covert strategies to avoid? Or do I use others as crutches to get me through difficult situations?	
What's the worst outcome if I face my struggle?	

Exposure activities allow you to practice challenging what you avoid in a way that you can emotionally manage. You start with activities that cause you to have a bit of distress, but not too much. There's no definite number of activities you should try out, but more than a couple. (Five to ten usually suffices.)

Recall the example of Jason, who was terrified of meeting women, being rejected, and making a fool out of himself. He rereads Worksheet 9-5 and then develops several exposure activities and rates them in terms of how uncomfortable they will be. He tries to include fairly easy activities and others that are more difficult. See Worksheet 9-7 for what he produces.

Worksheet 9-7   Jason's Exposure Activities

Uncomfortable Activity	Discomfort Rating (0–100)
Asking someone out on a date in person.	85 (terrifying)
Calling someone on the phone for a date.	75 (pretty darn scary)
Having a conversation with a woman I don't know.	65 (tough, but manageable)
Eating lunch in the staff lunchroom and talking with the people there.	35 (I can handle this)
Asking for help from a female salesclerk.	25 (piece of cake, but there's some tension)
Going to a party.	70 (very tough)
Volunteering at the food bank and talking with female volunteers there.	60 (not easy)
Volunteering to be on the social committee at work and going to the meetings.	55 (not my idea of fun, but I can do it)

Jason picks a few activities from his list and carries them out for a couple of weeks. He finds that the list pushes him to follow through and keeps him from his normal style of procrastination. When he finds himself too overwhelmed to do an activity that is difficult, he backs down and chooses an easier one. However, he understands that he must feel some discomfort for the exposure to work. As he does the exposure activities, he finds additional situations that expand his list and enjoys the pleasure of accomplishment.

Before I turn the task over to you, here are a few ideas for exposures for avoided situations or feelings. For example:

>> **For feeling dizzy, panic, rapid heartbeat:** Spin in a chair until you feel dizzy. Put your head between your knees for a minute, and then rapidly sit or stand up. Jog in place until you're out of breath.

>> **Getting dirty or messy:** Hold something sticky in your hands for two minutes. Run your hands through some dirt and don't wash them for an hour. Touch the inside of a waste basket and don't wash them for an hour. (Please don't touch contaminated surfaces during a pandemic.)

>> **Avoiding conflict:** Set a limit on a family member who tends to ask you for too much. Ask for things you need from others. Say no to unreasonable requests.

>> **Dealing with financial problems:** Start keeping track of all expenses. Organize your expenses into categories. Make a budget. Find ways to save money as needed. Set realistic financial goals.

Now it's your turn to develop an exposure activity list. Review Worksheet 9-6. Brainstorm all the possible activities that could propel you to avoid your problematic issue. Make a list in Worksheet 9-8, and rate your level of discomfort. Then plan to try out a few activities each week.

REMEMBER

You don't have to pick the easiest one first or the hardest one last. Just find something uncomfortable but manageable. The main idea is to go out and expose yourself. (But please leave your clothes on!)

Worksheet 9-8   Exposure Activities

Uncomfortable Activity	Discomfort Rating (0–100)

TIP

If you find the task of developing exposure tasks too difficult, consider seeking professional help. In addition, think about the following possibilities:

>> Ask a good friend or family member to give you some ideas.

>> Don't cater to mind chatter that tells you this won't help or the tasks are stupid.

>> Don't use crutches such as alcohol or drugs.

>> Treat yourself for accomplishing something difficult.

>> Expect and value experiencing discomfort.

>> Be patient and keep at it.

Chapter 10

Lifting Mood Through Exercise

Why devote a whole chapter to exercise in a book that deals with anxiety and depression? Well, because getting up and moving increases the naturally occurring feel-good *endorphins* in the human body. When endorphins, substances occurring naturally in the brain that are chemically similar to morphine, spread through your brain, you get a sense of well-being and pleasure. And it's hard to be depressed or anxious when you feel good inside.

This chapter tells you how much exercise you need to get those endorphins going and reviews most of the known benefits of exercise. You pick your top ten reasons for beginning or sticking with an exercise program and then figure out an exercise plan that fits your lifestyle. The final sections offer tips for finding the motivation to keep exercise going in your life.

How Much Is Enough?

The best time to get into an exercise habit is when you're young because exercise helps keep you healthy throughout your life. However, it's *never* too late to start. Even 90-year-olds benefit from starting a regular exercise routine!

WARNING

If you're in good health, it's okay to start an exercise program on your own. However, for men over 40, women over 50, and anyone with a chronic disease or other health concerns, it's best to check with a physician before beginning a vigorous exercise regimen.

Every few years, the United States government updates its guidelines for nutrition and exercise. The latest recommendations significantly increased the recommended amount of time for healthy people to engage in vigorous physical activity. So, what do the current guidelines recommend? Take a deep breath and relax. Here they are:

>> Children and adolescents should be physically active about an hour a day on most days. Activities can include vigorous play, dance, or organized sports. Some activities should include both high impact (jumping, jogging, running) and muscle strengthening (body weights, climbing, pushing, pulling).

>> Healthy adults should be physically active for at least 150 to 300 minutes a week. Activities should be at least of moderate intensity, such as fast walking or jogging. Alternatively, you can get the same benefit from 75 minutes of vigorous activities such as running, high-intensity aerobics, or biking. Whichever approach or combination you choose, two or more days a week should include muscle strengthening exercises such as weight training. In addition, the guidelines recommend that adults sit less during the day and get out of their chair more to benefit their health. The takeaway: More exercise is better than less for healthy adults.

>> Older adults should continue to exercise regularly. Their program should include muscle and bone strengthening as well as strategies to improve balance. Those older adults with chronic health conditions should consult their doctor or physical therapist for guidance on specifics.

>> Most pregnant women should be exercising 30 minutes per day. Check with your doctor to make sure this recommendation is right for you.

>> Adults with disabilities or chronic health conditions should also exercise for at least 150 to 300 minutes a week depending on their healthcare provider's advice. Inactivity should be avoided as much as possible.

Write down here how many minutes a day your guidelines suggest that you should be exercising:

REMEMBER

The point of exercise is to improve physical fitness. Fitness consists of the following:

>> **Cardiorespiratory endurance:** Your body's ability to pump blood and circulate oxygen, which improves from elevating your heart rate safely for increasing periods of time.

>> **Body composition:** Your body's ratio of fat and lean mass, which gets better with all types of exercise.

- » **Flexibility:** Your body's ability to move fluidly and with good range. Stretching, yoga, Pilates, dance, and swimming all help with flexibility.

- » **Balance:** The ability to remain stable while moving or standing still during various conditions and on different surfaces. Yoga and Tai Chi are especially good for balance.

- » **Speed:** The ability to move various body parts rapidly.

- » **Muscular strength:** Your body's ability to lift and push. Most people lift weights or engage in body weight exercises to increase muscular strength.

- » **Muscular endurance:** Your body's ability to sustain effort without getting tired. Consistent, regular exercise increases endurance.

The Case for Health Improvement

Hold on. The U.S. government gives you guidelines about what you should do exercise-wise, but what's with all the shoulds? Chapter 5 recommends that you stop "shoulding" on yourself. Now this chapter tells you that you should exercise. Am I just trying to make you feel guilty? No, not really. In fact, it would defeat the purpose of this book if you started feeling guilty!

However, exercise has so many benefits that everyone physically capable of moving around would feel better if they just did it. So, this section covers the many good things that can happen — as well as the bad things that can be prevented — when you exercise. You may find a few of these items surprising, but they're all 100 percent true and well documented.

You didn't think you'd get away with just reading a list of reasons for exercise, did you? Follow the instructions here to identify the ten reasons you should be exercising.

PRACTICE

1. **Read through the items in Worksheet 10-1. If the item is something that you're concerned about, check it off.** Some items may be relevant to just about everyone; others may be particularly important to you. For example, if you have a family history of diabetes or colon cancer, those items may be especially important and make it on your top ten list.

2. **When you finish checking off the items that pertain to you, spend a few moments deciding which ones are the most important and relevant to you.**

3. **Pick your top ten reasons for exercising and record them in Worksheet 10-2.**

Worksheet 10-1   Reasons for Exercising

- ❑ Is a source of fun
- ❑ Lowers risk of dying from almost any cause
- ❑ Improves energy
- ❑ Decreases risk of heart disease
- ❑ Relieves stress
- ❑ Improves immune system
- ❑ Reduces chronic pain
- ❑ Decreases blood pressure
- ❑ Boosts self-confidence
- ❑ Decreases risk of diabetes
- ❑ Decreases risk of breast cancer
- ❑ Improves lung capacity
- ❑ Reduces triglycerides
- ❑ Aids weight loss
- ❑ Decreases risk of colon cancer
- ❑ Improves appearance
- ❑ Decreases risk of falls in the elderly
- ❑ Improves flexibility
- ❑ Improves strength
- ❑ Decreases risk of osteoporosis

- ❑ Improves sleep
- ❑ Improves ratio of bad to good cholesterol
- ❑ Increases mental sharpness
- ❑ Decreases risk of gallstones in women
- ❑ Decreases risk of enlarged prostate in men
- ❑ Improves balance
- ❑ Improves quality of life
- ❑ Relieves symptoms of PMS
- ❑ Improves complexion
- ❑ Reduces medical and healthcare expenses
- ❑ Reduces varicose veins
- ❑ Allows you to eat more without gaining weight
- ❑ Reduces addictive cravings
- ❑ Reduces risk of dementia
- ❑ Aids digestion
- ❑ Improves academic achievement
- ❑ Reduces risk of depression
- ❑ Decreases anxiety
- ❑ Makes you taller— okay, maybe not!

Worksheet 10-2   My Top Ten Reasons for Exercising

1.
2.
3.
4.
5.
6.
7.
8.
9.
10.

Fitting Exercise into Your Life

You may have some surprisingly good reasons for exercising now, but wow, 30 to 90 minutes? Where will you find the time? You're probably way too busy as it is. Pay attention when those thoughts run through your head.

First of all, you don't have to find one big window of time for exercise. The government guide-lines state that it's just as useful to do your exercise in 10- or 15-minute segments. What mat-ters is the total accumulation per day. And it may help you to know that exercise consists of just about any type of activity that occurs at a *moderate level of intensity*. Moderate intensity means that you're increasing your breathing and heart rate, which you can do by mowing the lawn, dancing, taking the stairs, swimming, bike riding, jogging, or even walking at a rapid pace.

Thus, if your job is physically demanding, you may already be getting sufficient exercise every day. On the other hand, if you religiously take your dog on a leisurely walk every morning for 45 minutes, that probably won't do the trick. You need to pick up your pace because anything done without increasing your heart rate just doesn't cut it.

PRACTICE

Everyone is different. People have different schedules, habits, preferences, and lifestyles. Therefore, an exercise program that works for one person may not work for another. The fol-lowing instructions and checklist in Worksheet 10-3 are designed to help you choose exercise that will work into your life.

1. **Read through Worksheet 10-3, checking off all the exercise ideas that could conceiv-ably become part of your routine.**

2. **Add a few possibilities of your own at the bottom of the list.**

3. **Try each and every activity you select at least a couple of times.**

Worksheet 10-3   Exercise Checklist

❏ Get up 15 minutes early each day and take a brisk walk. Take the dog if you have one!

❏ Leave a little early for work and park your car a good 15 or 20 minutes away from your workplace. Walk quickly.

❏ Take the stairs rather than the elevator.

❏ Take a fast walk at lunchtime.

❏ Exercise during work breaks.

❏ Join a gym and go three or four times per week.

❏ Find an active sport you like, such as tennis, racquetball, basketball, rollerblading, swimming, and so on.

❏ Jog when you get home from work.

❏ Walk around the mall four or five times per week.

❏ Walk briskly when talking on your phone.

❏ Get a personal trainer.

❏ Take dance lessons.

(continued)

- ❏ Ride the bike that's been gathering cobwebs in your garage.
- ❏ Watch videos and work out at home regularly.
- ❏ Go to a yoga class.
- ❏ Take other classes such as spin, kickboxing, or high-intensity interval training (HIIT).
- ❏ Buy a treadmill, stationary bike, or elliptical trainer. (Try them out at a gym first to make sure you want to make the investment.)
- ❏ Exercise while watching television.
- ❏
- ❏
- ❏
- ❏
- ❏ Watch sports on TV. Nope! Sorry, that one doesn't count!

Setting your personal goal

Once you've tried out a few different exercise routines, it's time to set a personal goal. The health benefits from exercise are well known. However, you may not have realized how important exercise is for mental health. *If you struggle with anxiety or depression, consider exercise a vital part of your treatment plan.*

No amount is too small to begin with, but over the long term, it's important to put in adequate time. The good news: if you have a period in which your efforts wane, you can always step up and get right back at exercise. In fact, expect ups and downs in your success. It takes months to acquire a habit, and it's never too late to restart.

On Worksheet 10-4, jot down your personal exercise goals. Be specific. What activities will you do? How many minutes each week? Are you going to start small and build up?

Worksheet 10-4   My Reflections

_____

_____

_____

_____

_____

TIP

No matter what goals you start with, remember that you can always revise and rework them. It takes time and experimentation to develop your own exercise success. It will be well worth the effort for health and well-being.

Committing to health

If exercise came in a bottle prescribed as a medication, it would fly off the pharmacy shelves. No known drug prevents numerous diseases while improving both mental and physical health. Even better, there are almost no negative side effects. And the costs are much less than pharmaceuticals. No one charges you to walk in your neighborhood.

If you want to lead a healthy life, committing to exercise should be high on your list of priorities. Exercise pays off. People who exercise have more energy, better health, and fewer medical bills. Enough said. Just do it.

What to Do When Willpower Wilts

Working through the preceding section gives you some good reasons for exercising (ten, in fact!). And hopefully you've found a few types of exercise that fit into your life and have tried them out. Your intentions may be good, but what happens when your initial enthusiasm and commitment to do something positive for yourself fade? Or how do you get started if you haven't found that initial enthusiasm?

Fighting demotivating thoughts

The problem with finding and maintaining motivation to exercise lies in distorted, demotivating thinking. (See Chapters 5, 6, and 7 for more on distorted thinking.) Demotivating thinking keeps you from acting and puts you in a defeatist frame of mind, where you're doomed to fail. When your thinking is distorted, your mind is full of reasons you can't exercise. It's hard to get moving when demotivating thoughts take control. But here's a strategy for defeating defeatism. The following example gives you an idea of how you can give demotivating thoughts the one-two punch.

EXAMPLE

Janine, a busy mother of two, works as a bank teller. She rushes off every morning to drop her kids at day care and tries to fit in her errands during a 45-minute lunch break. By dinnertime, she's exhausted. It's no wonder Janine suffers from mild depression. When her doctor suggests she begin exercising to improve her mood and health, Janine laughs and says, "You've got to be kidding; I don't have an extra second in my day."

But fortunately for Janine, she has a copy of the *Anxiety & Depression Workbook For Dummies* and completes the Defeating Demotivating Thoughts exercise. Worksheet 10-5 shows what she comes up with, and Worksheet 10-6 has her reflections on the exercise.

PRACTICE

Most folks who struggle to work exercise into their lives have thoughts like Janine's. Just because you think something, though, doesn't mean it's true. Therefore, paying attention to the dialogue about exercise that runs through your head is important because you can argue with these thoughts and in turn increase your willingness and motivation to exercise.

Worksheet 10-5   Janine's Defeating Demotivating Thoughts Exercise

Demotivating Thoughts	Motivating Thoughts
I don't have time to exercise.	I could cut 30 minutes off my television watching each evening. And it wouldn't be that hard to get up 15 or 20 minutes earlier either. It's a matter of prioritizing what's important, I guess.
I don't have the money to get a babysitter so I can exercise.	I could watch exercise videos online or take the kids for a walk. They'd love it if I went bike riding with them more often.
I'm too tired to exercise.	Yeah, well as I think about it, exercise usually helps overcome fatigue.
I'm too depressed to exercise.	From what I've read, exercise actually helps defeat depression. Just because I don't feel like exercising doesn't mean I can't do it.

Worksheet 10-6   Janine's Reflections

I can see how my thinking is bogging me down on this exercise thing. Part of the reason I feel so down is because I haven't been able to lose the weight from my last baby. What I need to do is stop listening to all these thoughts and get moving. I think I'll ride my bike with the kids down to the library tonight.

To complete your own Defeating Demotivating Thoughts Exercise,

1. **Read the demotivating thoughts in the left column of Worksheet 10-7, and circle those that are relevant to you.** These are the most common thoughts people have that get in the way of exercise.

    If you have thoughts that aren't on the list, feel free to add them in the extra spaces provided.

2. **For each thought that you circle or that you add, develop a *motivating thought* that refutes and debunks the demotivating one.** Consider the following points in developing motivating thoughts:

    *   Is the demotivating thought exaggerated or illogical in any way?

    *   Is the thought just an excuse not to exercise?

    *   Is there a better way to think about this demotivating thought?

    *   If a friend of mine told me the thought, would I think it was completely legitimate, or would it sound like an excuse?

- Is the thought helping me?
- What would happen if I simply tried acting as though the thought weren't true?

If you struggle to come up with motivating thoughts, flip back to Chapters 5, 6, and 7 for myriad ways to defeat such thinking.

3. **Jot down your reactions to this exercise under My Reflections (see Worksheet 10-8).**

Worksheet 10-7   My Defeating Demotivating Thoughts Exercise

Demotivating Thoughts	Motivating Thoughts
I don't feel like exercising. I'll start doing it when it feels right.	
I'm not someone who exercises; it's just not who I am.	
It's not worth the trouble to exercise.	
Exercise is a frivolous pursuit.	
I don't have time to exercise.	
I'm too tired to exercise.	
I'm too old to exercise.	
I hate exercise.	
I'm too depressed or anxious to exercise; I'll do it when I feel better.	
I'm too out of shape to exercise.	
I have too much pain to exercise.	
Gyms and equipment cost too much; I just don't have enough money to exercise.	
Exercise just isn't worth the effort.	

Worksheet 10-8   My Reflections

_____

_____

_____

_____

_____

_____

Keeping track of your progress

An effective way to boost motivation is to keep an exercise calendar. On this calendar, track the physical activity you do every day, and write (or type) down your reactions to the activity. When you commit yourself to writing something down, you tend to pay more attention to what you do. That's just part of human nature. The following is a brief example of an exercise calendar; read it through before starting your own.

EXAMPLE

Randy is a unit secretary at a busy hospital. He feels like his life is out of control: He can't save enough money to go to school, his social life seems flat, and his mood is gloomy. On top of that, he notices his bulging belly. His pants are too tight, and he feels hopeless. Randy talks to a friend, who urges him to join a gym to get active again. Randy's therapist agrees with the recommendation, so Randy joins a gym and begins tracking his daily physical activity (see Worksheet 10-9).

Worksheet 10-9   Randy's Calendar of Physical Activities

Day	What I Did	How I Felt
Monday	I walked up and down the stairs at work instead of taking the elevator as usual.	I was surprisingly out of breath, but it felt like a step in the right direction.
Tuesday	I made it to a kickboxing class.	I stayed in the back and felt sort of foolish. But afterward, I was in a pretty good mood.
Wednesday	Nothing at all. I was a total couch potato.	Guilty, guilty, guilty.
Thursday	I went for a long walk with the dogs.	I felt really relaxed afterward. And it did my heart good to see how happy the dogs were.
Friday	Made it to the gym again.	I'm hopeful I can make this a habit. I feel good. Besides, there are some gorgeous women at this gym!
Saturday	I went hiking with some friends.	That felt great. It was good to be outside, and I enjoyed the company a lot.
Sunday	Nothing. Total couch potato.	Hey, it's okay to take a break here and there. Beating myself up won't help.

PRACTICE

Use Worksheet 10-10 to track your exercise progress. You'll be surprised at how the act of writing everything down keeps you focused on the goal.

Worksheet 10-10   My Calendar of Physical Activities

Day	What I Did	How I Felt
Monday		
Tuesday		
Wednesday		
Thursday		
Friday		
Saturday		
Sunday		

REMEMBER

Beating yourself up when you don't succeed at the task won't help you stay on track. Just acknowledge that you didn't do what you wanted to and recommit yourself to get moving. Recommit again and again until exercise becomes part of your routine.

Chapter **11**

Entertaining Enjoyment

t's hard to be anxious or depressed when you're having fun. Laughter, enjoyment, and pleasure interfere with feelings of sadness or worry, and pleasure actually causes your body to
release *endorphins*, brain chemicals that increase a sense of well-being. Unfortunately, when
you suffer from anxiety or depression, you tend to withdraw from pleasurable activities. Thus,
it's critical to bring pleasure back into your life as part of your healing process.

This chapter helps you choose from a variety of healthy pleasures: activities, people, and events
that are good for you and help combat anxiety and depression.

What's Your Pleasure?

Emotional distress interferes with thinking. If you're sad or worried, you may have difficulty
coming up with ideas about what sounds pleasurable. Not to worry. That's why I created the
Nifty Fifty Checklist of Pleasurable Activities (see Worksheet 11-1). As you can see, this list
doesn't consist of spectacular, intense pleasures. Rather, it contains a wide range of simple
pleasures. Research has found that frequent, simple pleasures actually provide more enjoyment
than occasional, spectacular pleasures anyway.

PRACTICE

1. **Review the Checklist of Pleasurable Activities in Worksheet 11-1.**

2. **Check off any items that sound appealing to you now or have been pleasurable to you
in the past.**

3. **In Worksheet 11-2, record the items that you believe you can bring into your life.**

Worksheet 11-1   The Nifty Fifty Checklist of Pleasurable Activities

- ❑ 1. Eating chocolate
- ❑ 2. Acting in community theater
- ❑ 3. Creating art
- ❑ 4. Traveling
- ❑ 5. Shopping
- ❑ 6. Listening to music
- ❑ 7. Drinking tea
- ❑ 8. Playing a sport
- ❑ 9. Camping
- ❑ 10. Eating spicy foods
- ❑ 11. Taking a hot bath
- ❑ 12. Gardening
- ❑ 13. Exercising
- ❑ 14. Going to the beach or visiting a waterfall
- ❑ 15. Reading a good novel
- ❑ 16. Finishing a small task
- ❑ 17. Going to a live sporting event
- ❑ 18. Dancing
- ❑ 19. Dining out
- ❑ 20. Getting a massage
- ❑ 21. Visiting a friend
- ❑ 22. Drinking a glass of wine
- ❑ 23. Having sex
- ❑ 24. Going to a bookstore
- ❑ 25. Sewing
- ❑ 26. Spending time with family
- ❑ 27. Sitting in the sunshine
- ❑ 28. Cooking something special
- ❑ 29. Hiking
- ❑ 30. Playing with your pets
- ❑ 31. Taking a walk
- ❑ 32. Playing cards or games
- ❑ 33. Smelling fresh flowers
- ❑ 34. Attending a social gathering
- ❑ 35. Taking up a hobby
- ❑ 36. Visiting a museum
- ❑ 37. Napping
- ❑ 38. Putting on your sweats after a tough day
- ❑ 39. Going to a movie
- ❑ 40. Attending a concert or play
- ❑ 41. Going to a comedy club
- ❑ 42. Taking a yoga class
- ❑ 43. Flying a kite
- ❑ 44. Meditating
- ❑ 45. Taking pictures
- ❑ 46. Sleeping in
- ❑ 47. People watching
- ❑ 48. Taking a scenic drive
- ❑ 49. Visiting a coffee shop and having a cappuccino
- ❑ 50. Learning how to spell cappuccino!

If this list doesn't provide you with a wide range of intriguing possibilities, you're having trouble accepting pleasure into your life. The later section, "Pleasure Busters," helps you deal with that issue.

Worksheet 11-2   Top Ten Pleasures That Work for Me

1. _____
2. _____
3. _____
4. _____
5. _____
6. _____
7. _____
8. _____
9. _____
10. _____

PRACTICE

Assuming you've managed to create your own list of pleasurable activities, it's time to schedule them into your life. Use the following instructions as well as Worksheets 11-3 and 11-4 to complete this part of the pleasure process.

1. **In Worksheet 11-3, for each day of the week, write down one or more pleasurable activities that you plan to engage in.** Try to pick different activities across the week. Ideally, choose some that you haven't done in a while.

2. **After you complete the pleasurable activity, circle it in the chart as a marker of your accomplishment.**

3. **Notice how you feel at the end of a week in which you've increased your simple pleasures.**

4. **Jot down your observations under My Reflections in Worksheet 11-4.**

Worksheet 11-3   Simple Pleasures

Day	Pleasurable Activities
Monday	
Tuesday	
Wednesday	
Thursday	
Friday	
Saturday	
Sunday	

Worksheet 11-4   My Reflections

_____

_____

_____

_____

_____

REMEMBER

Getting through depression and anxiety involves more than inserting pleasure into your life, as important as that is. For example, you need to stay active with exercise (Chapter 11), straighten out your thinking (Chapters 5, 6, 7), and solve problems competently (Chapter 12).

Poisonous Pleasures

Don't take this pleasure idea too far. Pleasure's great, of course, but some pleasures can get you into instant trouble, and other pleasures, when taken to extremes, can be dangerous or unhealthy. Thus, watch out for the dangers inherent in some pleasures, including:

>> Drug abuse

>> Prostitution

>> Alcohol to excess

>> Hanging out with bad company

>> Sleeping to excess

>> Excessively engaging with distressing social media

>> Overeating

>> Sexual promiscuity

>> Excessive caffeine consumption

>> Compulsive exercise

>> Shopping beyond your budget

>> Reckless driving

>> Excessive gambling

>> Thrill-seeking through risky behaviors

>> Shoplifting

>> Gobbling two gallons of cookie dough ice cream

WARNING

If you indulge in one or more of these poisonous pleasures, please consider seeking professional help. Even healthy activities like exercising or dieting, when taken to the extreme or overdone, can become a problem. Furthermore, these behaviors can greatly complicate the task of overcoming anxiety and depression.

Pleasure Busters

Ideally, you found a nice list of pleasurable activities from the Nifty Fifty Checklist (see Worksheet 11-1) and were able to insert them into your regular life without too much trouble. However, many people don't find this task so easy to do.

Emotional distress and especially depression cause distorted thinking. (See Chapters 5, 6, and 7 for the lowdown on distorted thinking.) This section zeros in on the thoughts that are most likely to interfere with your efforts to increase pleasure in your life. Three types of distortions typically get in the way: thoughts of undeservingness and unworthiness, thoughts that pleasure is a frivolous waste of time, and thoughts that deny the effectiveness of pleasurable activities.

Deciding to deserve fun

Depression and anxiety affect your self-esteem, and not for the better. When you're sad or anxious, you probably don't think too highly of yourself. And along with low self-esteem come thoughts such as:

>> I don't deserve happiness or pleasure.

>> I'm not good enough.

>> I'm not getting enough done as it is, so I certainly don't have time for pleasure.

>> I deserve punishment, not pleasure.

>> I've let everyone down. How can I justify having fun?

As you may imagine, these types of thoughts don't exactly result in a strong desire to seek pleasure and fun. They also increase emotional distress in general. Clearly, it's best to rethink those thoughts. The following example illustrates how pleasure-busting thoughts can be turned into pleasure-boosting thoughts.

EXAMPLE

Theresa suffers from depression. Her therapist suggests that she increase the pleasurable activities in her life. Theresa finds herself resisting the idea, so she and her therapist explore the reasons behind her reluctance. They discover two pleasure-busting thoughts standing in the way: "I don't deserve pleasure," and "I'm not getting enough done in my life as it is."

Theresa and her therapist work together to rethink her pleasure-busting thoughts. Worksheet 11-5 shows what they come up with.

Worksheet 11-5   Theresa Rethinking Pleasure Busters

Pleasure-busting Thought	Pleasure-boosting Thought
I don't deserve pleasure.	No one has to earn pleasure. Reintroducing pleasure into my life is partly how I can overcome my depression.
I'm not getting enough done in my life as it is.	Part of the reason I'm not getting enough done is because I'm so depressed. If I improve my depression, I'll be more productive.

PRACTICE

If you find that you're resisting increasing pleasure in your life, it's likely you have one or more pleasure-busting thoughts. The following exercise helps you identify the pleasure-busting thoughts you may have and develop more adaptive, pleasure-boosting thoughts.

1. **Read the pleasure-busting thoughts in the left column of Worksheet 11-6. These are the most common thoughts people have that get in the way of increasing pleasure. Circle those relevant to you.**

2. **Add any thoughts that aren't on the list in the extra spaces provided.**

3. **For each thought that you've circled or added, develop a pleasure-boosting thought that refutes the pleasure-busting thought.** Consider the following points in developing motivating thoughts:

   - Is this pleasure-boosting thought actually exaggerated or illogical in some way?
   - Is there a better way to think about this pleasure-busting thought?
   - If a friend of mine told me that thought, would I think it was completely legitimate, or would it sound merely self-defeating?
   - Is this thought helping me?

If you struggle to come up with pleasure-boosting thoughts, turn to Chapter 3 for ways to defeat the distorted thinking that's standing in your way.

Finding fun frivolous?

Common thoughts among the pleasure-challenged folks of the world are, "Having a good time is a waste of time," and "Fun is frivolous." These people usually think that work and accomplishments are acceptable activities, but fun, entertainment, or even relaxation are definitely unacceptable. Their leisure activities are typically ones that expand their knowledge or increase their skills.

Not to say that expanding your horizons is a bad thing, but trashy novels, silly movies, walks in the park, some time at a comedy club, dancing, and a little karaoke (mind you, you'll never, ever see *me* doing this one!) have many benefits.

Worksheet 11-6   Rethinking Pleasure Busters

Pleasure-busting Thought	Pleasure-boosting Thought
I don't deserve happiness or pleasure.	
I'm not getting enough done as it is, so I certainly don't have time for pleasure.	
I'm not good enough.	
I deserve punishment, not pleasure.	
I've let everyone down. How can I justify having fun?	

Benefits, you ask? Absolutely. Research shows that pleasure forms the backbone of a healthy life. For starters, pleasure decreases anxiety and depression because it releases endorphins that make you feel grrrreat. But it also has other important physical and emotional benefits, such as:

>> Improved immune function

>> Decreased feelings of chronic pain

>> Decreased risk of heart attack

>> Decreased stress

>> Prolonged life expectancy

>> Enhanced sense of well-being

>> Improved overall health

>> Increased productivity

Did you notice that last item, "Increased productivity"? Many people think that nonwork related activities are frivolous. Truth is, putting pleasure into your life actually makes you more productive when you're working. You have more enthusiasm for your work and more energy. In other words, you're very likely to get more done if you just take a break every once in a while!

PRACTICE

If you've fallen into the "fun is frivolous" mind trap, *seriously* consider the benefits of pleasure. Think about what pleasure and its benefits can mean to you and your life. Jot down your conclusions under My Reflections in Worksheet 11-7.

_____

_____

_____

_____

_____

Pleasure-pooping predictions

Minds riddled with depression and anxiety do a curious thing: they make predictions about how much you're likely to enjoy various activities. And with amazing consistency, these predictions, such as the following, are negative:

>> I'm not going to enjoy myself at all.

>> That sounds so boring.

>> I'll just look stupid.

>> I'm too depressed to like anything like that.

>> I'm too anxious to enjoy myself at that party.

Recognize any of these thoughts? Research has demonstrated rather conclusively that, especially when you're depressed or anxious, such predictions are worse than unreliable — they're actually *reliably* wrong! In other words, when you push yourself to engage in a potentially pleasurable activity, you're highly likely to discover that you enjoy it more than you think you will.

But if you believe what your mind tells you and take its negative predictions as the gospel truth, you'll follow the wrong road again and again — you'll avoid pursuing pleasure. Listening to your mind is a little like listening to the radio for the daily traffic report. Each and every day the reporter tells you to avoid taking I-40 because of construction delays. So, you choose the surface roads and spend an extra twenty minutes getting to work. The only problem is that the reporter is lying to you, and you'd be much better off not listening to their advice. Think of this conniving reporter as your mind, predicting that activities can't possibly cause you pleasure, and fire the reporter in your mind.

To help you overcome your mind's negative predictions, try the Pessimistic Pleasure-busting Exercise.

PRACTICE

1. **From Worksheet 11-1, choose five potentially pleasurable activities that you'd be willing to try.**

2. **List those activities in the left column of Worksheet 11-8.**

3. **Predict the amount of enjoyment or pleasure each activity may give you on a scale of 0 (no fun at all) to 10 (maximal pleasure). Write that number in the middle column.**

4. **Do the pleasurable activity.**

5. Rate how much enjoyment you actually felt from each activity on the same scale of 0 (no fun at all) to 10 (maximal pleasure).

6. Write about your observations and conclusions under My Reflections in Worksheet 11-9.

Worksheet 11-8   Pessimistic Pleasure-busting Exercise

Activity	Predicted Fun (0–10)	Experienced Fun (0–10)

Can you see a trend in Worksheet 11-8? Did you experience more pleasure than you expected for most of your activities? If you don't see it, keep trying.

REMEMBER

The pleasure you feel will likely increase slowly over time. And it's okay to come back to this exercise again later after you've worked on your depression and anxiety in other ways.

Worksheet 11-9   My Reflections

_____
_____
_____
_____
_____

Chapter 12

Moving and Tackling Life's Problems

Depression and anxiety steal energy, hope, and motivation. When negative emotions cloud your mind, it's hard to get moving. Everyday tasks seem overwhelming, simple problems appear complex, and molehills become mountains as a vicious cycle begins. In the end, not getting things done and not solving problems only make you more depressed and anxious.

In this chapter, you discover how to get going again. I warn you about the trap of waiting for motivation, and you get action plans for, well, umm . . . action. There's also a comprehensive, step-by-step game plan for untangling your problems and choosing good solutions.

The Motivation Myth

Especially if you're depressed, you may find yourself spending a lot of time spinning your wheels. In other words, you're not accomplishing what you want and you aren't even able to take the first step toward reversing your inactivity. You're likely to tell yourself, "I'll do these things when I feel motivated." Ahh, but that thought buys into a common myth that if you wait for motivation to arrive on your doorstep, you'll feel like taking action when it finally comes along. In actuality, action creates motivation — the more you do, the more you want to do. It doesn't work as reliably the other way around. The following example highlights the relationship between action and motivation.

EXAMPLE

It's Saturday morning, and I need to get six pages of writing done today to stay on schedule. I'm in sunny New Mexico, and — big surprise — I don't feel like writing right now. In fact, I really don't want to write at all today. The sky is so blue, the temperature outside is perfect, and the winds are calm. So, the thought of writing is more dreadful by the minute. Ugh. I'm getting kind of depressed just thinking about it. How about if I just put this task off until I'm more motivated?

There are problems with that plan. Not only will I fall behind, I'm also not entirely sure that the motivation will come along. Ever. If I wait for motivation that never comes, I'll never finish the book, you'll never read it, and the publisher will be really, really unhappy with me. Now I'm beginning to feel a bit anxious. The momentary relief from not writing on this beautiful Saturday morning leads to a whole lot of misery. It's not a pretty picture.

What's the alternative? To sit down and write, of course! When I do, something miraculous happens. I actually start to feel like doing it. In fact, I have fun with it by writing about this example of action creating motivation rather than the other way around.

One way to jump-start action is through the creation of an *activity log* (see the following example). An activity log is an action plan that plots out at least one small activity to accomplish each day and includes space to record how the task went and how it felt to complete it. Keeping track of the activities and small tasks you accomplish gives you incentive to keep going. Motivation slowly but surely rises, and you do even more than you expected.

EXAMPLE

Carmen looks around her house and feels self-loathing and disgust. She sees dishes piled everywhere, magazines tossed haphazardly, and a week's worth of junk mail strewn across her kitchen countertop. She hasn't cleaned the house in over a month, and the job of straightening up completely overwhelms her. Carmen manages to drag herself to her women's support group that meets Wednesday evenings. She relates her difficulty in tackling basic, daily chores. One member suggests that Carmen fill out an activity log. Worksheet 12-1 shows Carmen's result.

Worksheet 12-1   Carmen's Activity Log

Day	Activity	Outcome
Monday	Wash just the few dishes lying in the sink and leave the rest	Once I started, I ended up doing them all. That felt great!
Tuesday	Pay a couple of bills	It took me all day to get around to it, but I did it. It didn't make me feel much better though — probably because I waited so long.
Wednesday	Change my bed and do the laundry	I just couldn't do it; I got too discouraged.

Day	Activity	Outcome
Thursday	Stop by the grocery store on my way home from work	I've been eating way too much cold cereal for dinner, so this helped.
Friday	Vacuum the house	It's not my favorite thing to do, but it felt like I did something useful.
Saturday	Clean the kitchen and do the laundry	I really went to town on this one. I'm starting to feel a little better.
Sunday	Get my car washed	This really perked me up. My car hadn't been washed in five months!

Carmen notices that after she gets started doing an activity, she usually feels better. Overall, the activity log helps Carmen get going again.

If you've been feeling stuck lately and overwhelmed by all that you need to do, create your own activity log to get back on track.

PRACTICE

1. **Think about the various tasks and chores you've been putting off.**

2. **In the middle column of Worksheet 12-2, jot down one task or chore for each day of the week.**

TIP

   Start with small tasks and break big tasks into smaller parts. For example, don't take on cleaning out the entire garage on a single day; instead, tackle one messy shelf at a time. Make tasks doable!

3. **On each day, complete the corresponding task and, in the right column, write down how it went and how it made you feel to do it.** If you don't complete a given task, don't beat yourself up; just move onto the next one.

4. **After you finish a week's worth of tasks, jot down your observations of what you've learned under My Reflections (see Worksheet 12-3).**

If you find this exercise useful, continue it for several weeks. Once you start feeling motivation returning, you probably won't need it.

Worksheet 12-2   My Activity Log

Day	Activity	Outcome
Monday		
Tuesday		
Wednesday		
Thursday		
Friday		
Saturday		
Sunday		

_____

_____

_____

_____

Organizing Your Problem with S.O.C.S.

When people are emotionally distressed, many situations seem overwhelmingly difficult. Anxiety and depression make even small problems appear insurmountable because emotional pain interferes with clear thinking.

TIP

Systematic problem-solving helps you organize your thinking, use creative skills to come up with potential solutions, predict outcomes, and select a reasonable way to move forward. You can apply these strategies to everyday problems, to relationships, and even to problems with your career.

When feeling overwhelmed, most folks avoid the problem at hand as long as they can. This avoidance is unfortunate because problems usually grow rather than fade away. Avoidance eventually increases negative emotions.

Because avoidance isn't the answer, there's a way to break problems down and figure out what to do with them. The plan involves four steps, and to make it simple, I call it *S.O.C.S.* Here's what S.O.C.S. stands for:

>> **S:** *Situation,* meaning the nature and causes of the problem as well as your beliefs and feelings about the issue.

>> **O:** All possible *options* for addressing the problem.

>> **C:** The *consequences* or results most likely to occur with each option.

>> **S:** *Selecting* which option to go with and executing it.

The following sections review each of the S.O.C.S. steps in detail. To give you a complete picture of how this process works, you follow one example subject, Derrick, who solves a problem about his work. You see how he completes each component of the S.O.C.S. problem-solving process and then see how to do the same for yourself.

REMEMBER

The S.O.C.S. system is useful regardless of whether you're feeling emotional distress. Even if you feel great, you can employ this plan for tackling some of life's most vexing issues.

Sizing things up (S)

Rather than bury your head in the sand, take a hard look at your problem. Gather information about it and think about the causes and the relative importance of the problem to your life. Believe it or not, you're not the first person to experience your problem. You can obtain information by talking to others, reading books and articles, or searching online. Finally, reflect on what feelings this problem stirs up in you.

EXAMPLE

Derrick feels frustrated at work as a mechanical engineer. He hasn't been given the level of responsibilities he feels capable of taking on, and he hasn't received the bonuses or recognition he's expected. His frustration grows as he ruminates about his dilemma in the early morning hours. He realizes that the situation contributes to his mounting depression. Derrick goes online and researches comparable jobs; he also reads articles about career advancement. Derrick decides the first step in tackling his problem is describing it (see Worksheet 12-4).

Worksheet 12-4 Derrick's Problematic Situation: S.

I'm not happy with my job. I want more responsibility and the pay and recognition that go along with it. I've been here for six years, and I'm still doing the same things I was when I was hired. I don't think the problem is a lack of skills because I'm pretty confident about my talent. One of the articles I read suggests that I haven't been assertive enough and made myself known around here. This issue keeps me up at night, so it's quite important.

After describing his problem in great detail, Derrick is ready to go on to the next step: figuring out his options.

Using Derrick's description as a guide, take the time to describe your problematic situation.

PRACTICE

1. In Worksheet 12-5, describe your problematic situation.

2. Consider reading articles for helpful insights, and record any relevant information you find.

3. Include information about possible causes of your problem.

4. Include your emotional responses to the problem. Does it make you feel depressed, frustrated, anxious, or something else?

5. Indicate how important the problem is to you.

Worksheet 12-5 My Problematic Situation: S.

_____

_____

_____

_____

Collecting options (O)

After you lay out your problem, it's time to let the creative juices flow. This step asks you to brainstorm any and all ways of tackling your problem. Be sure to list all the ideas you have, even if they sound silly. Put your internal critic on hold, and let loose.

TIP

If you're stumped for solutions, consider other sources of information. Talk to trusted friends or colleagues. Read articles or books that may have relevance to what you're dealing with.

EXAMPLE

Derrick learns more about the job market and continues to read about career advancement in his field. He talks with friends and coworkers so he can brainstorm his options. After a lot of research and thought, he lists his ideas (see Worksheet 12-6).

Worksheet 12-6   Derrick's Situation and Options: S.O.

<u>Situation:</u> I'm not happy with my job. I want more responsibility and the pay and recognition that go along with it. I've been here for six years, and I'm still doing the same things I was when I was hired. I don't think the problem is a lack of skills because I'm pretty confident about my talent. One of the books I've read suggests that maybe I haven't been assertive enough and made myself known around here. This issue keeps me up at night, so it's quite important.

Options
I can look for another job.
I can work on my assertiveness skills by taking a class or going to Toastmasters.
I can ask for a meeting with my supervisor and discuss my concerns.
I can do nothing about work and try to find pleasure in outside pursuits.
I could go into business for myself.
I could tell the boss off.
I could get even more education and training to impress the higher-ups.
I could network at work more than I do. I could start by attending all those stupid company picnics and parties.

Derrick feels he's covered all bases with his possible options. He's now ready for the next step in the S.O.C.S. problem-solving process: recognizing consequences.

PRACTICE

Complete your own options step by following these instructions:

1. **In Worksheet 12-7, write down the situation you describe in Worksheet 12-5.**

2. **Gather data from books, online sources, friends, basically anywhere.**

3. **Develop a list of options for dealing with your problem, and write them down in the space provided.** Don't forget that one option is to not solve the problem and deal with the status quo.

Worksheet 12-7   My Situation and Options: S.O.

Situation:
_____
_____
_____
_____
_____

Options
_____
_____
_____
_____
_____
_____
_____

TIP

Don't censor your ideas; put down anything that's even in the ballpark of helping your situation.

Considering consequences (C)

After you list all the possible options for solving your problem, you need to contemplate the most likely outcomes for each of those options. I'm not asking you to be a fortuneteller. Obviously, you can't "know" how your solutions will turn out, but you can make a reasonably good guess. So, take your best shot at evaluating what you think is most likely to happen. Worksheet 12-8 shows what Derrick comes up with.

Fill out your own situation, options, and consequences form.

PRACTICE

1. **Write down your problematic situation in Worksheet 12-9.** (This time, feel free to abbreviate your situation — you're probably pretty familiar with it by now.)

2. **Briefly list your options from Worksheet 12-7 in the left column.**

3. **Contemplate what you think are the most likely consequences or outcomes for each option, and write them in the right column.**

Worksheet 12-8   Derrick's Situation, Options, and Consequences: S.O.C.

<u>Situation:</u> I'm not happy with my job. I want more responsibility and the pay and recognition that go along with it. I've been here for six years, and I'm still doing the same things I was when I was hired. I don't think the problem is a lack of skills because I'm pretty confident about my talent. One of the books I've read suggests that maybe I haven't been assertive enough and made myself known around here. This issue keeps me up at night, so it's quite important.

Options	Likely Consequences
I can look for another job.	I could, but this is actually a good company. I would lose my seniority here, and I'm not sure I'd find something a lot better.
I can work on my assertiveness skills by taking a class or going to Toastmasters.	It took me a while to realize this, but learning assertiveness and speaking skills may help a lot. The people who've done well here are a lot more sociable than I am.
I can ask for a meeting with my supervisor and discuss my concerns.	I've done a little of this, and it got me nowhere. Maybe after I learn to be more assertive it will work better.
I can do nothing about work and try to find pleasure in outside pursuits.	I spend more time at work than anywhere else, and that's how I like it. I need to solve the work problem first.
I could go into business for myself.	Someday this would be nice, but right now, I'd run a high risk of going bankrupt without better financing.
I could tell the boss off.	Sounds very, very tempting, but this could easily get me fired. Not a smart idea.
I could get even more education and training to impress the higher-ups.	I already have a master's degree. I haven't seen evidence of more education getting people that far here.
I could network at work more than I do. I could start by attending all those stupid company picnics and parties.	This fits in with my other idea about assertiveness. I think it actually has a good chance of working. I won't particularly like doing it, and I'll feel uncomfortable, but it's likely to pay off.

Worksheet 12-9   My Situation, Options, and Consequences: S.O.C.

Situation:

_____

_____

_____

_____

_____

Options	Likely Consequences

Selecting the most reasonable options

To make a choice about how to handle your problem, you need to carefully consider each option and its most likely outcome (see Worksheet 12-9). Reflect on how each option would make you feel if you were to carry it out. Some options may seem pretty difficult. And some options, you would obviously not select. When you make your selection, commit to it even if it seems difficult. You may want to tell others what you plan to do because spreading the word often makes the commitment firmer and makes you think twice before backing out or giving up.

It may not seem so, but deciding to make no choice is really making a choice. Doing nothing has its own set of likely outcomes.

Derrick sizes up his options and their potential consequences. He decides to work on his communication, assertiveness, and social skills. He signs up for a class, reads books, and goes to company functions.

EXAMPLE

To make your own choices, follow these instructions and use Derrick's example as a guide.

PRACTICE

1. **Review your S.O.C. form (see Worksheet 12-9).**

2. **Select the option or options that make the most sense to you — the ones most likely to get you what you want.**

3. **Jot down your selection in Worksheet 12-10.**

Worksheet 12-10   My Selection: S.

_____

_____

_____

_____

_____

Reviewing your work

Many people make decisions to do something but procrastinate when it comes to carrying out those decisions. Why? Because many actions arouse anxiety, fear, worry, or distress. If your choice of options makes you tremble, consider the following tips:

» **Role-play and rehearsal:** Using imagery in your mind, you can rehearse carrying out your solution. Or even better, rehearse aloud by yourself or with a trusted friend. The more times you repeat your rehearsal, the more you're likely to feel prepared and calm.

» **Self-talk:** Think of positive statements you can repeat to yourself as you carry out your plan. Consider writing them on a card to carry with you as a reminder. Positive statements may include:

- This is the right thing to do.
- I can tolerate the discomfort; it won't last long.
- I worked hard to consider other alternatives; this is the best shot.
- I have the absolute right to carry this out.

Running your solution and reviewing its effectiveness are crucial to your success. You've gone through the problem-solving process; now it's time to turn all that work into action. Decide when would be a good time to execute your plan and do it! Afterward, evaluate how your plan worked.

Reflect on your success, or make changes and try again. Record your thoughts on Worksheet 12-11.

Worksheet 12-11   My Reflections

_____

_____

_____

_____

TIP

Many people like to lay out the S.O.C.S. problem-solving process in a single form, like the one shown in Worksheet 12-12. You can use this form after you've already chosen your best option(s).

Worksheet 12-12   My S.O.C.S. Plan

Situation	
Option	
Consequences	
Selection	

4

Focus on Physical Feelings

Chapter **13**

Sleeping Soundly for Emotional Health

You're running late. You dash to the car and drive a little too fast. Your phone rings, and you glance at the screen to see who's calling. When your eyes return to the road, you see that the car ahead of you has come to a dead stop. You stomp on your brakes and barely avoid an accident. An enormous parking lot looms ahead on the freeway. You feel every muscle in your body tighten up, your heart pounds, and you begin to sweat. Drat! Another rotten start to the day.

Modern life supplies a never-ending string of opportunities for revving up your entire system. Your body prepares you to react to perceived dangers and stressors by orchestrating a complex response:

» Your brain sends messages to your nervous system to go into high gear.

» Your eyes widen to let in more light.

» Your heart beats faster.

» Your digestion slows so that energy is available for large muscles, which tighten.

» Blood flow increases to your arms and legs so that you can run or fight.

» Sweating increases to keep your body cool.

All these responses are pretty handy if you need to physically defend yourself or run away. But typically speaking, most folks don't jump out of their cars to beat up other drivers or abandon their cars and run to work. Well, okay, maybe in LA they do.

The costs of chronically revving up your body's fight or flight response include high blood pressure, chronic muscle spasms, tension headaches, suppressed immune system, irritable bowel syndrome, ulcers, and on and on. That's a high price for responses you rarely need. Furthermore, the stress and strain of daily hassles disrupt sleep for millions of people. Insomnia involves difficulty falling asleep, staying asleep, or waking up too early. These difficulties interfere with daily living. Rates of at least occasional insomnia among adults vary from 30 to 50 percent.

This chapter looks at aspects of sleep and emotional well-being. Sleep is essential for effective stress management. Specific suggestions give you ways to improve sleep. The bulk of this chapter describes techniques derived from Cognitive Behavioral Therapy for Insomnia (CBT-I). CBT-I includes education about sleep as well as changes in thinking and behaving regarding sleep. Sleep specialists agree that CBT-I is the preferred and most effective treatment for insomnia.

Recognizing the Importance of Sleep

During sleep, the body and mind recharge, repair, and heal. After a good night's sleep, you feel refreshed, replenished, and ready to face the day. Sleep improves memory, mood, attention, productivity, and even immunity. Sleep is essential for both physical and mental health.

How many hours of sleep do you rack up on a typical night? Although people differ in their sleep needs, most people function pretty well on seven to eight hours of sleep a night. The bottom line, however, is that if you feel rested, you're getting enough sleep. If you don't feel rested, you may be getting too much or too little sleep.

TIP

The strategies and tips found throughout this chapter help you track sleep, prepare for sleep, think helpful thoughts about sleep, and deal with insomnia. Many people find these strategies sufficient to improve regular sleep. However, some may need more specialized help.

WARNING

People with chronic sleep disorders are at higher risk of heart disease, high blood pressure, weight gain, and stroke. Therefore, if you have problems with sleep, you should really take them seriously. If you have insomnia for more than a couple of weeks, consult with your health care provider to check out likely causes of your sleep problems. The provider may also refer you to a sleep specialist.

WARNING

Waking up once on most nights is typical and not a problem to be concerned about. However, waking up frequently or being unable to get back to sleep after waking is a problem. This problem should be checked out with your physician because it may indicate:

>> Prostate problems (that is, if you're a guy)

>> Hormonal problems (typically, if you're female)

» Restless leg syndrome, a condition in which you feel an uncomfortable feeling in your legs or feet and an urge to keep moving them

» Medication issues

» An emotional disorder (for which this workbook can help, but you need a professional's opinion, too)

» Other physical conditions of various sorts

WARNING

If you don't feel rested after seven or eight hours of sleep, you may have a serious sleep problem known as *sleep apnea*. Sleep apnea involves a series of episodes in which your breathing stops momentarily while you sleep. Sleep apnea results in very poor quality sleep. Snoring can be a sign of sleep apnea, but that's not always the case. If you think you may have sleep apnea, your physician can refer you to a sleep clinic where the condition can be accurately diagnosed.

Depression and anxiety disrupt sleep and can cause insomnia. Some people have trouble falling asleep, others wake up in the early morning hours and can't get back to sleep, and some suffer from both problems. On the other hand, a few people with anxiety or depression sleep too much, and their sleep isn't refreshing.

If you have trouble sleeping, fatigue probably adds to your emotional distress. And as your emotional distress mounts from lack of sleep, your sleep problems deepen. Talk about a vicious cycle!

TIP

Health care providers have noticed substantial upticks in insomnia that some now call *coronasomnia* because it's related to the pandemic. Their patients report increased worry, disrupted schedules, anxiety, fear, and depression added to their sleep woes.

Tracking Your Sleep

A helpful first step in dealing with insomnia is taking time to gather information about the nature of your sleep. A sleep log or sleep diary is one way that you can take charge of this process. A sleep diary tracks much more than the time you spend in bed. Sleep is often affected by what you do during the day. For example:

» Did you drink coffee in the afternoon or evening?

» Did you take a nap?

» Were there particular stresses during the day?

» Did you get any exercise?

» What medications do you take?

One purpose of tracking your sleep is to discover patterns. Perhaps you have sleep problems only during the week when you work. You sleep perfectly fine on the weekends. Or maybe you have trouble sleeping after a late evening meal. A carefully filled out sleep diary will reveal the nature of these issues.

PRACTICE Fill out the Daily Sleep Diary, Worksheet 13-1, in the morning. Think about your sleep and the activities on the day prior. Complete sleep diaries daily for one week or more. If you have a sleep tracker on a device such as a watch or phone, feel free to include that information as well. You can obtain extra copies of these forms at www.dummies.com/go/anxiety&depressionworkbookfd2e.

Worksheet 13-1   Daily Sleep Diary— Date: _____

Questions	Answers
What time did you go to bed?	
Approximately how long did it take you to fall asleep?	
Did you wake in the middle of the night? What time(s)? How long did you stay awake?	
What time did you get up in the morning?	
How many hours did you sleep? What was the quality of your sleep?	
Do you feel rested?	
Did you nap during the day? How long? What time?	
Did you drink caffeinated beverages during the day? What time?	
Did you exercise?	
What time did you eat your last meal or snack before bed?	
Did you drink alcohol? At what time? How much?	
What medications do you take either prescription or over the counter?	
Do you take anything to help you sleep?	
Are you currently in a stressful situation, or do you have significant worries?	
Do you have other thoughts or concerns?	

After completing a week or so of sleep diaries, you may see some relationships between your behaviors during the previous day and the quality of your sleep. Or perhaps you may not. If sleep appears to be a problem, read on for more information about getting the rest you need.

TIP If you decide to check out your sleep problems with a health care provider, be sure to bring along your sleep diaries. They provide a wealth of information.

Sleep Guidelines

The following guidelines apply to anyone who's interested in improving sleep, whether or not they suffer from insomnia. Making simple changes in what you do before bed can lead to a better night's sleep.

WARNING Many people use prescription or over-the-counter sleep aids. Although these medications are helpful in the short term, they're not recommended for long-term use. There are serious downsides to using medications for sleep, such as memory loss, poor daytime concentration, and addiction. A better strategy for addressing sleep problems is detailed in the sections that follow.

Drinking and eating before bed

You probably know that caffeine is a stimulant and, as such, keeps many people awake. Some folks don't seem to be all that affected by caffeine, but others lie awake for hours after a single cup of java. Coffee isn't the only culprit though; other sources of caffeine include tea, many soft drinks, chocolate, and some pain relievers. Read the labels of what you're consuming, or you may be wide awake all night.

You may think that alcohol is the opposite of caffeine, so it should do the trick and put you right to sleep, right? Well, not exactly. Some people find a glass or two of wine relaxing and a helpful inducement of sleep. However, too much alcohol interferes with restful sleep. For that matter, too much of anything, such as rich foods or an especially late dinner before bed, can mess with your sleep.

TIP

When it comes to eating and drinking before bed, if you just have to have something, try an herbal tea without caffeine, such as chamomile or valerian. Or have a small glass of milk or a light snack. And don't drink gallons of fluids before you go to bed, or you'll be up all night for different reasons.

Bedtime routines

One key to restful sleep is going to bed somewhat relaxed. Strenuous and aerobic activities tend to stimulate the body, so avoid any such activities for at least an hour before you hit the sack. Also, don't call your mother and have a big argument before hitting the pillow. While you're at it, don't call your ex or anyone else who's likely to get you worked up.

Instead, develop a regular wind-down routine prior to bed. A warm bath (not overly hot, which can be stimulative for some), quiet music, an enjoyable book (probably not a horror novel), and limited screen time can all help you wind down.

TIP

Experiment with what you personally can or can't do prior to bed. For some, the horrors on the evening news don't have any stressful effects. Others find a murder mystery quite calming. Still others aren't bothered by aerobic exercise. Go figure.

Sleep setting

The environment you sleep in plays a key role in determining the quality of your sleep. For most people, sleep comes more easily when it's dark. But what if your work shift requires that you sleep in the daytime? Consider getting blackout curtains or wearing a sleep mask because darkness tells your brain it's time to sleep.

How about that mattress you've had for twenty years? Is it comfortable? For some, the floor or couch is good enough. For others, a really comfortable mattress is worth every dime. You may want to invest in high-quality sheets as well to make your sleep setting even more inviting.

When it comes to your sleep setting, noise matters, too. Find a way to keep your environment relatively silent. If you can't do that, you can mask noises with a sound-generating app, sound machine, or fan.

Finally, temperature matters. For most people, cool is better because they can always pile on the blankets. Sleep researchers have found that core body temperature tends to decrease during good sleep.

Associations and Sleep

Have you ever walked through a mall and smelled fresh cookies or bakery goods in the air? You might have noticed a small amount of saliva forming in your mouth. There's an instant association between the smell of something delicious and the desire to eat. That smell is no accident. It's intended to tempt you.

There are many such associations in life. You hear a song you loved in high school, and your mood lifts. A smile from a stranger brings a smile to your face. You stop at a red light without thinking. You hear a beep and immediately look at your phone.

An important association for good sleep is that you associate sleep with your bed. When you see those soft pillows and warm comforter, your brain immediately begins to shut down. Sweet sleep is coming soon.

What prevents you from associating your bed with sleep? See the following for examples of what does *not* help:

>> Eating or drinking in bed

>> Tossing and turning awake in bed for more than 15 minutes

>> Screen time in bed

>> Fighting in bed

>> Texting or talking on the phone in bed

>> Working in bed

Have sex and sleep in your bed, but save the rest for somewhere else if you want to strengthen the association of sleep with your bed. Note that a few people can fall asleep easily even after doing other activities, such as watching television or reading. If that's true in your case, no worries. Continue on.

TIP

Associating your bed with sleeplessness is counterproductive. If you're awake in bed for more than 15 minutes, get up and do something else. Read a book, do the dishes, look through a magazine, and go back to bed when you feel sleepy. (Stay away from screens, though. They wake you up.)

Relaxation and Sleep

Relaxing before bed helps you drift off to sleep. You can use a variety of methods. For example, you might choose to meditate before bed (see Chapter 8). Use your phone and download an app with sleep stories for adults. Sleep stories tend to be softly and slowly read passages that relax you. Be sure to try out any app before you buy one. I found some stories so annoying that they were the opposite of relaxing.

One of the most thoroughly researched methods for teaching your body to relax is called *progressive muscle relaxation*. In the beginning, this technique will take you about 15 or 20 minutes. As you practice the exercise, you'll be able to accomplish relaxation in a shorter period of time. After a while, some people are able to relax their bodies within just 2 or 3 minutes.

TIP

Feel free to record these instructions on your phone. Be sure to speak slowly and calmly.

PRACTICE

Progressive muscle relaxation involves systematically tensing various muscle groups and holding that tension for five or ten seconds. Then release the tension and allow relaxation to take over. The procedure starts with your hands and arms, moves through the neck, back, and face, and progresses down the legs and feet. You can do this in bed, on the sofa, or on any comfortable surface.

1. **Take a deep breath from your abdomen, hold it for a few seconds, and slowly exhale, letting the tension go.**

TIP

Imagine that your whole body is a balloon losing air as you exhale and release tension with the air. Take three more such breaths, and feel your entire body become limper with each one.

2. **Squeeze your fingers into a fist and feel the tension. Release your hands and let them go limp, allowing the tension in your hands to flow out.**

3. **Raise your arms until they're almost even with your shoulders and tighten the muscles. Hold the tension, and then drop your arms as though the string holding them up has been cut.**

4. **Raise your shoulders toward your ears. Hold the tension, and then let your shoulders drop.**

5. **Pull your shoulders back, bringing your shoulder blades closer together. Hold that tension . . . and let it go.**

6. **Scrunch up your entire face by squeezing your forehead, bringing your jaws together, tightening your eyes and eyebrows, and contracting your tongue and lips. Feel the tension, and then relax.**

7. **Gently drop your head back, and feel the muscles tighten in the back of your neck. Notice that tension, hold it, let go, and relax.**

8. **Gently move your chin toward your chest. Tighten your neck muscles and let the tension increase. Maintain the tension, and relax.**

9. **Tighten the muscles in your stomach and chest. Hold the tension, and let it go.**

10. **Arch your back, hang on to the contraction (but don't push too far), and relax.**

WARNING

Be gentle with your lower back, and skip this step entirely if you've ever had trouble with this part of your body.

11. **Contract your buttocks muscles. Hold the tension, and then let it go.**

12. **Squeeze and relax your thigh muscles.**

13. **Contract the muscles in your calves by pulling your toes toward your face. Hold the tension, and then relax your calves.**

WARNING

If you're prone to muscle cramps, don't overdo this exercise. Only contract your muscles as much as you feel comfortable with.

14. **Gently curl your toes, maintain the tension, and then relax.**

15. **Take time to tour your entire body, noticing if you feel different than when you began.**

TIP

If you find any areas of tension, allow relaxed areas to come in and replace the tense ones. If that doesn't work, repeat the tense-and-relax procedure for the tense area.

16. **Spend a few minutes enjoying the relaxed feelings. Let relaxation spread and penetrate every muscle fiber in your body. You may feel warmth, or you may feel a floating sensation. Perhaps you'll experience a sense of sinking down. When you wish to do so, open your eyes or tuck yourself in for a relaxed start to sleep.**

TIP

Spend 15 or 20 minutes on the muscle relaxation procedure at first, and then you can shorten it considerably. With practice, you'll be able to tense up several muscle groups at once. For example, you may tense hands and arms at the same time. Eventually, you may tense all the muscles in your lower body at once, followed by all the muscles in your upper body. If you carry all your tension in your neck, shoulders, or back, try tensing and relaxing just those muscles. Repeat the tense-and-relax cycle once or twice on especially tight muscles if that helps.

Use Worksheet 13-2 to track your thoughts and observations about using progressive muscle relaxation.

Worksheet 13-2   My Reflections

_____

_____

_____

_____

Dream Demons

Do nightmares invade your sleep on a regular basis? Everyone has the occasional nightmare, but if they routinely plague your nights and leave you feeling upset or unable to get back to sleep, try the strategy in Worksheet 13-3, which was developed by sleep specialists Drs. Krakow and Neidhardt.

PRACTICE

Worksheet 13-3   Nightmare Elimination Exercise

1. Write down your nightmare. Dreams tend to fade quickly from memory, so keep a pen and paper ready at your bedside.

_____

_____

_____

_____

2. Write down your thoughts and feelings about your nightmare.

_____

_____

_____

3. Rewrite your nightmare with a happier, better outcome.

_____

_____

_____

4. Rehearse your new dream in your mind several times before you go to bed the next night. Record how your night goes.

_____

_____

_____

Thinking About Sleep

Sleep is important, right? It's so important that if you don't get enough, your day will be utterly ruined. If you don't sleep enough, you may make terrible mistakes and even get sick. You *must* get enough sleep!

Well, hold the phone. That kind of thinking will *surely* keep you awake at night and make the next day more miserable to boot. When you find yourself thinking such thoughts, turn to Worksheet 13-4 for some more reasonable ways of looking at your situation.

Now it's your turn. What thoughts go through your head when you can't sleep? Are they helpful? Are they catastrophizing thoughts? Write down your sleep-sabotaging thoughts and design some reasonable alternatives in Worksheet 13-5.

REMEMBER

Worries about things other than sleep can also mess with your ability to get a good night's sleep. If you're a worrier in general, read and carefully work through the exercises in Chapters 5, 6, and 7.

Worksheet 13-4   Sleep-Sabotaging Thoughts and Sleep-Inducing Thoughts

EXAMPLE

Sleep-Sabotaging Thoughts	Sleep-Inducing Thoughts
If I don't get enough sleep, my day will be utterly ruined.	I've survived hundreds of days after not getting enough sleep. I don't like it, but some of those days were downright okay.
It's horrible when I don't fall asleep right away.	I don't like not sleeping, but it's not the worst thing that's ever happened to me. Maybe I can use my relaxation skills and at least rest a little better. This isn't the end of the world.
It's dangerous not to get enough sleep.	I suppose there's a slight danger in driving too far without enough sleep, but I can monitor my fatigue and pull over if I have to. People don't generally die from insufficient sleep.
I can't stand not sleeping.	I'm just catastrophizing here. I simply don't like not sleeping, but there are many worse things. Worrying about it will only worsen the problem.

Worksheet 13-5   Sleep-Sabotaging Thoughts and Sleep-Inducing Thoughts

PRACTICE

Sleep-Sabotaging Thoughts	Sleep-Inducing Thoughts

Making Sleep More Efficient

People with insomnia sometimes stay in bed for long periods of time hoping to get in a few more minutes or hours of sleep. This habit is a problem. First, it leads to the bed being associated with being awake. (See the section "Associations and Sleep.") Second, it leads to poor sleep efficiency.

Sleep efficiency is the time you're asleep divided by the time you're in bed multiplied by 100. Sleep experts recommend that you maintain sleep efficiencies greater than 85 percent. Following are two examples of sleep efficiency scores.

TIP

Jimmy goes to bed at 11 p.m., falls asleep at midnight, and wakes up at 3 a.m. unable to sleep. He tosses and turns and then looks at his phone for a while. He finally falls back to sleep around 5 a.m. and stays in bed until 10 a.m.

>> Total time asleep: 8 hours

>> Total time in bed: 11 hours

>> Sleep Efficiency: 8/11 = .72 × 100 = 72 percent

Davina has a regular schedule. She goes to bed at 10 p.m., falls asleep by 10:30 p.m., and wakes up at 6:00 a.m.

>> Total time asleep: 7.5 hours

>> Total time in bed: 8 hours

>> Sleep Efficiency: 7.5/8 = .94 × 100 = 94 percent

Use your sleep diaries to calculate your own sleep efficiency scores. If you find that your sleep is inefficient (less than 85 percent over a period of days), you may benefit from sleep restriction. Sleep restriction involves spending less time in bed to improve efficiency.

Sleep restriction has been found to be an effective, though somewhat annoying, treatment for poor sleep efficiency. You can try sleep treatment on your own, but if you have trouble, consult a sleep specialist. Here's the basic plan:

1. **Determine the average amount of sleep you actually get at night. (Use your sleep diaries.)**

2. **Add 30 minutes to that time. That's your total allowed time in bed each night for two weeks.**

3. **Go to bed and set your alarm so that you get up after spending the total allotted time in bed.**

   Get up even if you didn't get sufficient sleep. (That's the annoying part.)

   There's no daytime napping allowed during this time (admittedly, also annoying).

4. **Stay on this sleep schedule for about two weeks.**

   Your sleep efficiency should improve. If you find yourself feeling good, stay on this schedule. If you desire more sleep, add 15 minutes at a time to your allowed time in bed until you reach an equilibrium.

This procedure may seem a bit harsh, but it pays off with improved sleep. However, if at any time you feel overwhelmed with fatigue, discontinue, and check with a sleep specialist.

My Sleep Plan

The goal of this chapter is to help those who suffer from insomnia get to sleep, stay asleep through most of the night, and feel rested upon awakening. You may have found that your sleep environment is perfectly fine but that you tend to stay in bed without sleeping far too long. Unhelpful thoughts may be disrupting your sleep, or drinking coffee too late in the day may keep you awake.

Whatever you've discovered about your sleep, take a few minutes to decide what you're going to do about it. In Worksheet 13-6, write down your sleep goals. And tonight, have a good sleep. See you in the morning.

Worksheet 13-6   My Personal Sleep Plan

_____

_____

_____

_____

Chapter **14**

Making the Medication Decision

oday, extensive research has concluded that emotional problems are caused by a combination of genetics, environmental, social, and biological factors. People with anxiety or depression have diverse histories, and there's simply no reasonable way that anyone can explain exactly what the cause or causes of their distress derive from. But if you believe the ads posted by pharmaceutical companies, you'd assume that the right drug can cure specific imbalanced brain chemistry that causes emotional pain. Voilà!

If only it were that simple, I'd be first in line to recommend medication for whatever emotions disturb you. And I probably wouldn't be writing this book because there'd be no need for it. The fact is, scientists don't really understand how or why medication works for some of the people some of the time. And other people have multiple trials of medication but have experienced little or no relief.

In fact, comprehensive reviews of research suggest that a good percent of the improvement may come from the placebo effect. A placebo effect occurs when a person taking a sham, inert drug gets the same benefit as someone taking an active drug. I'll let future scientists quibble about that argument.

The bottom line is that for the majority of us, medication alone doesn't eliminate emotional distress, and rare is the case when medication is the only strategy that one would want to employ. Nevertheless, medication does have an important role to play, so this chapter helps you make a good decision about whether you want to consider medication for your anxiety or depression. It also prepares you for discussing medications with your doctor. If you and your doctor decide that medication is right for you, then a form helps you track any side effects so that you can keep your doctor accurately informed about your condition.

REMEMBER

Whether or not you take medication to alleviate your emotional distress is a decision that you'll make in collaboration with your health care provider. One purpose of this chapter is to make you an informed consumer. Ultimately, your doctor will determine if you have a condition that's treatable with medication. And ultimately, you'll have to agree to take medication or not. The more information you and your doctor have, the better informed your decision will be.

To Take or Not to Take

One question I frequently encounter is, "What works best: medications or therapies?" The answer is both. For depression, most research suggests that medication and therapy work about equally well. But for some types of anxiety, cognitive behavior therapies, such as the ones covered in this book, may hold a slight edge. Some folks obtain a better outcome when they combine medication with therapy.

REMEMBER

Studies show that cognitive behavior therapy helps prevent relapse, so it's strongly recommended that you don't rely on medications as your sole approach to treatment. (Much of what you're reading in this workbook is based on the principles of cognitive behavior therapy.)

PRACTICE

How do you make the medication decision? First you need to understand that some situations or experiences support taking medication. Worksheet 14-1 lists the reasons for considering medication. All the items suggest a need for professional evaluation. Check off the situations or items that pertain to you; each additional statement you select increases the likelihood that medication will be part of your treatment plan.

PRACTICE

Now use Worksheet 14-2 to reflect on the items you've checked. In the space provided, elaborate on the statements that apply to you. Use specifics to describe how these problems appear in your life. Include your thoughts, feelings, and observations.

Every coin has two sides. Worksheet 14-1 reveals the possible reasons for considering medication, but there are also reasons you may not want to take that route. Consider the following reasons that lead some people to opt out of taking medications:

>> **Side effect concerns:** Different medications have various side effects. Side effects are reviewed in detail in the section "Sizing Up Side Effects" later in this chapter, but common ones include dry mouth, gastro-intestinal problems, sexual difficulties, weight gain, and headaches. Some people suffer side effects more than others, and although your doctor can usually find ways around the worst of them, side effects are a real concern.

Worksheet 14-1   Indications for Medications

- ❑ 1. I seriously think about or plan to hurt myself or others.
- ❑ 2. I feel out of touch with reality. I hear or see things that aren't there.
- ❑ 3. I have severe mood swings from high to low.
- ❑ 4. I feel totally hopeless that things could ever improve.
- ❑ 5. My thoughts are constantly racing and feel out of control.
- ❑ 6. I've experienced a severely traumatic event and can't stop thinking about it.
- ❑ 7. My emotional distress is causing serious disruptions in my life.
- ❑ 8. I've tried therapy for six months or more and feel no improvement at all.
- ❑ 9. My doctor says that medical conditions are primarily causing my depression.
- ❑ 10. I've been depressed or seriously anxious most of my life.
- ❑ 11. I can't stand the thought of talking with someone about my problems.
- ❑ 12. I feel totally overwhelmed by my emotional problems.
- ❑ 13. I have a problem with alcohol/drug use in addition to depression or anxiety.
- ❑ 14. I feel highly suspicious or paranoid.
- ❑ 15. Lately, I've made really impulsive, terrible, outrageous decisions.

Worksheet 14-2   My Summary of Medication Indications

_____

_____

_____

_____

_____

>> **Worries about long-term effects:** Most medications for emotional problems appear to have relatively little short-term risk. However, some medications haven't been around long enough for doctors to know for sure if problems may show up after many years of use. And because medications often must be taken for a lifetime, long-term effects can be a serious concern.

>> **Addiction:** Some medications for anxiety, such as benzodiazepines, are addictive. That means if you take them for more than a few months, you could become dependent on them and experience withdrawal symptoms if and when you discontinue them. However, most antidepressants don't appear to be addictive in the usual sense. And some antidepressants treat anxiety as well as depression.

>> **Pregnancy and breastfeeding:** Under careful medical review, some medications for emotional distress appear relatively safe for pregnant or breastfeeding mothers. However, the safety data isn't comprehensive, and controversy exists around their use in this special case.

WARNING

Postpartum depression, depression that follows giving birth, is relatively common but can become quite serious if left untreated. If you experience symptoms of depression following the birth of a baby, you should get an evaluation.

>> **Personal preference:** Because of religious reasons, philosophical viewpoints, or strong personal preferences, some people simply prefer not to take medication. If that's the case for you, please get treatment for your problems through self-help exercises or through a qualified mental health professional.

REMEMBER

Although valid reasons exist for choosing to not take medications for anxiety or depression, if your distress is extremely severe, hasn't improved from therapy, or involves serious suicidal or homicidal thoughts, I hope you'll reconsider your treatment decision and consult with your doctor.

PRACTICE

1. **Review your reasons for and against taking medication.**

2. **Consider talking about your concerns with your primary care provider or a mental health professional.**

3. **Decide how you want medication to factor into your treatment and write out your reasoning process in Worksheet 14-3. Include your thoughts, feelings, and observations.**

Worksheet 14-3 My Medication Decision

_____

_____

_____

_____

_____

Preparing Your Prescriber

If you decide to take medication (hopefully you're planning to do so only in conjunction with therapy or self-help exercises), it's important to give your health care provider complete and truthful information so that he or she can make an accurate recommendation for your treatment. Most people forget what they want to say to health care providers during hurried appointments. So here's a questionnaire for you to fill out and give to your provider during your visit. Your health care provider may need additional information, but the questions in Worksheet 14-4 are a good start to expressing the particulars of your condition.

If you don't want to tear this questionnaire out of this book or lug the whole book to your health care provider's office, you can download extra copies at www.dummies.com/go/anxiety&depressionworkbookfd2e.

Worksheet 14-4   Important Information for My Health Care Provider

1. Describe your emotional symptoms. (See Chapter 1 for ideas.)

_____

_____

_____

_____

2. About how long have these symptoms been occurring, and how frequently do they appear? Have you had these feelings in the past?

_____

_____

_____

_____

3. Describe how severe your symptoms have been and how they've affected your life. Be sure to discuss whether you've had thoughts about harming yourself or others.

_____

_____

_____

_____

4. Describe any significant changes that have recently occurred in your life. Include deaths, job changes, divorces, injuries, chronic pain or illness, retirement, or financial upheaval.

_____

_____

_____

_____

5. Describe any physical symptoms you've been experiencing. (See Chapter 1 for ideas.)

_____

_____

_____

_____

6. Describe the frequency and severity of your physical symptoms and how long you've experienced them.

_____

_____

_____

_____

(continued)

Worksheet 14-4 *(continued)*

7. List illnesses you've had recently and any medications (and their dosages) that you're currently taking. Include any chronic conditions you're being treated for, including high blood pressure, diabetes, kidney or liver disease, or asthma. Don't forget to mention birth control pills.

_____

_____

_____

_____

8. Do you have a family history of significant emotional problems? Include mental health information for any close relatives.

_____

_____

_____

_____

9. List any herbs, supplements, vitamins, or over-the-counter medications that you take.

_____

_____

_____

_____

10. Write down your current and past use of cigarettes, alcohol, and drugs. Include frequency and amounts.

_____

_____

_____

_____

11. List your allergies. Have you had any bad reactions to medications, herbs, or foods in the past?

_____

_____

_____

12. Are you pregnant, planning to get pregnant, or breastfeeding?

_____

_____

_____

_____

Sizing Up Side Effects

Close to half of those who take medications for anxiety or depression stop because of disagreeable side effects or because they don't feel they're benefiting from the drug. These people may not be aware that:

>> Many medications can take a number of weeks to achieve a beneficial effect.

>> Side effects often decrease or disappear over time.

>> The prescriber probably knows about alternative medications with fewer side effects.

>> Another medication may be added to reduce side effects.

WARNING

Stopping any medication for emotional difficulties needs to be carefully supervised because even medications that aren't addictive in the usual sense can cause troublesome reactions if stopped abruptly. Please don't stop taking prescribed medication without consulting your health care provider.

If you're experiencing problems with your medication, the decision to continue with medication, try an alternative medication, or add another drug to the regimen to reduce side effects is best made in tandem with your health care provider. You guessed it — that means you must communicate with your prescriber on a regular basis about the specific side effects you're experiencing.

PRACTICE

Because it's so important for your health care provider to know about your experience with side effects, Worksheet 14-5 is a Side Effect Tracking Form for you to fill out and take to your consultations (or use as a guide during your telephone conversations). Complete these forms weekly after you start a new medication for depression or anxiety.

1. **In the middle column, each day of the week, place a check mark next to each symptom you experience to a noticeable degree.**

2. **After a week, in the right column, add up the number of check marks. Be sure to date the weekly chart.**

3. **Complete these checklists for the weeks between your health care appointments.**

4. **Be prepared to discuss these with your provider.**

TIP

You always have the option of alternative treatments for depression and anxiety. Many people take herbs and supplements for minor emotional distress, and your health care provider can tell you about other options for especially severe depression. For more information about alternatives to medication, see the latest editions of two of my other books, *Anxiety For Dummies* and *Depression For Dummies* (Wiley).

Worksheet 14-5   My Weekly Side Effect Tracking Form Date:

Symptom	Check Marks	Totals
Restlessness		
Fatigue		
Euphoria for no reason		
Vision problems		
Constipation		
Sleeplessness (or even feeling little need for sleep)		
Trembling		
Diarrhea		
Sharp decrease in mood for no reason		
Increase in anxiety		
Dry mouth		
Headaches		
Sexual problems		
Nausea or stomach upset		
Overwhelming apathy		
Memory problems		
Weight changes (rate once a week)		
Changes in appetite (up or down)		
Racing heartbeat		
Skin rash		
Sweating		
Dizziness		
Feeling revved up		
Problems urinating (too much or too little)		
Muscle spasms or twitching		
Nightmares		
Swelling of feet or hands		
Numbness		
Any other bodily or unexpected emotional changes (list them)		

5

Relationship Therapy

IN THIS CHAPTER

» Discovering the connection between emotions and relationships

» Examining your relationship

» Enhancing your relationship with positive actions

» Dealing with endings

Chapter **15**

Restoring Relationships

Supportive relationships provide a buffer against all types of emotional distress. Numerous studies show that good relationships and social support improve both mental and physical health.

Humans are social animals, biologically programmed to function better when friends, family, and neighbors are available for a cup of tea, a drive to the doctor, or an afternoon walk. Like gorillas, birds, and ants, people thrive in close-knit colonies. Therefore, working to improve your relationships can help boost your moods, increase your ability to manage stress, and create a sense of well-being.

Yet, distressing emotions get in the way of attempts to improve your relationships. Such emotions harm friendships, intimate relationships, and even relationships with coworkers or relative strangers. So, along with the obvious ways of working to alleviate your anxiety or depression, shoring up your relationships will improve your moods.

This chapter reviews strengthening strategies that you can apply to almost any type of relationship. However, intimate relationships are emphasized because disruptions in these types of relationships cause the most harm and because repairing them is enormously beneficial to your mental health. In addition, coping strategies are offered if you're dealing with the loss of a relationship because such an event can be quite traumatic and trigger intense feelings of anxiety or despair.

TIP

Loneliness and isolation during the COVID pandemic are thought to be partially responsible for huge increases in depression and anxiety worldwide. Of course, other pandemic stressors, such as financial uncertainty, loss of family members, and fear about catching the virus, also contribute to mental health problems.

Revealing the Emotion-Relationship Connection

Whether you like it or not, when you're anxious or depressed, you become more self-absorbed. That doesn't mean that you become conceited, but your attention focuses on your personal problems and concerns. Although the shift in focus is quite understandable, relationships are likely to suffer when your problems consume most of your energy. Because you're mentally and emotionally drained, you don't pay much attention to nurturing your relationships, and relationships need careful nurturing.

In addition, when you're anxious and depressed, those who care about you are likely to make attempts to cheer you up or help you. When their efforts fall short, they often feel frustrated and helpless. Eventually, they feel exhausted and may pull away from you. Frankly, after a prolonged time, it's a downer to be around someone who's constantly bummed out.

The following example shows you how depression can easily erode a good relationship.

EXAMPLE

John slips in and out of depression with the seasons. When daylight diminishes in the winter, his moods darken. (See *Depression For Dummies* [Wiley] for more about Seasonal Affective Disorder.) After a whirlwind romance last summer, John marries Gia, the woman of his dreams, in a beautiful fall wedding. He's never been so happy.

John warns Gia about his winter blues. However, both hope that their love and her presence in his life will help him ward off depression during the dark months. Unfortunately, depression overtakes John as the days become shorter. He withdraws from Gia, who tries to understand but becomes hurt and frustrated with her inability to cheer him up. John feels guilty that he's hurting his wife but feels powerless to do anything about his predicament. The relationship suffers.

PRACTICE

In Worksheet 15-1, answer the questions about an important relationship in your life to see if depression or anxiety has been inflicting harm.

TIP

Although depression and anxiety often cause problems in relationships, they're not the only culprits. Some relationships deteriorate in the presence of severe emotional problems, and other relationships are simply unhealthy. If you wonder why your relationship isn't doing well, or if you suspect you're being abused, check with a mental health professional who specializes in working with couples.

Worksheet 15-1   The Relationship Impact Questionnaire

1. Have I withdrawn or pulled back from my relationship? If so, in what ways?

_____

_____

_____

_____

2. Am I less affectionate than I used to be? If so, in what ways?

_____

_____

_____

_____

3. Am I more irritable or critical than I used to be? If so, in what ways?

_____

_____

_____

_____

4. Am I being less caring, giving fewer compliments, or being less empathetic? If so, in what ways?

_____

_____

_____

_____

Enhancing Your Relationship

Have you ever received or given flowers at the start of a new relationship? Ideally, relationships continue to supply "flowers" of many varieties — compliments, companionship, good times, caring, affection, laughter, and more. Most good relationships start out with enthusiasm and a bouquet of good feelings. But too often, complacency seeps in, and life interferes. After a while, it's easy to forget to send flowers.

When you stop cultivating a garden, ugly weeds choke out the healthy plants. The same is true of a relationship, which wilts from inattention. You can fertilize your relationship by increasing:

>> Positive talk

>> Positive actions

Whether your relationship is really suffering or is doing pretty well but isn't quite what you'd like it to be, the strategies in this section can help make it better.

Talking together

Communication is the foundation of a good relationship. Everyone receives help from having safe people to express their thoughts and feelings to. To help you create the right climate for such positive communication, here are two exercises: the Daily News and the Top 12 Things I Appreciate About My Partner.

TIP

If your communication with your partner is conflictual, jump to Chapter 16 for a fix. And if the following exercises don't go over well, see a therapist for couples counseling.

Perusing the Daily News

PRACTICE

The Daily News (Worksheet 15-2) is a way of making sure that you and your partner spend time talking and listening to one another. The purpose of this exercise is to enhance intimacy. Make this exercise a high priority, and perform it often.

Worksheet 15-2   The Daily News

1. **Work with your partner to decide on a time when you will sit and talk about the day's events for 20 minutes. You may choose to chat at the same time every day, or you may want to vary it. Daily is best, which is why it's called the "Daily News," but you'll benefit from talking this way at least three or four times a week.**

2. **Commit to your meeting times and write them down here:**

_____

_____

_____

3. **Let your partner begin and speak for ten minutes.**

4. **Show interest by:**

   - **Asking a few questions for greater understanding**

   - **Nodding your head**

   - **Making brief comments**

   - **Expressing empathy or understanding for how your partner feels**

TIP

Don't give advice or solve your partner's problem at this time. And avoid criticism or stirring up conflict.

5. **After your partner shares the events of his or her day, try to summarize what he or she said in a positive manner.**

6. **Ask your partner if your understanding of what he or she said is basically correct. If not, ask for clarification.**

7. **Take your turn to talk about your day, asking your partner to follow these same rules.**

After you work through the Daily News exercise a few times, reflect on how it went and record your thoughts in Worksheet 15-3. How did you feel before and after the exercise? Do you know more about your partner now, and does your partner know more about you? Do you feel closer?

Worksheet 15-3   My Reflections

_____
_____
_____
_____
_____

Putting compliments to good use

Compliments, when sincerely offered, enhance communication and positive feelings. When you feel anxious or depressed, you may not think about all the things you appreciate about your partner. But when you don't express what you cherish and admire, your partner is likely to feel unappreciated. Work through the following exercise, the Top 12 Things I Appreciate About My Partner, to get back on track when it comes to complimenting your partner.

PRACTICE

1. **In Worksheet 15-4, write down all the things you appreciate, value, admire, and cherish about your partner.** Include attributes such as intelligence, caring, warmth, attractiveness, talents, help with daily life (such as cooking, cleaning, finances, and so on), sense of humor, and anything else you can think of. Only include items you feel sincerely apply.

   Be specific in your assessment of your partner. For example, rather than saying, "You're the best person in the whole world," narrow it down and say, "I love the way you play with the baby." Also, avoid "buts;" for example, don't say, "I really like your hair, _but_ it would look better shorter." That's really just a backhanded compliment — it could go either way.

2. **Compliment your partner at least once a day from your list (or come up with something new).**

3. **Create a strategy for remembering to express these compliments.** For example, make a note in your calendar, set a reminder on your phone, or put sticky notes in various places around the house.

Worksheet 15-4   The Top 12 Things I Appreciate About My Partner

1. _____
2. _____
3. _____
4. _____
5. _____
6. _____
7. _____
8. _____
9. _____
10. _____
11. _____
12. _____

Get into the habit of handing out genuine compliments to everyone, not just your partner. Doing so will improve your popularity by making people notice you. It may even get you a raise!

Some people dismiss compliments by saying, "Oh, you don't mean that," or "That isn't really true." If your partner responds in this way, keep complimenting. People dismiss compliments not because they don't want to hear them but because they have trouble accepting them.

After you spend a couple of weeks increasing the compliments you give your partner, reflect on any changes in your relationship (see Worksheet 15-5). Do you notice any increased warmth, affection, or communication? Are you or your partner in a better mood?

Worksheet 15-5   My Reflections

_____

_____

_____

_____

_____

If you can't think of anything to genuinely appreciate about your partner, your relationship is in serious trouble. Seek help from a professional trained in couples counseling.

Delightful doings

If communication is the foundation of a good relationship (see the "Talking together" section), sharing pleasurable activities is the house that sits on top. This section reviews an important technique for increasing positive times with your partner: the Positive Sharing System.

The Positive Sharing System is designed to give you an easy way of showing your partner that you care. The system involves making a list of small caring actions that you and your partner can do for each other often. After making a list, each person keeps track of what the other has done. Review this strategy with your partner so that both of you participate. Although this technique may look simplistic, research shows that it works and builds surprisingly positive feelings. Before you get started on your own Positive Sharing System, consider the following example.

Trisha and **Michael** decide to try Positive Sharing because they've noticed that their relationship has gone stale. They discuss specific actions they can take to increase the pleasure they get from one another. Michael asks Trisha to stop complaining about their finances, but in talking, they realize that his request is both negative and focused on something they frequently argue about. So, they think of other, more positive actions to take to increase pleasure. For example, Trisha asks Michael to be nicer to her mother. But upon reflection, she realizes that her request is too vague, so she asks him to spend one or two minutes speaking to her mother on the phone when she calls. Worksheet 15-6 shows what they finally settle on and the results of their first week of taking the decided actions.

Worksheet 15-6   Trisha and Michael's Positive Sharing System

Desired Actions	Dates Carried Out
Michael brings in morning newspaper.	7/16, 7/20, 7/21
Trisha rubs Michael's back.	7/16
Michael rubs Trisha's back.	7/16
Trisha starts dinner before Michael gets home.	7/17, 7/18, 7/21, 7/22
Michael buys Trisha a small gift.	7/22
Trisha texts Michael at work just to chat.	7/16, 7/18, 7/19
Michael talks to Trisha's mother when she calls.	7/21
Trisha helps the kids with homework while Michael watches the news.	7/16, 7/20
Michael puts gas in Trisha's car.	7/22
Trisha mows the front yard.	7/18
Michael makes coffee in the morning.	7/16, 7/17, 7/19, 7/20, 7/22
Trisha pays the bills.	7/20

Trisha and Michael discover that, to their surprise, this strategy actually leads them to feel closer and warmer with each other, and they stop arguing as often. In fact, they enjoy the results so much that the following week, they add several more items to their list. Both notice an increased desire to please the other.

PRACTICE

1. **Talk with your partner and develop a list of small actions that either of you would interpret as a sign of caring or affection.** These actions must be

   Stated positively

   Clear and specific (so you will know for sure if it happens)

   Easily done

   Able to be carried out frequently

   Not something you've been fighting about

2. **List these actions in the left column of Worksheet 15-7.**

3. **Each day, in the right column, write the date when you notice your partner doing one of the items for you. Your partner should do the same.**

4. **At the end of each day, briefly discuss the progress of your exercise with your partner.**

5. **Commit to doing at least three to five of these actions every day, whether your partner does the same or not.** Don't feel obligated to do any particular item, but carry out a variety of them.

Worksheet 15-7   Our Positive Sharing System

Desired Actions	Dates Carried Out

TIP Consider taping this list to your refrigerator or some other obvious place in the house so that it's easy for you and your partner to keep track of each other's actions and see the progress you're making.

You can download as many copies of this form as you need at www.dummies.com/go/anxiety&depressionworkbookfd2e.

REMEMBER When you and your partner work on this exercise, one (or both) of you will inevitably slip from time to time by forgetting about the positive sharing exercise. Simply recommit yourself each time that happens. Resist the temptation to be critical when that occurs. In other words, don't let something positive turn into a negative because of unavoidable human slips.

After you've tried the Positive Sharing System for a week, reflect on its effects on your relationship and record your thoughts in Worksheet 15-8.

Worksheet 15-8   My Reflections

_____
_____
_____
_____

Dealing with Relationship Loss

It would be nice if people lived forever and relationships always endured. But life isn't a fairy tale, and everyone doesn't live "happily ever after." Relationships break up, marriages dissolve, circumstances cause prolonged separations, and people die. And loss, whether from death or happenstance, causes disturbing distress.

REMEMBER

In fact, loss sometimes leads to depression. When you lose someone, it's natural to grieve and feel sad. However, grief isn't quite the same thing as depression. The main difference is that depression includes feelings of inadequacy and low self-esteem, while grief centers around feelings of loss and loneliness. Also, most people find that grief decreases with time, unlike depression. Loss or fear of loss can also create anxiety. You may think you can't handle life without your loved one; you may feel dependent and overwhelmed.

If you've lost someone, first and foremost, take care of yourself. Be sure to eat healthy, stay away from abusing drugs and alcohol, and exercise regularly, whether you feel like it or not — even if you just take a 30-minute brisk walk each day. And try to get enough sleep. Grieving takes a physical and mental toll, and you need all your resources to get through it.

In addition, you may want to turn to other sources of support. Don't be afraid to ask for help. Such sources can include:

>> Religious or spiritual resources

>> Grief support groups

>> Friends and family

>> Mental health professionals

WARNING

If you lose someone and believe that you can't go on, or if you have thoughts of hopelessness or suicide, seek professional help promptly.

Moving on

When you're grieving, it's natural to feel like staying in bed and pulling the covers over your head. And there's a tendency to avoid thinking about the lost person or relationship. Some folks even turn to drugs or alcohol to blunt their pain. However, all those strategies merely make things worse.

PRACTICE

A better approach is to explore your thoughts and feelings about the lost person. Yes, you should actually spend some active time reviewing and reconstructing the relationship and what the person meant to you. This process eases moving on.

To get the most out of this Grief Exploration Questionnaire (see Worksheet 15-9), set aside at least an hour to answer the questions. Don't rush the process. Also, you should expect to feel intense sadness or grief; in fact, you're likely to cry. If you have a trusted friend or family member who wants to support you through this process, that can be helpful. But if you feel overwhelmed or that you can't handle this exercise even with a supportive friend, seek professional help.

Becoming active

You'll never fully replace someone you've lost because people and relationships are unique and, in one sense, irreplaceable. Nonetheless, you can pick up the pieces, move on, and refill your life with meaningful relationships and activities. Explore the following after you begin to recover:

>> **Volunteer work:** A great way to regain a sense of meaning in your life is to help others. Plus, volunteer work often leads to friendships and a new social circle.

>> **Pleasurable activities:** Even if you feel sad and unenthusiastic, putting pleasure back into your life is possible. (See Chapter 11 for more about healthy pleasures.) You won't feel like you "should" indulge in pleasure, but after you start to recover from your loss, allowing yourself to enjoy things can accelerate your healing.

>> **Socializing:** Whether it's visiting with friends and family or starting to date again, being with other people helps you get through tough times. Sometimes starting to date or making new friends can feel frightening at first. However, both are steps in learning to love and set up new connections. Venturing back into the world is part of the healing process.

Worksheet 15-9   Grief Exploration Questionnaire

1. What was my life like when I was with this person?

_____

_____

_____

_____

2. What did I value about this person?

_____

_____

_____

_____

3. What was difficult about this person?

_____

_____

_____

_____

4. What lessons did I learn from this relationship, both positive and negative?

_____

_____

_____

_____

5. What is different about my life now?

_____

_____

_____

_____

6. What am I most angry or resentful about?

_____

_____

_____

_____

7. What aspects of this relationship am I most grateful for?

_____

_____

_____

_____

8. What did I enjoy about this relationship?

_____

_____

_____

_____

9. Compose a letter to the person you've lost. The purpose of this letter is to provide you with closure. Review questions 1–7 for material you may want to include in your letter, and feel free to be emotional and express anything that's on your mind.

_____

_____

_____

_____

_____

_____

_____

_____

Chapter 16

Smoothing Out Conflict

onflict with someone you care about hurts, and when you're depressed or anxious, you tend to be more irritable, which leads to more conflict. Like so many other problems related to depression and anxiety, a vicious cycle ensues.

This chapter helps break the negative cycle of conflict. It explains what's called the *malicious assumption*, which leads to defensiveness and counterattacks. You then track the malicious assumptions and defensiveness in your relationships. You see how identifying and understanding your hot buttons and those of your partner help depersonalize what you previously considered criticism. Finally, this chapter offers tips for dealing with conflict constructively.

Overriding Defensiveness

When people feel emotionally vulnerable, whether from depression, anxiety, or conflict in a relationship, they start making the *malicious assumption* in response to things their partners say or do. The malicious assumption refers to the tendency to automatically interpret communications or actions in the most negative, critical way possible. More often than not, the malicious assumption grossly misinterprets the true meaning of the message.

Here's a common, concrete example of the malicious assumption in everyday life. Suppose you're driving on the freeway, and someone cuts you off. You interpret the driver's motive in one of two ways: as the result of careless inattentiveness or as a hostile action aimed at you directly. Which reaction is the malicious assumption? The belief that the driver cut you off deliberately and with hostility. Thus, if you make this assumption, you may respond by opening your car window and giving the other driver a good look at one of your fingers. (You know the one.) This action, in turn, may lead to a dangerous escalation of violent action, also known as road rage.

Defensiveness occurs when the malicious assumption causes you to perceive a communication or behavior as an attack. In defensive response, you say that you aren't to blame in any way for the problem, or you counterattack. Saying that something's not your fault *assumes* that your partner had hostile intentions. And when you counterattack, all you accomplish is an escalation of conflict. Either reaction is likely to provide fuel for an argument.

TIP

Sarcasm usually indicates defensiveness. Pay particular attention when you hear yourself being sarcastic, and reflect on a more reasonable response.

EXAMPLE

The examples in Worksheet 16-1 help you see how the insidious process of malicious assumptions and defensiveness works.

Worksheet 16-1   Examples of Malicious Assumptions and Defensive Responses

Initial Communication or Action	Malicious Assumption	Defensive Response
"You look tired today."	She's saying I look horrible.	"You don't look so great either."
"Where's the checkbook?"	He's saying I didn't put it back where it should be.	"Hey, I didn't lose it; you had it last!"
"Did you fill the car up with gas?"	She's criticizing me for not getting gas.	"No, but why can't you get gas sometimes?"
Your partner forgets your birthday.	Obviously, she doesn't care about me anymore.	That's just fine; I'll get back at her.
Your partner tells you to change some wording in a book you're writing together.	He must think I'm stupid.	"It's not like everything you write reads like Hemingway!"
"The house is a mess."	He's saying I don't keep the place clean like I should.	"So, what am I, your maid? Clean it up if you don't like it."

REMEMBER

Notice that in Worksheet 16-1, all the initial communications and actions are at least somewhat ambiguous. In other words, you can't tell with certainty whether the person had hostile intentions. Besides, whether or not a message or behavior is clearly hostile, it doesn't do much good to respond defensively — unless, of course, all you want is a good fight.

Shining light on your defensive behavior

PRACTICE

Before you can stop making the malicious assumption and following it with defensive responses, you need to see how these behaviors play out in your life. Start by tracking events in which these behaviors crop up. Use the following instructions as your guide. (After you identify your own defensive behaviors, you'll read about an alternative to defensiveness and an explanation for dealing with truly hostile criticism in a way that may lead to better outcomes.)

1. **Whenever your partner says or does something that you feel may have been intended as hostile, write it down in the left column of Worksheet 16-2.**

2. **In the middle column, write down how you interpret what happened.** Try to be honest; don't clean up your reaction — or your language! Say how you really feel about what your partner said or did.

3. **In the right column, jot down how you responded, and analyze your response for defensiveness. Did you try to absolve yourself of all blame, or did you counterattack in some way?**

Worksheet 16-2   My Malicious Assumptions and Defensive Responses

Initial Communication or Action	Malicious Assumption	Defensive Response

Review your malicious assumptions and defensive responses. In Worksheet 16-3, reflect on how they may be causing problems in your relationship.

Worksheet 16-3   My Reflections

_____

_____

_____

_____

Check, please

Hopefully the exercise in the preceding section has made you more aware of when you get defensive. But what's an alternative when you perceive your partner's actions or words as hostile or malicious? Try checking it out.

Checking it out involves first catching the urge to be defensive. Then, when you're ready, you make a gentle inquiry about your partner's true intentions.

EXAMPLE

Max promises to pick up **Teva** for dinner and a movie at 6:30. He arrives breathless at 6:50, saying, "Sorry, traffic was horrible." Teva immediately makes a malicious assumption, believing that Max was purposely late, which proves that Max is losing interest in her. She almost says, "That's what you said last time, you jerk," but she decides to check it out. She stops herself and takes a deep breath or two. After she calms down a little, she asks, "Max, I'm a little worried that you might be losing interest. Is that possible?" Max is quite surprised by the question and says, "Gosh, no. I'm really sorry if it seemed that way to you. There really was a terrible accident. I really care about you and enjoy every second that I'm with you."

PRACTICE

When you find yourself in a potentially hostile situation, take a moment to practice the checking it out technique by following these instructions:

1. **The moment you feel attacked or criticized, close your mouth.**

2. **Take a slow, deep breath in, and exhale very slowly. Repeat once or twice until you feel a little calmer.**

   While you're breathing, remind yourself that if you speak while you're upset, the odds of saying something useful or productive have been precisely calculated at 1 in 5.86 billion.

3. **When you feel calmer, inquire about your partner's actual intentions. Gently explain what your worry or concern is about, but don't accuse or attack.**

4. **Keep track of your exchange so that you can work through it with less emotion involved. In Worksheet 16-4, record the initial communication or action in the left column.**

5. **Write down your malicious assumption in the middle column.**

6. **In the right column, jot down how you checked out your assumption.**

Worksheet 16-4   My Malicious Assumptions and Checking It Out Responses

Initial Communication or Action	Malicious Assumption	Checking It Out

Don't refuse to defuse

Another alternative to defensiveness or counterattacking is *defusing.* You use this technique when your partner clearly is engaging in criticism. Basically, defusing consists of saying something downright counterintuitive — finding at least a sliver of truth in your partner's statement. When you acknowledge part (or sometimes all) of your partner's concerns, you keep the dialogue going and take the emotional charge out of the interaction. Don't completely capitulate or lie to your partner, but genuinely work to discover your partner's perspective on the problem at hand. Usually, you and your partner can find at least something to agree on.

TIP

This technique doesn't work for dealing with flat-out verbal abuse. For that kind of situation, you need to get help. Sometimes it's difficult to know if you're being emotionally abused. So, if you're not sure if your partner is being abusive, consult with a mental health professional.

PRACTICE

Worksheet 16-5 contains examples of criticisms with corresponding defusing responses. In each defusing response, a section appears in italic to show you which part of the criticism is valid and acknowledged by the person being criticized. For the last three criticisms in the worksheet, fill in the defusing responses that you think would be most effective.

Worksheet 16-5   Defusing Criticism

Criticism	Defusing Response
You spend too much money.	Sometimes I probably do, but I'm not sure what you're referring to right now.
You yell at the kids too much.	You may have a point. I'll try to be more aware of when I yell.
The house is a mess; you never clean it.	I understand how you might feel that way, but I don't think I value a pristine house as much as you do. Can we figure out a compromise here?
You're always telling me what to do. You're way too controlling.	I agree that I sometimes fall into that habit, although I think I let you have your way on a lot of things. What is your specific complaint?
I don't want to spend so much time over at your mother's place.	
You're a mouse; you let your boss walk all over you.	
You need to lose weight.	

REMEMBER

Practice defusing whenever you can. It's not the type of reaction that comes naturally, but all your relationships will go more smoothly if you master the technique.

After you put the defusing technique as well as the checking it out technique (see the preceding section) to the test in your own relationships, reflect on how these alternatives to defensiveness and counterattacking have worked for you. Did you find that checking it out revealed that your partner indeed was being hostile? Or did you discover that your partner wasn't intending to inflict hurt or criticism? In either case, did checking it out keep things from escalating like they usually do? When you tried to defuse your partner's comments, did the potential conflict seem to deflate? Record your reflections in Worksheet 16-6.

Worksheet 16-6   My Reflections

_____

_____

_____

_____

_____

Discovering the Problem Isn't All About You

When someone you care about is angry or distraught, you may think that the upset relates to you in some way. This reaction is natural but not always correct. When you wrongly take responsibility for your partner's emotions, you engage in *personalizing*. And when you personalize, you're likely to feel distressed and may become defensive or counterattack. (See "Overriding Defensiveness" for more on those reactions.)

When people get upset, it often has very little to do with you — even if they say it does. How can that be? Truth is, most of the time, people have intense emotions about events because one or more of their personal hot buttons have been pushed. These hot buttons are usually based on views or assumptions that people have about themselves, other people, and the world. (See Chapter 7 for information about problematic assumptions.)

If you can identify what your partner's hot buttons are, you understand what triggers their anger and other heightened emotions. It also helps to know that your partner's upset has more to do with problematic assumptions than with you. Understanding problematic assumptions allows you to *depersonalize* the event, which in turn leads you to feel a little empathy rather than defensiveness.

PRACTICE

If the person you're having conflict with is willing, consider having them take the Problematic Assumptions Questionnaire found in Chapter 7. Then take time to discuss both of your problematic assumptions with each other. This process should lead to enhanced understanding of how problematic assumptions contribute to your conflicts.

Reflect on your discussion on Worksheet 16-7. If your partner resists or gets defensive during these discussions, consider couples counseling to get you started.

Worksheet 16-7   My Reflections

_____
_____
_____
_____
_____

Talking About the Tough Stuff

As explained in Chapter 15, communication forms the foundation of any good relationship. That chapter gives you tools for sharing experiences and positive feelings. This chapter tells you how to talk about dicier issues, such as concerns, disagreements, and dissatisfactions. Sometimes people just need to discuss this stuff. Unfortunately, most people don't know how to have difficult but successful conversations. Two useful strategies for helping you express the tough stuff are *I Messages* and *buffering*.

Shifting the focus with I Messages

When you want to communicate concerns or dissatisfaction, the language you use makes a big difference in how heated your communication becomes. If you're critical or blaming, you're likely to produce defensiveness or a counterattack in your partner. *I Messages* state your concerns in terms of how they affect you and don't blame or accuse your partner of anything. To use this technique, you clearly state how *you* feel about an issue; you know you're giving an I Message when you start your communication with the word *I* instead of *you*.

Don't expect to master the I Message technique quickly or easily. The natural, perhaps instinctive response, is to lash out. Thus, I Messages take lots of rehearsal and practice.

PRACTICE

Worksheet 16-8 lays out examples of blaming messages accompanied by alternative I Messages. Read the examples, and then come up with your own I Messages as alternatives to the blaming messages in the blank spaces at the bottom of the list.

Of course, it's possible that I Messages could lead to a negative response by your partner. They simply improve your odds as compared to blaming and complaining You Messages.

Worksheet 16-8   The I Message Technique

Blaming Messages	I Messages
You don't love me anymore.	I'm feeling a little insecure. I'd sure like a little more affection.
You never cut the grass unless I bug you about it over and over again.	I don't like being a nag about the grass. I would like it if you could find a way to do it more regularly so I wouldn't feel a need to bug you.
You complain about everything.	I worry sometimes that you're not happy because you have so many complaints.
You really tick me off.	I'm feeling a little annoyed with you.
You charge way too much on the credit cards.	
You never put your dishes in the dishwasher!	
You're always late.	
You don't appreciate all the things I do around here.	

TIP

You can make your I Messages even more effective by not only expressing what you feel but also stating your concern gently.

Softening the blow through buffering

When you communicate negative or critical concerns, you have two choices: you can smash your partner over the head, or you can soften the blow. Guess which one works best? Like buffered aspirin, *buffering* reduces the acidity in your communications. To buffer, you add a phrase that conveys the possibility that your position may not be entirely correct or that your reaction may be a little excessive. You may feel you're undoubtedly 100 percent correct, but it never hurts to cover your confidence a bit. Even if you're totally in the right, buffering helps.

PRACTICE

Take a look at buffered and unbuffered examples in Worksheet 16-12 and decide for yourself which approach is more likely to lead to a *productive exchange* — one in which you have possible compromise and useful conversation. After reading the examples, fill in your own buffered alternatives for the unbuffered concerns in the blank spaces at the end of the list.

TIP

Combining your buffering with an I Message (see "Shifting the focus with I Messages" earlier in the chapter) can convey your point even more effectively. The Buffering Strategy in Worksheet 16-9 includes I Messages and buffered phrases that suggest your position may not be entirely, 100 percent correct.

Worksheet 16-9   The Buffering Strategy

Unbuffered Concerns	Buffered Concerns
You're messing up the checking account.	I probably overreact to the checking account problem, and I'd like us to come up with a better system.
You were rude to our neighbors.	I may be seeing this wrong, but it felt like you were a little rude to the neighbors.
You were flirting with that woman at the party.	I could be off on this, but it seemed like you were flirting with that woman at the party, and I felt hurt.
You're working way too many hours at the office lately. Your priorities are out of whack.	Help me understand what's keeping you at the job so many hours. I miss you when you're not around.
You're spending way too much on clothes.	
You're always screaming and yelling at the kids — they can't stand to be around you.	
You spoil the kids. They're becoming brats because of you.	

6
Looking Beyond Anxiety and Depression

Chapter **17**

Reining in Relapse

The good news about anxiety and depression is that they're both highly treatable disorders. Typically, you can expect treatment efforts, either on your own or in conjunction with professional help, to improve your emotions. The bad news is that relapse is common. Fortunately, there's a lot you can do to prevent relapse and get better quickly should it occur.

If you've made a substantial improvement in your anxiety or depression and want to hold onto your gains, this is the chapter for you. This chapter helps you figure out if you're at risk for relapse. Watching for relapse signs allows you to nip problems in the bud before you feel overwhelmed. The chapter also gives you a couple of strategies for preventing relapse from occurring in the first place.

WARNING If you've worked (*really* worked, that is) through the rest of this book and your moods remain anxious or depressed, this is not the chapter for you. Seek professional help if you haven't improved or you're struggling more than you'd like. However, if you've improved but not gotten to the point of recovery you'd like to be at, keep doing more of what you've been doing.

Sizing Up Your Risk of Relapse

If your main problem is depression, your risk of relapse is particularly high. In fact, if you treated your depression only with medication, your risk of relapse exceeds 50 percent over the next couple of years. Anxiety poses a lower relapse risk.

Studies indicate that cognitive behavior therapies (those that focus on changes in thinking and behaving), which are the basis for most of this book, work. Not only do these therapies work, but they significantly reduce relapse risk. So, the bottom line is that if all you've tried is medication, embrace the skills throughout this book or see a therapist trained in cognitive behavior therapy.

PRACTICE

You're probably wondering how much risk you actually have for relapse. To figure out your risk, check off the items in Worksheet 17-1 that pertain to you.

REMEMBER

You may think that checking off the first statement in the list reduces your risk of relapse. Wrong. Surprisingly, overconfidence has been found to be a risk factor for relapse. In other words, a little optimism is a good thing, but you need to temper that optimism with realism. Knowing that you have some risk of relapse is vital to helping you deal with early signs.

If you checked any statements at all in the Relapse Risk Quiz, you're at increased risk for the return of emotional distress. Checking more than two or three statements puts you at extremely high risk.

TIP

Treat depression and anxiety until symptoms almost completely subside. Extend therapy for at least six or eight weeks after you experience a return to full energy, appetite, sleep, and pleasure levels. Continue medication even longer — 6 to 12 months after full remission of symptoms.

Worksheet 17-1   Relapse Risk Quiz

❏ 1. I'm completely over my anxiety or depression. I have no fear it will return.

❏ 2. I've been previously depressed more than once in my life.

❏ 3. I've had bouts of anxiety off and on for years.

❏ 4. I've only taken medication for my problems.

❏ 5. I suffer from a chronic illness.

❏ 6. I've had some big financial problems lately.

❏ 7. I recently lost someone I care deeply about through breakup or death.

❏ 8. I recently experienced a traumatic event.

❏ 9. I lost my job not long ago.

❏ 10. I just retired.

❏ 11. There's been an increase in family conflict lately.

❏ 12. I just graduated from high school or college.

❏ 13. When I get depressed or anxious, I know it's entirely my fault.

❏ 14. I can't control my moods.

❏ 15. To be happy, I need people to like me.

REMEMBER If you work through the exercises in this chapter and a relapse still occurs, don't catastrophize. You're not starting at square one. You have skills, and you can apply them anew. Or you can try one of the exercises that you haven't gotten around to. If you can't get out of your funk on your own, you can always turn to professional help. You *can* feel better; don't just sit around and feel miserable.

Not Letting Relapse Sneak Up on You

With relapse, subtle signs may appear and go unnoticed. Then, suddenly, you find your problems have returned, possibly even worse than before.

Don't let relapse get the best of you. After you've recovered from anxiety or depression, conduct a review of your emotions and feelings on a weekly basis. Over time, you can reduce the frequency of these reviews to once every month or two as your risk of relapse gradually lessens.

PRACTICE To review your emotions and feelings, complete the Early Warning Signs: Emotion Relapse Review in Worksheet 17-2. Take your time to think about each question regarding specific warning signs and describe in writing what's been going on with you.

Worksheet 17-2   Early Warning Signs: Emotion Relapse Review

1. Have I started avoiding people lately? If so, who, what, when, where, and why?

_____

_____

_____

_____

2. Have my thoughts been dark and pessimistic? If so, what are they, and how intense are they?

_____

_____

_____

_____

3. Have I noticed any changes in my appetite? If so, how long has it lasted, and have I lost or gained any weight?

_____

_____

_____

_____

(continued)

4. Have I been avoiding activities or places lately? If so, what, where, when, and why?

_____

_____

_____

5. Have I noticed any changes in my sleeping patterns? If so, what are the changes, and how often do they occur?

_____

_____

_____

6. Have I been more irritable than usual? If so, when, and under what circumstances?

_____

_____

_____

7. Has someone close to me said that I've been out of sorts in any way? If so, what was said?

_____

_____

_____

_____

8. Have I noticed changes in my memory, concentration, or energy? If so, what are these changes?

_____

_____

_____

_____

9. Have I been feeling excessively guilty or down on myself about anything? If so, what's that been about?

_____

_____

_____

_____

10. Have I been sad or worried about anything recently? If so, what, where, when, and why?

_____

_____

_____

_____

Visit www.dummies.com/go/anxiety&depressionworkbookfd2e to download and print as many of these forms as you need for your own use.

TIP

If you fill out the Emotional Relapse Review form regularly, relapse isn't likely to overtake you unexpectedly. The moment you spot significant signs of relapse (as described in Worksheet 17-2), read and work through the next two sections of this chapter. In addition, go back and do more of whatever it was that reduced your emotional distress previously.

REMEMBER

Changes in energy, appetite, or sleep may be due to a physical problem. If you're experiencing these types of changes, check things out with your primary care provider.

Having a Fire Extinguisher Ready

Don't wait for a fire to start before making a plan. If you don't have one, buy a fire extinguisher now. In addition, fire drills save lives, as do rehearsals of how you'll deal with relapse. Approaching the potential of relapse as you would the potential for fire can save you a lot of grief and prevent relapse.

PRACTICE

Worksheet 17-2 lays out the early warning signs you should look for. Worksheet 17-3 lists a few of the common events that trigger emotional distress. Read through the list, thinking about which events you fear may cause you trouble at some point in the future. For each item, jot down the specifics of your concern. (At the end of the list, add any likely future events that you worry about.)

Worksheet 17-3   Fuel for Emotional Fires Questionnaire

1. Loss of someone important to me

_____

_____

_____

_____

2. Being rejected

_____

_____

_____

3. Getting sick or hurt

_____

_____

_____

(continued)

Worksheet 17-3 *(continued)*

4. Money problems

_____

_____

_____

5. Major political changes

_____

_____

_____

6. Humiliation, shame, or embarrassment

_____

_____

_____

7. Societal issues such as discrimination, poverty, pandemics, climate change, and so on

_____

_____

_____

8. My additional concerns

_____

_____

_____

So, should you worry about all the bad things that could possibly happen to you? What about the advice in Chapter 8 about the value of staying centered in the present? Well, you raise a good point. Staying in the present is a good idea, but so is being reasonably prepared for the future.

To be prepared, try the Fire Drill Strategy. Take each event that you list as worrisome in Worksheet 17-3 and figure out how you would cope if that event occurred. First, review this example of the Fire Drill Strategy.

EXAMPLE

David recovered from a combination of anxiety and depression about two months ago. He's planning to stop seeing his counselor, who worked with him over the past six months. Before ending their sessions, David's therapist suggests that David prepare for possible fire, or the flare-up of one of his fears. The therapist has David fill out the Fire Drill Strategy (see Worksheet 17-4) on one of his worries. David's father and uncle both died of colon cancer in their 50s, and David's now 51, so the fear of developing colon cancer is very real for him.

Worksheet 17-4   David's Fire Drill Strategy

<u>Situation:</u> Fear of colon cancer

1. How would someone else cope with this situation?

    I can't deny that it would be incredibly tough. However, my father used the last years of his life to get his affairs in order and spend time with his family. He also was very helpful to many people in his cancer support group. I could do that. I remember my uncle was very angry and seemed to suffer a lot more. I'd rather be like my father.

2. Have I dealt with something like this in the past? How did I do it?

    When I was in college I came down with meningitis. I was really sick, and everyone was worried. I don't remember being terrified, though. I think I could use the same acceptance I had then.

3. How much will this event affect my life a year after it occurs?

    Actually, given that I get regular screenings, the odds are pretty good that any cancer will be caught early when it's treatable. I may be catastrophizing about this issue.

4. Is this event as awful as I'm making it out to be?

    Obviously not. There have been so many advances both in terms of catching it early as well as treatment that I think I'd be okay. As for the slim chance that I'd die, I guess I could deal with that, too. I'd have to.

5. Are there any intriguing, creative ways of dealing with this challenge?

    I've been meaning to participate in the cancer walk-a-thon. Maybe I'll get off my behind (so to speak) and just do it. If I am diagnosed, I'll join the support group like my Dad did. He seemed to really benefit and help others at the same time.

After completing this exercise, David realizes that he can cope with even his worst fears. Seeing the benefit of the exercise, he also fills out a Fire Drill Strategy on several other challenges that he may encounter down the road.

PRACTICE

Using Worksheet 17-5, complete your own Fire Drill Strategy. Simply list your specific fear at the top and answer the questions that follow. Fill out a questionnaire for each problematic concern you identified in the Fuel for Emotional Fires Questionnaire (see Worksheet 17-3).

How did you feel before you filled out your Fire Drill Strategy? Did answering the questions reveal anything about your fear? Take a few moments to reflect on what you've learned about preparing for future difficulties, and record your thoughts in Worksheet 17-6.

Worksheet 17-5   My Fire Drill Strategy

Situation:

1. How would someone else cope with this situation?

_____

_____

_____

2. Have I dealt with something like this in the past? How did I do it?

_____

_____

_____

3. How much will this event affect my life a year after it occurs?

_____

_____

_____

4. Is this event as awful as I'm making it out to be?

_____

_____

_____

5. Are there any intriguing, creative ways of dealing with this challenge?

_____

_____

_____

Worksheet 17-6   My Reflections

_____

_____

_____

Keeping the Ball Rolling

If you've worked hard and conquered your depression or anxiety, that's great! But you still probably experience minor bumps in the road. And some people fail to appreciate the things that are going well for them. Are you one of those folks? Do you notice the activities that increase your feelings of satisfaction and well-being?

Doing the right things

The technique in this section, the Satisfaction Tracker, is designed to track satisfying activities. Paying close attention to satisfying activities highlights what's going right in your life, and increasing your focus on your well-being improves your odds of preventing relapse.

EXAMPLE

Cindy has had a tough year. She broke up with her boyfriend and was diagnosed with breast cancer. Her physical recovery was excellent and rapid by most standards. However, as is common with breast cancer survivors, Cindy suffered from depression off and on during her ordeal. Now a year later, her depression has thoroughly abated. Cindy tracks her satisfying activities as a way of solidifying her gains and preventing relapse (see Worksheet 17-7).

Worksheet 17-7   Cindy's Satisfaction Tracker

Situation	Satisfying Thoughts	Satisfaction Intensity (0–100)
I took pictures at a wedding.	My hobby has turned into a second career. That was my dream!	80
I was chosen to teach a continuing education class in digital photography.	I love teaching. I must be getting pretty good at what I do.	70
I went on a cruise with friends.	This was great. I was never able to treat myself like this before.	85
I took a long walk in my neighborhood and noticed the scenery.	I appreciate things like this more than ever.	60
I paid my bills.	I'd been putting that off for too long. It wasn't a major high, but it felt nice.	40
I went to my first party since my recovery.	I felt a little on-stage, but it was nice to see my friends there.	65

PRACTICE

Using Cindy's Satisfaction Tracker as a guide, complete your own Tracker in Worksheet 17-8 to keep track of the good stuff going on in your life. Remember to include major as well as minor events.

1. Note a particular event in the left column.

2. In the middle column, write down your thoughts and feelings about the event.

3. In the right column, rate the sense of satisfaction you experienced from that event on a scale of 0 (no satisfaction) to 100 (total ecstasy).

4. Following the exercise, use Worksheet 17-9 to reflect on what you've discovered about your recovery and current well-being.

Worksheet 17-8   My Satisfaction Tracker

Situation	Satisfying Thoughts	Satisfaction Intensity (0–100)

Worksheet 17-9   My Reflections

_____

_____

_____

_____

_____

Disrupting satisfaction interrupters

Sometimes, activities that you anticipate being wonderful turn out to be just okay, blah, or downright downers. This kind of outcome may indicate that your satisfaction was sabotaged by a *satisfaction interrupter*. The culprit is usually a thought that steals your initial or planned enjoyment of an activity. To understand satisfaction interrupters and their effects on your experiences, check out the following example.

EXAMPLE

Austin loves golf and looks forward to playing in a weekend charity game. It's a crisp, clear day, and the course is beautiful. Austin is clearly the best player in his foursome. He expects to have a really a great time. But as he plays, he finds himself having thoughts that interrupt his good feelings. After he finishes his round of golf, he fills out a Satisfaction Interrupter (see Worksheet 17-10) to get a better handle on what his thoughts have been doing to him. After completing the exercise, Austin realizes that he needs to do something about his satisfaction-interrupting thoughts and completes the Satisfaction-Interrupter Disrupter shown in Worksheet 17-11.

Worksheet 17-10   Austin's Satisfaction Interrupter

Event	Satisfying Thought	Satisfaction-Interrupting Thought
On the first tee, I drove the ball straight down the middle of the fairway.	Nice beginning! I could take this tournament.	The last time I started like this, I ended up getting a double bogey.
Nate said, "You're really on today!"	He's right; I am!	He's jinxed me. I feel like I'm going to start slipping.
I'm in the lead at the end of the first round.	My game is really improving. I should think about getting on the circuit.	Every time I have thoughts like this, I can hear my mother telling me that I'll never amount to anything.

Notice how Austin's initial, satisfying thoughts were zapped by his satisfaction-interrupting thoughts. These satisfaction-interrupting thoughts didn't make Austin feel depressed (like the thoughts discussed in Chapters 5, 6, and 7), but they robbed him of his good feelings. When the joy in your life is stolen in this manner, you're more susceptible to relapse.

So, what can you do to hold onto your joy? Well, here's a strategy for dealing with satisfaction interrupters. Check out Worksheet 17-11 to see how Austin uses the Satisfaction-Interrupter Disrupter.

Worksheet 17-11   Austin's Satisfaction-Interrupter Disrupter

EXAMPLE

<u>Satisfaction-Interrupting Thought:</u> Every time I have thoughts like this, I can hear my mother telling me that I'll never amount to anything.

1. What evidence do I have that either supports or refutes my satisfaction-interrupting thought?

   I'm doing fine. I have a good job with lots of potential for advancement. My mother has been wrong about so many things in my life that it's almost funny.

2. If a friend of mine told me that he or she had this thought, would I think it sounded reasonable or self-defeating?

   I've had friends who are good golfers, and I've encouraged them to compete. If my friend told me that he felt like a failure because of something his mother said, I'd tell him to grow up and get over it.

3. Do I have experiences in my life that could refute this thought?

   I've won several local golf tournaments. I can't be that much of a loser. I don't have to be the world's best golfer to get somewhere in life, but hey, I'm darn good.

4. Is this satisfaction-interrupting thought distorted, and can I come up with a more accurate replacement thought? (See Chapter 6 for more information on thought distortions.)

   Clearly, thinking that my mother's view has anything to do with reality is pretty darn distorted. I'm overgeneralizing and dismissing evidence that shows I'm doing great. I can replace my satisfaction-interrupting thought with, "I'm doing great with my golf game. I don't need to listen to my mother's voice anymore."

After Austin answers the Satisfaction-Interrupter Disrupter questions, he realizes that he's been allowing distorted thinking to interfere with his pleasure.

Now that you've seen how it's done, track your satisfaction-interrupting thoughts in Worksheet 17-12.

PRACTICE

1. **In the left column, use a few words to capture what should have been a satisfying event.**

2. **If you initially had satisfying thoughts about that event, record those in the middle column. If you didn't have such thoughts, leave this column blank.**

3. **Record your satisfaction-interrupting thoughts in the right column.** Remember, these are any thoughts that somehow took away the pleasure you may have otherwise felt.

Worksheet 17-12   My Satisfaction Interrupter

Event	Satisfying Thought	Satisfaction-Interrupting Thought

TIP

Some people automatically sabotage their satisfaction with general beliefs such as, "Fun is frivolous," "I don't deserve to have a good time," or "I should be working." These thoughts stop satisfaction before it even begins. Look out for such beliefs in your own thinking, and read more about them in Chapters 7 and 11.

Download as many of these forms as you need at www.dummies.com/go/anxiety&depression workbookfd2e.

PRACTICE

One at a time, subject your thoughts from Worksheet 7-12 to the Satisfaction-Interrupter Disrupter questions in Worksheet 17-13.

1. **Choose one of your satisfaction-interrupting thoughts and write it in the space provided at the top of the questionnaire.**

2. **Answer each of the questions that follow in relation to that thought.** If you have trouble answering these questions, please review Chapters 5 and 6.

3. **In Worksheet 17-14, reflect on what these exercises have shown you. Can you see how your satisfaction-interrupter thoughts are robbing you of joy? Can you see that replacement thoughts make a difference in the way you feel?**

Worksheet 17-13   My Satisfaction Interrupter Disrupter

Satisfaction-Interrupting Thought:

1. What evidence do I have that either supports or refutes my satisfaction-interrupting thought?

_____

_____

_____

_____

2. If a friend of mine told me that he or she had this thought, would I think it sounded reasonable or self-defeating?

_____

_____

_____

_____

3. Do I have experiences in my life that could refute this thought?

_____

_____

_____

_____

4. Is this satisfaction-interrupting thought distorted, and can I come up with a more accurate replacement thought? (See Chapter 6 for more information on thought distortions.)

_____

_____

_____

_____

Worksheet 17-14   My Reflections

_____

_____

_____

_____

Chapter **18**

Promoting Positives

The focus throughout this book is on ways to help you overcome depression and defeat anxiety. Working through the exercises and trying the strategies presented will improve your moods. You deserve to feel better, and if you already feel pretty good, this chapter is for you.

This chapter goes beyond depression and anxiety and reaches for true happiness. Why? Because science reveals that happiness doesn't just feel good — happy people have better immune systems, live longer, have lower blood pressure, and have more empathy for others. Happy people are also more productive and make more money. That's a pretty good argument for finding happiness.

If happiness is such a good thing, you may wonder what exactly makes people happy. Although happy people usually make a little more money than what's needed for bills and food, research shows that money alone doesn't lead to more happiness. Unless you're poor and struggling to put food on the table, studies indicate that even winning a big lottery payout doesn't increase happiness for very long. And, surprisingly, power, youth, and good looks don't seem to contribute much to people's reported happiness.

People with money, looks, and power suffer from depression and anxiety. In fact, rich, gorgeous, young, and powerful people are as likely to be as miserable as anyone else. You've probably seen recent examples of extraordinary athletes who admit to having mental health issues. That's not to say you should give away all your money, neglect your appearance, and quit your job. It's just that having all those things doesn't create happiness.

So, what does lead to happiness? Chapter 11 talks about the value of seeking *healthy pleasures*. Simple, healthy pleasures are helpful for kick-starting better moods, but they're somewhat transitory. This chapter gives you ideas for finding deeper, longer-lasting satisfaction and well-being.

Focusing on Gratitude

You may have a grandmother or mother who suggests that you think about good things and put aside the bad. That's pretty good advice. The commonsense advice of our elders usually has more than a grain of truth to it. Concentrating on the good things in your life and whatever fills you with a sense of gratitude can be surprisingly helpful to developing your sense of well-being.

Keeping track of the things that make you grateful

Studies show that keeping track of what you appreciate or are thankful for improves mood, sleep, and health. What's really amazing is how easy it is to enhance your life-satisfaction in this manner.

EXAMPLE

Janet had a bout of depression and recovered a few months ago. She carefully monitors herself for signs of relapse and feels grateful that she seems to have beaten the blues. Before terminating therapy, her therapist suggests that Janet count her blessings for a while. So, Janet fills out a Gratitude Diary; Worksheet 18-1 shows her first week's efforts.

Worksheet 18-1   Janet's Gratitude Diary

Day	What I Feel Grateful For
Monday	1) I found a great parking space this morning. 2) I lost two pounds. 3) Work went well today. 4) I love my dog! 5) My kids are terrific.
Tuesday	1) The same parking space was there today! 2) The weather is wonderful. 3) The kids did their homework without my nagging. 4) I'm so glad I have good health. 5) The traffic wasn't too bad today. 6) I don't have any money problems right now.
Wednesday	1) I like this town. 2) Nothing bad happened at work. 3) I went for a great walk. 4) I'm not depressed. 5) I like my car.
Thursday	1) The kids got off to school without their usual whining. 2) Traffic was pretty darn good today. 3) I got by that speed trap without getting caught! 4) I had fun in my spin class. 5) I had a good talk with my friend Lisa.

Day	What I Feel Grateful For
Friday	1) It's Friday! 2) It looks like I may get a raise. 3) I had a delicious lunch with my friend. 4) I'm not depressed. 5) I streamed a good movie.
Saturday	1) I enjoyed watching my daughter's soccer game. 2) I helped out a neighbor by watching her kids and felt great that I could do that. 3) The repair bill for the air conditioner wasn't as bad as I feared. 4) I'm not depressed! 5) I went out for dinner with my boyfriend. We had a nice time.
Sunday	1) I planted tomatoes. 2) I took the kids over to their friend's house and had a few hours to myself. 3) I talked to my mother, and she seemed in good spirits. 4) I lost another pound. 5) I felt a little down about starting the week again, but I pulled myself out of a bad mood. I couldn't do that before.

Janet is surprised at how good it feels to track what makes her feel grateful for a few weeks. She starts exercising more, and she feels a deeper sense of satisfaction with her life.

Using Janet's Gratitude Diary as a guide, fill out your own Diary in Worksheet 18-2.

PRACTICE

1. **On each day of the week, think of five things you feel grateful for that day.** These items can be very small, such as finding a great parking space, or more substantial, such as your good health.

2. **Write each item in the diary on its corresponding day and reflect on how appreciative you feel that day.**

3. **At the end of the week, use Worksheet 18-3 to reflect on what you've learned as a result of keeping tabs on what makes you feel grateful.**

Consider continuing this exercise every week for a month and from time to time in the future.

Download as many copies of this exercise as you need for your personal use at www.dummies.com/go/anxiety&depressionworkbookfd2e.

Writing testimonials

This strategy for bringing gratitude into your life by writing testimonials was developed by Dr. Martin Seligman. Dr. Seligman conducted research on this technique and found that participants felt great after completing it.

Worksheet 18-2   My Gratitude Diary

Day	What I Feel Grateful For
Monday	
Tuesday	
Wednesday	
Thursday	
Friday	
Saturday	
Sunday	

Worksheet 18-3   My Reflections

_____

_____

_____

_____

_____

EXAMPLE

Dustin has a lot to be grateful for. He conquered his social anxiety more than a year ago. His college roommate, Jack, was instrumental in helping Dustin overcome his anxiety. Now a junior in college, Dustin is taking an upper-level psychology class. His professor suggests a project called the Testimonial Exercise. The students are instructed to choose someone from their lives who made a real difference and write out a testimonial to that individual. The students are told to deliver the testimonial and read it to their selected person. In Worksheet 18-4, you can read what Dustin writes about his roommate.

Worksheet 18-4   Testimonial Exercise

Dear Jack,

I was given the assignment of writing a testimonial to someone who's made a difference in my life, and guess what? You're it. I felt pretty weird about this at first, but the more I thought about it, the more I liked the idea. I don't think I've ever told you how much I appreciate what you did for me in helping me overcome my social anxiety. That first year of college was brutal for me. Your friendship saved me from utter misery.

You took me under your wing and pushed me to do things I didn't think I could. And you were a role model for me. You taught me how to talk with women. We had some pretty good times, didn't we? But sometimes I would get pretty down about my problems, and you'd kick me in the butt. You told me I needed to get counseling. Oh, how I didn't want to hear that! But you were right. The whole first-year experience changed my life. I give you credit for so much.

My hat's off to you, buddy. They don't come any better than you. Your friendship is incredibly valuable to me. And now before I make myself totally sick, I'd better end this thing. But seriously, I appreciate all you did.

Your buddy,

Dustin

Use Worksheet 18-5 and the following instructions to complete your own Testimonial Exercise.

PRACTICE

1. **Choose someone from your life who's made a real positive difference in your life.** Ideally, the person you choose shouldn't be someone you're romantically involved with.

2. **Write at least two or three paragraphs expressing your gratitude and telling the person what he or she did for you.** Write out your testimonial in longhand — it's more personal that way.

3. **Arrange a time to meet with the person you wrote to and read your testimonial out loud to him or her.**

4. **Spend some time talking with your chosen person.**

5. **In Worksheet 18-6, reflect on this exercise and what it's taught you about the good people and things in your life.**

Worksheet 18-5   **Testimonial Exercise**

Dear   ,

_____

_____

_____

_____

_____

_____

_____

_____

_____

_____

_____

_____

_____

_____

_____

_____

_____

_____

_____

Worksheet 18-6   **My Reflections**

_____

_____

_____

Making the World a Bit Nicer

A powerful way of achieving happiness is by helping others. Being kind to others helps you in two ways. First, you're likely to enjoy the feeling you get from giving service or kindness to others. Second, doing something nice for another person takes your mind off your own problems.

To get you started, Worksheet 18-7 lists some possible good things you can do to help others. It's good to come up with your own list of things that are important to you, but for more ideas, consider checking out www.randomactsofkindness.org.

Worksheet 18-7   Nice Ideas

- Walk dogs at your local Humane Society
- Offer to take someone else's shopping cart back to the store
- Volunteer to tutor someone
- Volunteer to drive for a Senior Center
- Offer to run an errand for a neighbor
- Pick up litter in your neighborhood
- Let another driver merge into your lane
- Donate blood
- Donate food or clothing to a homeless shelter
- Write a thank-you note to someone

PRACTICE

This exercise helps you discover the personal benefits of small acts of kindness. Even in small ways, you make the world a better place while simultaneously enhancing your own well-being.

1. **Brainstorm a list of at least 20 small acts of kindness — things you could do almost anytime. Write them in the left column of Worksheet 18-8.** The key is to think of ideas that are truly gifts — in other words, you shouldn't expect something in return. If you want to include a few more substantial acts, that's fine; remember, the frequency of your actions is what really makes the difference.

2. **After you develop your list, start doing the things you've listed!**

3. **Track each act of kindness in the right column by recording the date when you complete the act.**

4. **In Worksheet 18-9, reflect on how this exercise affects you.**

Worksheet 18-8   My Nice Ideas

Acts of Kindness	When I Did It

(continued)

Worksheet 18-8 *(continued)*

Acts of Kindness	When I Did It

Worksheet 18-9 **My Reflections**

_____

_____

_____

_____

Letting Go

One way people ruin their chances for happiness is by holding on to resentments, anger, and rage. When you've been wronged, it's natural to feel upset, and anger can be useful, at least for a while. Anger helps you defend yourself when attacked because it revs up your body to right a wrong.

However, anger that's held for too long poisons your body and soul. Chronic anger leads to high blood pressure, emotional disturbance, and a decrease in common sense. Thus, when you're angry, you simply can't be happy.

But ridding yourself of chronic anger isn't an especially easy task. You must do something that feels counterintuitive: somehow find forgiveness for those who have wronged you.

TIP

There may be certain wrongs that you can't realistically forgive. For example, you may find yourself unable to forgive acts of severe violence or abuse. In that case, an alternative approach is to let go of the anger and rage by finding acceptance. See Chapter 8 for ideas on acquiring acceptance.

PRACTICE

Worksheet 18-10 guides you through a series of steps for finding forgiveness and the serenity that comes along with it.

Worksheet 18-10　　Finding Forgiveness

1. Write down what's happened to you to make you angry. Be specific. Try to avoid using words of rage and retribution. Instead, describe the person and event in dispassionate terms. Review what you've written over and over until your feelings about it begin to lessen.

_____

_____

_____

_____

2. Put yourself in the offender's shoes. Search for understanding as to why they may have carried out the offense against you. Was the offender or perpetrator afraid, misguided, depressed, defensive, lacking judgment, or purposefully hurtful? Write down your ideas.

_____

_____

_____

_____

3. Think of yourself as a forgiving person, not a victim. Describe how your life may improve when you let go of your anger and forgive.

_____

_____

_____

_____

4. When thoughts of revenge come into your mind, write down reasons for letting them go. Remember that ongoing anger and rage harm you more than the perpetrator.

_____

_____

_____

_____

5. Consider writing a letter of forgiveness in the space below. You don't have to send it to the perpetrator, but you may find comfort in discussing it with others.

_____

_____

_____

_____

REMEMBER

Forgiving isn't the same as saying that the wrong was okay. Forgiveness gives you back the peace you had before the event occurred. And letting go of your anger allows you to regain your previous happiness.

Exercising Self-Control

In pursuing happiness, avoiding the *quick fix* is important. Quick fixes come in all shapes and sizes — alcohol, drugs, chocolate, a new car, a better house, more clothes, blah, blah, blah. Such things are fine in moderation, of course, but they don't create lasting happiness.

In fact, studies demonstrate that, in the long run, self-control and the ability to delay gratification lead to better adjustment and greater satisfaction with life. Yet, the world promises and encourages instant gratification and suggests that you should be happy at all times. Those expectations can easily set you up for disappointment. The truth is that:

>> People aren't always happy.

>> Meaningful goals require effort and patience.

>> Overindulgence leads to satiation and depleted pleasure.

>> People who insist on instant gratification are inevitably frustrated and disappointed.

PRACTICE

Worksheet 18-11 starts you on the path to achieving greater self-control. Even small steps in this direction enhance your sense of well-being. Please realize you don't have to make major changes all at once. Most importantly, devote some serious time to this exercise to get the best results.

Worksheet 18-11   Strengthening Self-Control

1. Write a brief description of an area in your life in which you've given in to impulses or expected instant gratification.

_____

_____

_____

_____

2. Write your reflections on how increasing self-control may improve your long-term satisfaction.

_____

_____

_____

_____

3. Based on what you've written, develop a goal for change.

_____

_____

_____

_____

4. Record your reflections on how your life would change for the better if you were to achieve this new goal.

_____

_____

_____

_____

Discovering What's Really Important

What do you value? How much of your time do you devote to activities that are meaningful and consistent with your values? And do you live your life according to those values? If not, you're probably not as happy as you could be.

PRACTICE

The following Values Clarification Quiz can help you focus on what's really important to you. After you fill it out, you can use the results to redirect your life plan in a more meaningful way.

1. **Read through all the values listed in Worksheet 18-12.**

2. **Circle the eight items you prize most highly.**

3. **Of those eight, pick your top three most-prized items and write them in Worksheet 18-13.**

Ponder how you've spent your time in the past month. Estimate the amount of time you've devoted to activities that are concordant with your top three values (see Worksheet 18-13). If you notice a discrepancy between what you value and what you do, consider reprioritizing. In Worksheet 18-14, jot down how you plan to re-allocate your schedule and resources to better reflect what you deem as important. Making these changes is likely to improve your long-term life satisfaction.

Worksheet 18-12   Values Clarification Quiz

Money	Donating time or money to others
Pleasure	Cleaning up the environment
Independence	Political activism
Risk-taking or excitement	Competition
Creativity	Leisure time
Recognition	Honesty
Achievement	Winning
Variety	Family life
Entertainment	Recreation
Close friends	Status
A loving partner	Expensive possessions
Spirituality	Intellectual pursuits
Health	Looking good
Good food	Satisfying work
Having happy kids	Showing kindness
Art	Mental or physical stimulation
Economic security	Safety
Influencing others	Predictability

Worksheet 18-13   My Top Three Values

1.

2.

3.

Worksheet 18-14   My Reflections

Finding Meaning Before Your Funeral

Finding meaning and purpose in life is about connecting with ideas and concepts that are larger and deeper than yourself. For many, religion and spirituality are the primary channels for finding such meaning. But regardless of your spiritual beliefs, giving serious consideration to what you want your life to be about — in other words, the legacy you want to leave behind — can be an enlightening exercise.

In this section, think about your funeral or memorial service and the thoughts and feelings that those in attendance may experience when contemplating your life. What do you want people to remember about your life? The following exercise helps you discover the traits, characteristics, and values you hold most dearly. By reminding yourself to live the rest of your life accordingly, you'll feel more enriched and fulfilled.

EXAMPLE

Roland completes the Eulogy in Advance exercise as a way of enhancing the sense of meaning and purpose he gets from his life. As he prepares to write his eulogy, Roland realizes that he hasn't been living his life in a way that justifies how he wants to be remembered. Nevertheless, he writes out how he wants people to think of him and his life after he's gone (see Worksheet 18-15).

Worksheet 18-15   Roland's Eulogy in Advance

We are gathered here today to say goodbye to our friend and family member, Roland. Roland was a wonderful father and husband. He loved and enjoyed spending time with his family. Roland's children grew up to be successful and happy. He loved and cherished his wife throughout their marriage. He was careful to keep the romance alive, even until the end. Roland was a true friend to many of us here today. When someone needed help, Roland was the first to offer. His door was always open. Whether or not people needed his time or even his money, Roland was generous. Roland also gave to his community; he organized members of his congregation to pick up seniors who were unable to drive so that they could attend church services and functions. Truly, he made the world a little better place.

Roland sees a painful contrast between the life he's been living and the one he wants to be remembered for. Thus, he realizes that he spends far too much of his time working and buying unnecessary "stuff." He doesn't want people to recall that he was the first on his block to have the latest gadget or the most expensive car. Roland vows that in the future, he'll spend more time with his friends and family, and he makes a plan for contributing more to his community. He cherishes these values far more than all the material prizes in the world.

PRACTICE

Use the space in Worksheet 18-16 to write your own Eulogy in Advance. Remember to be honest about how you'd like to be remembered, regardless of your current activities and behaviors.

1. **Sit back and relax for a few minutes.**

2. **Ponder how you'd like to be remembered at the end of your life.** Think of loved ones and friends. What do you wish they'd say or think about you?

3. **Write down your thoughts.** Your Eulogy in Advance should reflect the things you value most — in other words, what you want the rest of your life to be about.

REMEMBER

Starting at this moment, right now, you're beginning the rest of your life. Whether you're 15 or 84, it's never too late to start living a life with meaning and purpose.

Worksheet 18-16   My Eulogy in Advance

_____

_____

_____

_____

_____

_____

_____

_____

_____

_____

_____

_____

_____

_____

_____

_____

_____

_____

_____

_____

_____

_____

_____

_____

_____

_____

_____

7

The Part of Tens

Chapter **19**

Ten Reasons to Seek Additional Support

Many people benefit from reading and learning about treatments for anxiety and depression. They're able to take actions on their own without outside professional mental health treatment. If that person is you, great!

However, a good percentage of people may need to seek guidance from a health care provider or a mental health therapist. Tips and warnings throughout this book suggest that you get help when you're stuck or feeling overwhelmed. The following sections offer some specific instances when getting professional evaluation and treatment is best.

If you decide to get professional help, check with your insurance company for a list of providers that accept your insurance. Ask your primary health care provider for recommendations.

You Feel Hopeless

Everyone feels hopeless from time to time. For example, you may feel hopeless when your teenager refuses to take your advice or when you watch the daily news. Those feeling are understandable. But when hopelessness invades your thoughts, when you believe that life is never going to get better, it's time to ask for help.

Hopelessness, left untreated, often leads to suicidal thoughts. Don't wait. Even when life looks bleak, strive for hope. If hope isn't realistic in the direst of circumstances, you can achieve acceptance. Acceptance gives you the strength and grace to live peacefully with whatever it is you're struggling with.

You Feel Like Ending Your Life

If you have thoughts of killing yourself, you need immediate help. If you have a specific plan and the means of carrying it out, call 911. If your thoughts don't include the method or the means, call the national suicide hotline at 1-800-273-TALK (1-800-273-8255).

Trained counselors will help you decide what plan of action you need to take so you don't do something that lands you in the hospital or in the morgue. Be truthful with the counselor, and don't gloss over the seriousness of your thoughts. Suicide remains one of the most common ways that people die. Suicide is almost always a permanent solution to a fixable or temporary problem.

TIP

The National Suicide Hotline phone number plans to change in July 2022. The new number will be 988.

You're Getting into Trouble at Home

People with anxiety and depression are often good actors. They're able to pull themselves together when necessary and act *as if* all is well. Some who suffer significant emotional problems carry off this act pretty reliably in public. But when they open the door to their homes, the disguise falls away and their despair emerges.

Acting is exhausting, so add fatigue to the mix of sadness or worry if you're anxious or depressed. The result is often an irritable grouch. The grouch often takes out frustration on family members or roommates. The resulting conflict only increases bad feelings for all involved.

If you hold it together until you get home and then become grumpy with those you're close to, consider getting professional help. It's only a matter of time before family members become weary of serving as punching bags for your unhappiness.

You're Having Trouble at Work or School

Depression and anxiety interfere with completion of work, attention and concentration, short-term memory, and interactions with others. Making even simple decisions can seem impossible. No wonder many people with significant emotional problems run into trouble at work or school.

If emotions are hurting your performance, you should seek professional help. Many times, working with a therapist for a while is all you need to feel good enough to get back to meeting your responsibilities. Don't lose your job or fail at school because of reluctance to admit that you need help.

You Want to Isolate from Others

Some people are born recluses and rarely find other people easy to be around. However, depression and anxiety can turn an extrovert into a reclusive introvert. Over time, a depressed or anxious person can withdraw, not finding pleasure in the company of others.

Isolation is not good treatment for emotional disorders. If you find yourself turning down invitations, staying away from family or friends, or even missing important responsibilities because of anxiety or depression, it's time to seek professional help.

You're Abusing Drugs or Alcohol

For many people, a glass of wine in the evening can be quite relaxing. People suffering posttraumatic stress disorder often turn to medical marijuana for relief. Drugs can be quite effective for treating anxiety or depression. That means prescription drugs that a health care provider prescribes.

The problem with using drugs or alcohol is that they tend to numb bad feelings. What happens when a substance makes you feel better? You want to use it again and again, which can result in dependency and addiction. If you find yourself going down that slippery slope, talk to your health care provider. Substance abuse is not a sign of character weakness or disgrace. Human beings are susceptible to addiction.

You Feel Overly Agitated

Maybe you find yourself getting more and more agitated. You're unable to sit still, and you start pacing. You find it impossible to concentrate and can't get anything done. You might have rapid, irrational thinking. This agitation doesn't appear one evening and go away. It lingers.

This may be a sign of a more complicated disorder, such as posttraumatic stress disorder, bipolar disorder, or another physical problem. You need to get a professional consultation to help figure out the cause and treat it effectively.

You Can't Control Your Temper

Irritability is normal with anxiety or depression. However, if your temper spirals out of control frequently, you need help. Temper outbursts do nothing but make your emotional well-being worse than before.

First, get a physical assessment to rule out medical problems or medication side effects. Then seek a professional with experience in anger management treatment. You may also want to take a look at *Anger Management For Dummies* (Wiley).

You Can't Get Motivated to Do Anything

Apathy often tags along with anxiety or depression. Most people push themselves through apathy and at least do enough to get by. If your dishes are overflowing in the sink, your laundry is piled up, your bills are unpaid, and you forget to feed the dog, you need professional help. Start with a checkup by your primary care provider, and then get a referral for mental health treatment.

Family and Friends Worry About You

Friends and family care about you and want what's best for you. Some may be worrywarts, anxious about small things. However, if most of those who know and care about you express concern about your emotional well-being, listen to them. Start by thanking them for their concern, but don't expect friends and family to be your counselors. They may be "there for you," but even the closest family can get burned out by listening to your troubles, especially if your issues are serious and chronic.

WARNING

Avoid making your loved ones feel responsible for your mental health. Doing so may jeopardize your relationship and won't help you in the end. You must take charge of getting better on your own or with help from a mental health provider.

Chapter **20**

Ten Ways to Help a Loved One with Anxiety or Depression

When someone you care about suffers from emotional distress, it's natural to want to help. This chapter gives you a few tips on how to help without hurting. It's important to realize that you can lend a hand but can't solve the complicated issues that cause someone to have anxiety or depression. Friends can coach, cheer, and buffer, but they can't take responsibility.

Listening without Judging

Have you ever been on the phone or at a coffee shop with a friend who dominates the conversation, complaining about this or that, without seeming to care what you have to say? Then after 30 minutes of your listening to the monologue, the friend turns to you and says, "Thank you so much. I feel better."

You might think that you did nothing, but you really did one of the most healing of all interactions. You listened to your friend without offering opinions, judgments, or criticisms. The simple act of listening can help anyone who suffers from anxiety or depression.

The gift of listening is essentially a free and easy way to support your loved ones. You don't need to offer solutions or suggestions, just a kind and nonjudgmental ear.

Learning More

Listening is a start, but you might also want to learn a bit more about the symptoms your loved one is dealing with. If they are agreeable, ask questions about what they are feeling and thinking. Then find out how those thoughts and feelings influence their day-to-day behaviors.

You can also learn more about depression and anxiety by reading Chapter 1 in this book. Don't try to diagnose the problem; leave that to professionals. But you can use the information you discover to support your loved one in striving to find ways of coping with distressing thoughts and feelings.

Staying in Touch

People with depression or anxiety sometimes feel ashamed of their emotions. They isolate themselves from others, sometimes shutting out the very people who could support them. If your loved one is backing away from interactions, it's okay to give them some space, but still be present. Communicate softly and frequently that you're available when they need someone to talk to.

Send a weekly text letting the person you care about know that you're thinking of them. Tell a joke or send a happy emoji. Texts are nonintrusive and don't require an immediate response.

Separating the Emotion from the Person

People who suffer from depression or anxiety can become rude, irritable, and sometimes dismissive of friends and family. What can be even more irritating is when those same people may act perfectly fine with colleagues or strangers. Don't take their moodiness around you personally.

Those with emotional problems often pull themselves together in some interactions and then fall apart with exhaustion when they're home or with close friends. Don't take this as disrespectful. It's a manifestation of their trust in you that allows them to misbehave.

TIP This doesn't mean you have to accept abuse or neglect from a family member or friend. Try to have patience and give it time. If your loved one is in treatment, you may want to ask for a joint session to address some of these relationship issues.

Offering a Hand with Finding Help

When people are overwhelmed by emotion, even small tasks seem almost impossible to carry out. Finding a psychologist, psychiatrist, social worker, or counselor can be daunting for even the most persistent, capable consumer. Getting involved in the tangled web of insurance companies, copays, networks, and availability takes incredible mental stamina. That may be difficult or almost impossible for someone who's already feeling fragile or overwhelmed.

Offer to help make initial phone calls to insurance companies and providers if your loved one allows you to. Perhaps you can find two or three providers who take your loved one's insurance and are available and willing to take them on. When you've found some options, stick around to support your loved one in making those phone calls, and help schedule the first appointment. You might even offer to drive and wait in the lobby for support.

Providing Hope

For the majority of people with depression or anxiety, treatment works. Many benefit from psychotherapy, some from medication, others from self-help. The great news is that few people can't find a treatment to relieve their symptoms at least partially.

However, people in the throes of depression and anxiety may believe that their situation is uniquely hopeless. Help your loved one by gently reminding them to have hope for the future. You can show your optimism by encouraging them to never give up and reminding them that help is available for those who are willing to pursue it.

Taking a Walk

Maybe you've listened and been present for your loved one, but they can't reach out of their despair to respond. Sometimes a slow walk around the neighborhood or park can be extremely beneficial for someone suffering from anxiety or depression. You can be the catalyst for a better day by inviting them out for a stroll. There's no need to talk; just walk together. A pat on the shoulder or a small hug might be just what they need.

Of course, if your loved one agrees, getting out and exercising a bit more strenuously is even better than a leisurely walk. Exercise can be an effective treatment for symptoms of both depression and anxiety (see Chapter 10).

Helping with Daily Chores

High emotional arousal takes energy, so exhaustion often follows. Offer to help your loved one with some simple daily chores. Even small tasks may seem overwhelming to someone with high levels of anxiety or depression. Offer to:

>> Bring over a frozen casserole or dinner

>> Run an errand

>> Pick up their kids from school

>> Organize papers or bills

>> Call a helpline to solve a computer problem

Be assertive. Most people won't ask for help, but they really could benefit from some assistance. Explain that helping them will actually make you feel better.

Not Blaming Yourself

I've worked with many family members who blame themselves for their loved one's emotional distress. That's especially true of parents and their children. While in some circumstances, relationship problems do contribute to emotional stress, trying to figure out who did what to whom doesn't solve problems. Shift from blame to curiosity, acceptance, and assistance.

Sitting with blame does nothing to heal, but taking action does. Now that emotional problems are present, what can you do to help? Don't dwell on past mistakes or your personal contribution to the problem. Rather, plan on future goals, strive to forgive yourself and others, and look for a better tomorrow.

Taking Care of Yourself

Don't burn yourself out by the troubles of those you care about. Most humans have had interrupted sleep worrying about others. But rarely do your sleepless nights solve anything except make you fatigued. Be there, and support and offer to help, just don't take ownership of the problem.

Take care of your own physical and emotional self by getting enough sleep and exercise, eating a healthy diet, and resisting unhealthy temptations. You need to stay healthy to have the energy for helping others.

Index

S

Y

About the Author

Laura L. Smith, PhD, is a clinical psychologist. She is a past president of the New Mexico Psychological Association. She has considerable experience working with children, adolescents, and adults with anxiety and depression. She recently completed *Anger Management For Dummies*, 3rd Edition (Wiley). She has presented workshops on cognitive therapy and mental health issues to national and international audiences.

Dr. Smith has worked on numerous publications together with her husband Charles Elliott, PhD, who is now retired. They are coauthors of *Quitting Smoking & Vaping For Dummies; Borderline Personality Disorder For Dummies*, 2nd Edition; *Child Psychology & Development For Dummies; Anxiety For Dummies*, 3rd Edition; *Obsessive Compulsive Disorder For Dummies; Seasonal Affective Disorder For Dummies; and Depression For Dummies*, 2nd Edition (all published by Wiley).

Dedication

I dedicate this book to the millions of people who suffer from symptoms of anxiety and depression. I hope you find this workbook beneficial. I expect you will. Keep on working; you will get better.

Authors' Acknowledgments

Once again, I want to thank the outstanding team at Wiley. As usual, their expertise, support, and guidance was of immeasurable help. Thank you to Kelsey Baird for her encouragement during the initial planning for the book. Project manager extraordinaire, Tim Gallan, answered questions, helped with formatting, and kept the content on point. I appreciated the input of talented copy editor Karen Davis. Thank you also to technical editor, Joseph Bush, for his particularly insightful comments.

A special acknowledgment to Charles Elliott, coauthor of the first edition of *Anxiety & Depression Workbook For Dummies*. His voice is always present in my writing. Even though he has retired, he continues to edit, critique, and cheer me on.

Publisher's Acknowledgments

Acquisitions Editor: Kelsey Baird

Development Editor: Tim Gallan

Copy Editor: Karen Davis

Technical Reviewer: Joseph P. Bush, PhD

Production Editor: Mohammed Zafar Ali

Cover Image: © Dmitry Rukhlenko/Shutterstock